A Nervous Man Shouldn't Be Here in the First Place

A Nervous Man Shouldn't

The University of Georgia Press • Athens

Be Here in the First Place

THE LIFE OF BILL BAGGS

Amy Paige Condon (signature)

Amy Paige Condon

This publication is made possible in part through a grant from the
Bradley Hale Fund for Southern Studies.

Epigraph is from *Letters to a Young Poet* by Ranier Maria Rilke,
translated by M. D. Herter Norton. Copyright 1934, 1954 by
W. W. Norton & Company, Inc., renewed © 1962, 1982 by
M. D. Herter Norton. Used by permission of W. W. Norton
and Company, Inc.

Designed by Erin Kirk
Set in Minion Pro

Most University of Georgia Press titles are
available from popular e-book vendors.

Printed digitally

Library of Congress Cataloging-in-Publication Data
Names: Condon, Amy Paige, author.
Title: A nervous man shouldn't be here in the first place : the life
    of Bill Baggs / Amy Paige Condon.
Description: Athens : The University of Georgia Press, 2020. |
    Includes bibliographical references and index.
Identifiers: LCCN 2020024342 | ISBN 9780820354972 (hardback) |
    ISBN 9780820358185 (ebook)
Subjects: LCSH: Baggs, Bill. | Journalists—United States—
    Biography. | Newspaper editors—United States—Biography.
Classification: LCC PN4874.B233 C66 2020 | DDC 070.4/1092
    [b]—dc23
LC record available at https://lccn.loc.gov/2020024342

To Bill
and his "impossible dream" for peace

Be patient toward all that is unsolved in your heart and try to love the *questions themselves* like locked rooms and like books that are written in a very foreign tongue. Do not now seek the answers, which cannot be given you because you would not be able to live them. And the point is, to live everything. *Live* the questions now. Perhaps you will then gradually, without noticing it, live along some distant day into the answer.

Rainer Maria Rilke
Letters to a Young Poet

CONTENTS

Part IV. From There to Here

AUTHOR'S NOTE

A few thoughts on how I approached writing Bill Baggs's life story:

Fifty-plus years ago, Baggs and his cohort of white southern newspaper editors worked and wrote with language we deem offensive and inappropriate today. When referring to African Americans, the word "Negro," most often uncapitalized, was the prevailing journalistic style of the 1940s through 1970s. Baggs was one of the few newspapermen in the country to capitalize the word and to use honorifics out of respect for black citizens. When he did not use proper names, it was out of an abundance of caution to protect people who feared, with good reason, economic and physical reprisal. I have not sanitized any of his or his colleagues' quotes, even though some may make readers cringe.

In the halls of academia and in creative spaces, heated discussions take place regarding who has the right to tell whose story. I have not presented Baggs as a white savior, nor have I overplayed his friendships with world leaders and those unsung champions of Miami's civil rights struggle. What I have endeavored to illuminate through Baggs's life is that none of us makes progress alone. Our stories are intertwined, interdependent. In our becoming, we learn from one another. Baggs relied on the friendships he forged across racial, ethnic, and religious backgrounds to get to the truth of the human condition, just as much as those friends depended on him to use his platform to raise and amplify their voices.

In the years following World War II, many reporters and editors who worked at southern newspapers found themselves covering the biggest stories of their lives right in their own back yards. Because Baggs landed in Miami, he also confronted and covered the front lines of the Cold War as it played out across the Florida Straits, in the Caribbean Basin, and throughout South America. Communist instigators, organized crime, exile and rebel groups, and the newly formed CIA all found in South Florida a fertile ground for operation. This unique intersection of people, place, time, and circumstance drew Baggs into the orbit of both powerful politicians and future Watergate "plumbers," a universe few of his colleagues in the news business would ever experience. To get the story for his readers, Baggs undoubtedly crossed lines clearly drawn decades later by professional journalism's ethics and standards. Baggs often had to construct rules of engagement between reporters and sources on the fly because the situation was so new, the stakes so high (imminent nuclear war), the enemy so clear (communism), and the lines between friend and informant so blurred. Today, the public would not truck with a journalist who spoke on behalf of a president or who agreed to carry a diplomatic message to a foreign leader.

There is no way to truly know whether Baggs held any sway with President Joh F. Kennedy on Cuba. But had Baggs not ventured into uncertain territory, the president would have missed a powerful voice calling for restraint in October 1962. Because Baggs broke with his peers and took a lonely stand against the Vietnam War, he provided cover for Walter Cronkite, then "the most trusted man in America," to remove his reporter's hat and call for a peaceful and negotiated end to the Vietnam War, as he did during the final three minutes of his newscast on February 27, 1968. Did these events lay the groundwork for Daniel Ellsberg to entrust a reporter with the Pentagon Papers? Would Kay Graham have stood behind Bradlee, Woodward, and Bernstein in their use of an anonymous FBI informant to follow the Watergate story?

Baggs loved to say, "This is not a simple life, my friend, and there are no simple answers." When political tensions ran high and people sent him hate mail, he replied to each letter with a white postcard on which he pressed those words in black ink. We continue his search for answers, simple and otherwise. It is my fervent hope that by sharing Baggs's story we may find a few.

MAIN CHARACTERS

William Calhoun "Bill" Baggs: editor of the *Miami News*, 1957–1969

FAMILY

Crawford Collins "C. C." Baggs and Kate Bush Baggs: parents
Joan Orr "Frec" Baggs: wife
Craig Baggs: oldest son
Mahoney Baggs: youngest son
Charles Crawford Baggs: brother
Billie Baggs Beers: sister
William Beers and Robert Beers: nephews
Grace Bush Dancer and W. R. Dancer: aunt and uncle with whom Bill
  Baggs lived in Colquitt, Georgia
Charles "Sis Charlie" Bush: aunt

PROFESSIONAL PEERS AND ASSOCIATES

Harry S. Ashmore: former editor, *Arkansas Gazette*, and executive vice
  president, Center for the Study of Democratic Institutions
James M. Cox: three-term governor of Ohio, 1920 U.S. presidential candi-
  date, owner of the *Miami Daily News* and the *Atlanta Constitution*
James M. Cox Jr.: son of Governor Cox and president, Cox Media Group
Al Daniels: president, Burdine's Department Stores
Rev. Canon Theodore Gibson: president, Miami chapter of the
  NAACP, leader of Miami's Christ Episcopal Church, and Miami city
  councilman
Harry Golden: editor, *Carolina Israelite*

Robert Maynard Hutchins: founder, Center for the Study of Democratic
   Institutions
Howard Kleinberg: news editor and managing editor, *Miami News*
Dan Mahoney: publisher, *Miami (Daily) News*
Ralph E. McGill: editor and publisher, *Atlanta Constitution*
John Popham: southern correspondent, *New York Times*, and managing
   editor, *Chattanooga Times*
Harrison Salisbury: managing editor, *New York Times*
Jack Tarver: publisher, Atlanta Newspapers, Inc.
Sander Vanocur: NBC news correspondent
Hoke Welch: managing editor, *Miami Daily News*

U.S. GOVERNMENT

William Bundy: assistant secretary of state for East Asian and Pacific
   affairs
LeRoy Collins: 33rd governor of Florida, 1955–1961
William O. Douglas: U.S. Supreme Court justice
J. William Fulbright: Democratic senator from Arkansas
Averell Harriman: U.S. ambassador-at-large
Nicholas Katzenbach: undersecretary of state, Johnson administration
Luis Quintanilla: former Mexican ambassador to the United States

VIETNAMESE

Ho Chi Minh: president of North Vietnam
Mai Van Bo: North Vietnamese ambassador to France
Luu Quy Ky: vice chairman, Committee for Cultural Relations with
   Foreign Countries
Hoàng Tùng: Ho Chi Minh's spokesperson and editor, *Nhân Dân*
Col. Hà Văn Lâu: military high command, North Vietnam

A Nervous Man Shouldn't Be Here in the First Place

And then he said he had very bad news for us.—"Notes on Missions to North Vietnam"

Bill Baggs, editor of the *Miami News*, had not slept much over the last few nights in Hanoi, what with the incessant air-raid sirens and the earth-shaking detonations in the suburbs surrounding North Vietnam's capital. Here, in a guesthouse on a farm in the countryside, he could at least rest and, he hoped, ease some of the back pain and the constant ache that persisted because of chronic kidney problems. Just as he was drifting off, a banging on the door startled him awake again. His colleague, Harry Ashmore, remained dead asleep, exhausted from trying to get around Hanoi on a bum leg.

The breathless runner on the other side of the door said he had been looking for them all over Hà Nam Province and had finally thought to look here. Baggs tried to explain that the bombing near the city of Nam Dinh had forced them to turn around, but the boy talked over him. He had more urgent news: their contact Hoàng Tùng, the editor of *Nhân Dân*, the Communist Party of Vietnam's official newspaper, and spokesman for President Ho Chi Minh, had sent him. The Central Committee had prepared its response to President Lyndon Johnson's message, and they needed to return to the city immediately. It was April 3, 1968, 12:30 a.m., Hanoi time.

Baggs shook Ashmore awake. The two men dressed, packed, and drove northeast through the dark and the rain over the rough two-lane highway between My Trung and Phu Ly. Unlike the pastoral countryside they had encountered the year before, trucks were parked all along the road. The silhouettes of antiaircraft stations rose every few yards in the adjoining rice paddies.

Once they reached Hanoi, just before 4:00 a.m., they understood the urgency. Awaiting them was a statement by the Democratic Republic of Vietnam (DRV) confirming that the North Vietnamese were ready to sit down and talk with the U.S. government.

A day and a half later, when Baggs and Ashmore were set to leave Hanoi, Tùng met the men for lunch with the official secret aide-mémoire in hand. After all the back-and-forth negotiations of the last several hours, Tùng settled into a "philosophical mood," according to Baggs's notes.

He had one son in the army and another heading to war after graduation, Tùng told them, and he wished that the people of the United States could understand that his people fought because they believed in their country. He apologized for the poor condition of the Russian car they had been driving, and then he paused before saying he had some bad news.

Just before leaving his office, Tùng had received word that Rev. Martin Luther King Jr. had been shot and killed in Tennessee. Baggs, who had a habit of turning quick goodbyes into long stories, was stunned. He asked a few questions, but Tùng offered no specifics. Ashmore spoke of the last time he had seen King, in Geneva at a conference where the civil rights leader had delivered a moving speech in support of the North Vietnamese people, of finding a peaceful settlement to the war.[1]

Tùng suggested it was time to depart for the airport, or they would miss the only flight out for several days. Baggs folded his six-foot-one-inch frame into the back of the GAZ Volga, shut his eyes, and rested his head against the seat. The sedan was already cramped, laden with a driver, a "lousy interpreter," banged-up luggage, souvenir rice-paddy hats, and two comely "ceremonial greeters" embellished, in his own words, with too much makeup, both carrying bouquets of delicate pink sweet peas and magenta-colored larkspur.

The flowers inside the car bobbed in stark contrast to the day workers in dark, loose clothing outside. They pedaled bicycles and rode motorcycles alongside military vehicles and young men—boys, really—who walked with Soviet rifles slung across their slim shoulders. The car lurched past the wasted industrial zone, pockmarked by craters and the ragged teeth of warehouses and factories destroyed by Operation Rolling Thunder, the American bombing campaign. Ashmore attempted to make conversation with the young women by drawing comparisons to his own college-aged daughter. When he ventured into realms doctrinaire, one of the greeters launched into a tirade about the "capitalist warmongers."

Once the party reached the airport and the designated International Control Commission area, the two men said quick farewells. After stops in Laos and Cambodia on a rickety aircraft, they flew to Tokyo, where Baggs called Howard Kleinberg, the *Miami News'* managing editor. Half a world away, Kleinberg was still asleep.[2]

He asked Baggs about Hanoi, but all the editor wanted to talk about was King. "He had been shattered by the news," Kleinberg recalled two decades later.

Baggs ordered Kleinberg to meet him at the Jefferson Hotel in Washington, D.C., the following night, April 5, to collect the film and articles Baggs had produced in Vietnam.

Kleinberg balked. "I don't know whether you know it or not, but Washington is on fire."

"If I can go through American air raids on Hanoi and then fly to Washington," Baggs barked, "you can pick your ass out of your cushy chair in Miami and meet me there."

Kleinberg arrived in the nation's capital not long after Baggs's own flight had touched down. Baggs handed over the unprocessed Russian film cartridges and the raw copy he had pecked out on a portable typewriter, marked up with handwritten edits.

The two men stood on the balcony overlooking a city still smoldering from the riots, the pain and protest of lost hope among D.C.'s Black residents.

"My god, Brat," Baggs said, exhausted. "What has happened to this country? Are we all animals?"[3]

Kleinberg, thirty-six and nearly a decade younger than Baggs, offered only silence. With the sun setting, he still needed to get past the barricades and roadblocks to make it to the airport and meet the afternoon paper's deadline.

Baggs called in a favor from Senator J. William Fulbright, who sent a car to ferry Kleinberg to Baltimore just in time for the flight.[4] Baggs stayed up the rest of the night preparing for the long and inevitable State Department briefings to come. As he took a drag from one of the dank and foul-smelling Erik cigars he smoked unceasingly, Baggs wondered if he was entering a more hostile war zone than the one he had just left.[5]

PART I

From Colquitt to Miami

CHAPTER 1

1923–1936

Your Highness and gentlemen, I can tell you one thing—we're a long way from
Colquitt, Georgia.—To a group of dignitaries, Paris, 1967

It's hard to know whether William Calhoun Baggs would have bumped
elbows with world leaders and marquee names as a newspaper editor had
his father lived. Chances are strong that he would have inherited the family business, a chain of Ford dealerships—some of the first in Georgia. Or
he might have gone on to the Ivy League and become a statesman. But
fate wrote a wry twist into the story, as Baggs often did in his newspaper columns. Less than three weeks following his birth on September 30,
1923, Baggs's father, Crawford Collins "C. C." Baggs, a prominent Atlanta
businessman and city alderman being groomed to run for mayor, died
of spontaneous peritonitis—the result of either an intestinal blockage, as
was written on the death certificate, or "poisoned whiskey," as Baggs would
later claim.[1]

Attendees of C. C.'s funeral read like a veritable *Who's Who* of Atlanta
society—current and past Georgia governors, judges, and members of
the prestigious Capital City Club. He was buried at Westview Cemetery,
the largest memorial park in the Southeast at the time and the final resting place for the area's most notable individuals, among them Henry W.
Grady, the pro-industrial and racist "New South" editor of the *Atlanta
Constitution*, and Joel Chandler Harris, journalist and curator-author of
the Uncle Remus folktales.[2]

With three children to care for, Baggs's mother, Kate Bush Baggs, could
have returned to her hometown of Colquitt, Georgia, a small agricultural
community in Miller County near the Alabama border. There, she would
have been surrounded and supported by a large extended family. But Kate,
it seems, was not a conventional woman.

Instead, she remained in the Virginia Highlands neighborhood of Atlanta (not far from author Margaret Mitchell's home) where she had lived for the past seven years. There, her three children—eldest son Charles Crawford, age ten, daughter Billie, age three, and newborn Calhoun, as he was called throughout childhood—could receive a stellar education and the cultural influences of a burgeoning, cosmopolitan city, such as museums, libraries, and the theater. With financial support from C. C.'s successful business ventures, Kate, college educated, found work as a clerk at the gold-domed state capitol so that she could provide for her brood and stay connected to the life to which she had grown accustomed.[3]

Still, all of her planning and striving to raise her children outside of the limited prospects of rural southwest Georgia, which was steeped still in the morass of the Depression, ended when Kate died from a sudden heart attack in January 1936. She was forty-seven years old.[4]

Charles Crawford, by then age twenty-two, worked as an auto mechanic and pilot in Alabama. Sister Billie remained in Atlanta, where she enrolled in boarding school to finish her junior and senior years of high school. Baggs, just twelve years old, was placed into the guardianship of the family attorney, Judge Alex W. Stephens (great-nephew of Confederate vice president Alexander H. Stephens), and sent to live with his mother's two younger sisters in her hometown.[5] As Baggs would later say, "Colquitt could not have been more different and still be in the same state as Atlanta."[6]

Baggs's lineage ran deep in these parts. He was a descendent of Isaac Bush, who founded Colquitt and designed its layout, including the quaint town square that was designated a historic landmark district in 1983.[7] His grandfather, Charles Callaway Bush, was the town's judge off and on for more than thirty years. His grandmother, Alice "Cappie" Calhoun Bush, was a distant relative of John C. Calhoun, the ardent defender of slavery from South Carolina and vice president to Andrew Jackson. Cappie was a pillar of Colquitt Methodist Church, which put the family, in her estimation, a touch above the Baptists in town.

Colquitt remains today the only incorporated area of Miller County and harbors one-third of the county's six thousand residents—which is nearly three thousand fewer people now than when Baggs first called it home in the winter of 1936. Bushels of peanuts, soybeans, cotton, and corn still spring from the verdant fields that sprawl far and wide in all directions along U.S. 27 and State Road 91. More than half of the nation's peanuts, mainly runners, are harvested in the state of Georgia, and of that, Miller County is responsible for one-fifth of the total haul.

Were it not for the vision of the Colquitt/Miller County Arts Council, however, the city might have died out years ago. One of its hallmarks is *Swamp Gravy*, a semiannual folk-life play based on the oral histories of longtime white and Black community members.[8] Another is the Millennium Mural Project, a series of ten murals throughout the town center that illustrate its history, economy, and people. Inside Cotton Hall, an early New Deal–era warehouse, folk artist Henry Lee Gorham captured a Depression-era scene of a busy Saturday morning along a stretch of East Main Street in front of the hall, right around the time when Baggs would have had the run of the place. The mural depicts Blacks and whites going about their business side-by-side at the post office, the old Pruitt Grocery, the barber shop, and Nug's Café, which was run by a large Black woman named Johnnie Mae who served up southern comfort foods by day and ran a juke joint at night.[9] It's an idyllic scene for a small town in the Jim Crow South.

Around the block from Cotton Hall on Pine Street, Baggs settled into the home of his aunt and uncle, Grace Bush Dancer and W. R. Dancer. Their young daughter Alice Jane lived there, too, as did Grace's older sister, "Sis Charlie." Baggs's grandparents, Charles and Cappie Bush, had wanted a boy so badly, they named their middle daughter Charlie—and she lived up to the masculine moniker, wearing Army boots, smoking cigarettes, driving fast, and packing a pistol when necessary. She was a teacher at the local high school and never married. According to grand-nephew William Beers, who wrote a brief recollection of his Colquitt relatives for family, Grace was on the other end of the spectrum. She prized her girlish figure, worried about her standing within the community, was prone to exaggerated emotions, and often fell victim to "the vapors."[10]

The Dancer house stood out from the rest of the neighborhood. W. R. had painted the ramshackle one-story on brick piers an olive-drab shade amid a sea of whitewashed houses. The paint came cheap, he later admitted to his nephew William. Indoor plumbing had been a relatively recent add-on to the high-ceilinged antebellum abode, and the additions stuck out on either side like oversized knobs. The backyard pecan orchard served as a second income for the family, necessary for trying to make ends meet in the middle of the Depression. Within the grove's confines stood an old cabin, purportedly former slaves' quarters, filled with odds and ends that

Baggs, and later his nephews, would rummage through. Among their finds were rough-hewn furniture, an ancient spinning wheel, and a flintlock rifle.

W. R., whom Baggs would affectionately call "Pa" in time, ran a mobile lumber mill from a trailer outfitted with equipment that he could move from leased property to leased property to cut down pine trees, plane the wood, and sell off the pulp to the paper mills. Steeped in this milieu, Baggs carried with him a lifelong love for the scent of freshly cut wood and the velvety feel of newsprint.

When Georgia summers grew hotter than the hinges on the gates of hell, Pa would take to stripping down and lying in a cast-iron tub. His clients and contingent of Black and white workers—all men—seemed to have no qualms talking leases and dollar figures with him as he reclined buck naked in the bathroom.

Grace and Sis Charlie were kind, smart, and witty, but there were certain nonnegotiable rules by which the Bushes and Dancers were expected to live.

They came from "good families," and good families went to church every Sunday, preferably a Methodist one. People of "good breeding came from old families established in the ways of refined southern living." Considering that their lineage extended for more than three hundred years across South Carolina, Georgia, and Florida, the Bushes and Dancers and Baggses (who hailed from nearby Camilla) certainly could be considered "old" South—even if their bank accounts reflected reduced circumstances. Refinement meant you were "proud, but not boastful." You always dressed appropriately—never in the denims of manual laborers—and you spoke with precise diction. According to Grace, a good southern soul was not allowed to drop his *g*'s. Sis Charlie rarely allowed a split infinitive or double negative, and the use of the word "nigger" sent you to the sink to have your mouth washed out with "the foulest soap imaginable," though the word slipped from adults' lips from time to time in a spasm of anger or in the shock of humor.[11]

Baggs obliged on all accounts.

When Baggs entered Colquitt Elementary School, there existed a class distinction between city kids, like him, and those who lived in the country. A fellow student of his, Laverne Kimbrel Shaw, now ninety-three, recalls that Baggs launched a school newspaper during his first year in town. He sold once-a-month subscriptions to the *CES Flashes* for ten cents. This was a lot of money for children during the Depression, Shaw says, but they scooped the brief up anyhow. On four to five sheets of mimeographed paper, printed front and back, Baggs gathered gossip, reported the latest news and information about sports and clubs, and listed the names of honor-roll students. When he advanced, he served as the editor of the *Milcohi Spectator*, the monthly student newspaper of Miller County High School, which covered eighth through eleventh grade. (According to Shaw, twelfth grade was not added until the 1950s.)[12] There, he tried his hand at "political cartooning," according to his application for the United States Army Air Force.

By all accounts, Baggs excelled at just about anything he tried. When he missed nearly a year from school because of whooping cough and a case of the mumps, he maintained his grades and read so many books that he developed an affinity for self-education. Every year of high school he made honor roll, and he lettered in tennis, basketball, and six-man football, playing an integral part on the 1940–42 team.[13] He served as secretary for the senior class, president of the Spanish and Beta clubs, and captain of the Schoolboy Patrol Group.[14]

"He was an outstanding kid," says Shaw.

Baggs's seemingly boundless energy, wide-ranging intellectual curiosity, and affability hint at a preternatural drive for achievement. Yet he very well could have been motivated by something deeper, something unnamed, like an internal clock that propelled him to pack in as much life in as few years as possible. Or perhaps he possessed the fearlessness often experienced by people who have already lost everything.[15]

CHAPTER 2

1936–1939

If you wish to know the truth, and I would gather that you do, the only man I am emulating is my grandfather, now a dead man but one who lived a long and vigorous life, and whose motto to me was: When you get out of bed in the morning, get down on your knees and pray, but in the kind of world we live in, after you have finished the prayer, you had better come off those knees hustling. —To G. S. P. Holland, December 30, 1957

Baggs's awakening to matters of race in the Jim Crow era began early during childhood when his mother, just two generations removed from the Civil War, tried to explain why there were "colored" and "whites-only" water fountains. When he moved to Colquitt, the separate-but-equal doctrine that ruled southern society by custom and law was even more apparent. His own family history was complicated, enmeshed as it was with the founding of the Confederacy. The middle name "Calhoun" by which he was called was handed down like an inheritance from the Lost Cause. Throughout the city cemetery, long-dead uncles and cousins twice-removed lay beneath markers embossed with the Stars and Bars. Sis Charlie would tell Baggs that "slavery, of course, was horrible," yet she still revered a southern "gentility and civility" that few Blacks were ever shown.[1] Instead, like elsewhere in the South, Blacks were constantly reminded of their otherness.

Baggs grew up with a fondness for many of the town's Black citizens, however, a respect that remained with him throughout his life. He developed a deep work ethic by helping Pa's crew chop stumps for the lumber mill, and he picked cotton for a penny a pound when he wasn't in school.[2] He met an elderly Black man named Alec who had been born into slavery and was a child laborer when word "drained slowly down into the South" that he was freed. Baggs held the elderly man, in his late eighties by then, in high regard. Alec's hard-earned and practical wisdom ennobled him. "He could tell a boy in October if the winter was going to be long and severe. On the banks of the creek, he could make an awful noise and 'call up' an alligator."

Even as a young boy, though, Baggs recognized that Alec's life had been marked by the limitations of crushing poverty and illiteracy imposed on him because of his skin color. The memory of Alec's indelible sadness never left Baggs.[3]

Like many white families of the period, the Dancer-Bush household ran smoothly because of the help. Miss Jean was the family's cook. Baggs adored her and her homemade breads slathered with freshly churned butter and mayhaw jelly.[4] Her turnip greens were the high-water mark by which all greens would be measured the entirety of his life. In fact, he longed for the comfort of them in tough times and corrected the way others prepared theirs when they did not meet Miss Jean's soupiness.[5] He and his cousins, and later his nephews, were fascinated by Miss Jean's daily habit of chewing on a long kitchen match until it turned into a soft, splintered brush for rubbing snuff on her gums. There, also, "a tall, gentle black man, who everyone called Boll Weevil," worked odd jobs for Pa when the sawmill sat dormant. Baggs often was found in his company, following him around, peppering him with questions.[6]

Although Pa paid decent wages and would bail out any of his crew if they got in trouble for public drunkenness, Aunt Grace saw no Christian hypocrisy in the fact that the shanties provided at a low rent for Pa's Black employees, which her nephews dubbed "Aunt Grace Estates," had no running water or electricity.

"She pointed out that the roofs didn't leak and there was glass in most of the windows," her great-nephew William Beers later wrote. She also was proud that the general store for the Black citizens in town had goods that were "every bit as high quality as the goods available in the stores that served whites," never once questioning why the stores were separate in the first place.[7]

That Black children did not attend the same schools or churches that Baggs did was evidence enough that their lives were far different from his own. There also were the rumors, stories passed around by Baggs's classmates, of hangings down by the creek and across the county line.[8]

All across America, but particularly so in Mississippi, Georgia, and other southern states, a rise in racial terror and killings grew in direct proportion to the economic, political, and social gains of Black citizens. It was not uncommon for the murder or disappearance of a Black person to go unreported or undocumented by newspapers, the police, and the courts, because the authorities or their proxies, the white businessmen and land owners, community and church leaders—folks they saw and worked with daily—were also the perpetrators. Sometimes sheriffs were overwhelmed by angry mobs and did not stand in their way. Sometimes they were complicit. Rarely would law enforcement investigate and prosecute mob members, and if they did, the accused were rarely convicted in the courts by juries of their peers. The daily fear experienced by Blacks often resulted in their silence and acquiescence.[9]

When Baggs was sixteen and already writing about high school sports for the local newspaper, the *Miller County Liberal* prominently featured an extract from a speech Congressman E. E. Cox delivered on the floor of the U.S. House of Representatives, which had just passed anti-lynching legislation. The congressman, a former circuit judge who represented Miller County from Georgia's 2nd District for almost thirty years, said that as long as Negroes "maintained their proper relationship and performed their rightful functions in the South," then this law would be unnecessary. He went on to recount and defend the extralegal execution of a Black man in a neighboring county, who had been accused of killing a young white girl but was never tried or convicted in a court of law.

"Lynching is not a cause, it is an effect," Congressman Cox continued. "It will disappear entirely when the cause for it disappears."[10]

The anti-lynching bill Congressman Cox opposed later died in the U.S. Senate, the same fate as nearly two hundred similar bills introduced between the end of the Civil War and the beginning of the 1970s.[11] (The U.S. Senate finally passed the Justice for Victims of Lynching Act in early 2019. As of this writing, the bill still has not passed the U.S. House of Representatives and lynching still is not recognized as a federal hate crime.)

According to family members, at some point during the formative years between 1936 and 1941 when Baggs lived with his mother's kin in Colquitt, he witnessed scenes of injustice and terror that would forever reframe his sense of humanity. The details of these indelible moments are few, for Baggs did not talk or write much about his childhood and told only a few members of his family bits and pieces.

Before his death in 2013, Robert Beers, one of Baggs's nephews who followed him into journalism, began writing a biography of his uncle. In it, Beers tells of a heart-racing moment that took place one afternoon after football practice when Baggs was around the age of fourteen or fifteen. The following is based on his account.

Baggs had taken the long way home so he could dip into the grocer's and get a bottle of RC Cola. From the direction of the courthouse, he heard a man scream, "Somebody, please help me!" Baggs turned and walked closer, to see a Black man with his head up against the iron bars of the second-floor holding cell.

"They going to kill me," the man cried again.

From all corners of the square, the roar of car engines bounced off the buildings. Two cars came from the west and two more from the east, shot-guns extended out of their windows. The cars circled the courthouse and parked, and three men emerged and marched into the building. One wore a suit and tie, another had his jacket off, the third wore bib overalls. More men stepped out of the cars and looked around. One focused on Baggs.

"Go home, boy," the man warned. "This ain't got nothing to do with you."

Baggs disappeared from view, but he could still see the scene of a Black man fighting as he was dragged from the courthouse. The men threw him into the back of a dark-blue Chevrolet and the caravan of cars sped out of town. When Baggs arrived home, he asked his aunts and uncle whether they knew why the man was in jail and what was going to happen to him. They advised that he had best forget what he saw. Two days later, he over-heard a fellow student talk about a lynching out on Dothan Road, just over the Early County line. Without an obituary or a report to go on, Baggs never knew if it was the same man he had seen taken from the courthouse.[12]

Later, to his wife and sons, Baggs confided that he had witnessed the lynching of a young Black man whom he knew and considered a friend. Again, he offered them few details, whether to protect them or himself from the memory, but they recognized that it was one of the most signifi-cant turning points in his young life. The murderers wore robes and hoods and did not see Baggs, but he saw them, and one man in particular who had removed his mask.

A Sunday following, Baggs sat at the end of the family pew at Colquitt Methodist Church, as was expected. When he looked up to take the of-fering plate, he recognized the man from the lynching mob. In that mo-ment, Baggs's easygoing obedience turned to doubt. The pleasing young man he had been questioned everything, especially authority, from then on. In that moment he lost some measure of faith, even as he clung fast to his humanity.

CHAPTER 3

1939–1943

He was, maybe, 40 years of age, but he was old. In rural Panama, in the years before World War II, the land he worked was obstinate, and he had to claw it hard to make it yield enough for a family of ten.—"Life's Purpose," *Miami News*, November 23, 1963

With brother Charles Crawford a full decade older and overseas training pilots for the Polish Air Forces, Baggs grew close to his sister Billie, who spent her summers and holidays off from Brenau University in Colquitt.[1] In February 1939 she became engaged to a Georgia Tech graduate named William Howard Beers from Birmingham, Alabama, who had accepted a position with the U.S. Army Corps of Engineers in the Panama Canal Zone—an exotic locale that sounded as far from the flat Georgia plains as one could get.

The couple married on June 7 at Colquitt Methodist Church, with Pa giving away the bride and Aunt Grace serving as the matron of honor. Alice Jane sang "I Love You Truly," while Baggs ushered guests to their seats.[2] The newly minted Beerses honeymooned at the 1939 New York "World of Tomorrow" World's Fair, where their future shone as brightly as the inventions—among them, the first automatic dishwasher and a seven-foot-tall robot by Westinghouse, General Motors' concept for the interstate highway system, DuPont's clingy cellophane, and the first mass-market television broadcast in the RCA pavilion.[3]

Two years later, in May 1941, the couple returned to the States for an extended three-month vacation that coincided with Baggs's graduation from Miller County High School. Elected by his forty-seven other classmates, Baggs delivered the valedictory address during the May 29 ceremony. Delivered as the tremors of a world war grew ever stronger, he spoke of the challenge of life ahead of them.

We, the youth of America, must give our all to meet the eventualities that this crisis may offer. How can we do it? . . . First, education. This is essential in the development of a vigorous country. . . .

The second and probably the most important factor in the building of power is cooperation. . . . Without it, we cannot have a great and respected national defense, and without this we cannot defend our land, where men are born equal, and their success depends upon their later actions and achievements.[4]

Baggs's speech about American ideals and patriotism contrasted with his own post–high school plans. He declined an appointment (by Congressman E. E. Cox, the voice of anti-anti-lynching) to the U.S. Naval Academy. And his staunch defense of literacy and knowledge belied his choice to postpone, possibly permanently, university. He opted instead for adventure and experience. He kicked off Colquitt's cloying clay, packed the few clothes and prized books he owned along with a couple of glowing reference letters from the school superintendent and principal, then traveled with his sister and brother-in-law to New York City, where they hopped the USS *Ancon* and set sail for Cristobal, Panama Canal Zone.[5]

In what would become a defining theme of Baggs's life, he arrived on the scene—this time in Panama—at an opportune moment. The U.S. government viewed the tropical isthmus of Panama as the most important strategic outpost in Latin America. Within the zone territory, which measured only ten miles wide and fifty miles long, the United States had invested more than $500 million (nearly $9 billion in 2019 dollars) to support canal construction and other public works, as well as agricultural, banking, and commercial development. The military investments, including airfields and warning stations, allowed "a one-ocean Navy to fight in two oceans," according to a brief, uncredited article in the March 17, 1941, issue of *Life* magazine. Not only did work in the Canal Zone test America's industrial ingenuity, it aided the country's emergence from the Great Depression on the cusp of the United States' growing role in the Allied war effort, which was much more apparent in this small stretch of paradise than it ever was on the U.S. mainland. With naval ships in the ports and antiaircraft stations, radio communication centers, and airstrips springing up in the surrounding jungle, the threat of battle hung heavy on the humid, salty breezes.

Once the Beerses settled back into the steamy enclave of Diablo Heights, near Balboa on the southernmost end of the Canal Zone, Baggs began working as a file clerk at the U.S. Navy supply depot, then as a purchasing agent and a stevedore. He took side trips to neighboring Costa Rica and across the Caribbean Sea to Haiti. After a long day's labor, he used his earnings to pay for a smattering of classes in history, economics, political science, and literature. He devoured books—two or three a week—practiced conversational Spanish, and read as many different newspapers as he could get his hands on, reminiscent of the year in grammar school he spent laid up in bed. The Canal Zone was a true confluence of multiculturalism, where Latin American, North American, and Asian influences melded. It would be the ideal proving ground for Baggs's future in Miami.

Among the emigrants lived the *Nikkei*—the nearly four hundred Japanese nationals who resided between Colon in the north and Panama City in the south. As tensions between the United States and imperial Japan rose in the Pacific, the Nikkei came under increasing suspicion. The U.S. government had stopped allowing Japanese freighters through the canal in July 1941. U.S. Army personnel boarded fishing boats on a regular basis for impromptu inspections. By September 1941, the government of Panama had suspended all trading with Japanese shopkeepers and shippers.[6]

On a sunny Sunday afternoon, December 7, 1941, Baggs was with his sister and brother-in-law in front of the big radio in the living room when CBS announcer John Charles Daly broke into the news program: "The Japanese have attacked Pearl Harbor, Hawaii, by air, President Roosevelt has just announced. The attack also was made on all naval and military activities on the principal island of Ohau [*sic*]. We take you now to Washington."[7]

Rattled by the attack and swept up in the passion of the moment, Baggs and some friends raced toward Balboa's Japanese district, situated just outside of the protected Canal Zone. There, they harassed, punched, and kicked the Japanese men who crossed their path, bloodying a few noses, even as Panamanian police arrived to round up anyone of Japanese heritage for internment on nearby Taboga Island and at a military camp that already held German and Italian prisoners of war. Within the next few days, as the wounded from Pearl Harbor began to arrive for treatment at Gorgas Hospital, the majority of Japanese were behind barbed wire.

Baggs, who was shocked by how quickly and violently the prejudices he despised in rural Georgia so clearly overtook him in Panama, regretted his reaction for the rest of his life. Many years later, Baggs confided to his nephew Robert Beers that "it was a sneak attack and we were young and foolish and felt it was a way to make some type of crazed statement."

Like the other men around him, the just barely eighteen-year-old Baggs was gung-ho to sign up because he felt it was his duty as an American. His older brother Charles was, by then, a flight sergeant serving in England. Baggs wanted to be right there beside him.[8]

He applied for the U.S. Army Air Forces and continued to work, by then as a copy boy with the *Panama Star and Herald*. The nearly hundred-year-old English and Spanish broadsheet was helmed by a dedicated and long-serving editor by the name of Albert McGeachy, who penned a daily column and lived by the paper's motto, "open to all, controlled by none."[9] Here, Baggs got his first real taste of newsroom reporting right in the heart of conflict. He did whatever McGeachy and the senior reporters asked of him, separating carbons, setting type, fetching copy, and transcribing Associated Press cables from New York, sometimes translating them into Spanish. McGeachy called him "Little Genius" and eventually assigned Baggs to write local-interest stories and entertainment reviews—lightweight, feel-good stories while the war raged.[10]

By September 1942, Baggs's application to the U.S. Army Air Forces was accepted. He was nineteen, and his sister and brother-in-law finally agreed to sign off as his guardians. On March 10, 1943, after passing his physical and mental fitness exams, he was winging his way to Howard Field in Nashville, Tennessee, for basic training with the hope of earning his wings.

CHAPTER 4

1943–1944

> You just lie up in the nose of the Monster and wonder why men fight up here where it is so peaceful. There forms a heavy layer of clouds beneath now, cutting out view to the ground. It shuts you off from earth and in those moments, you feel nearer the firmament of heaven. . . . I rarely even think of turnips—that's how it is.—To Anne Nichols, July 16, 1944

Cadet William C. Baggs, or "Bill," as he was now called—the military having dispensed with Calhoun in favor of his given first name—measured a skosh over 6'1" tall and barely weighed 170 pounds when he arrived in Nashville. A deviated septum discovered through the standard physical seemed to explain the sinus headaches he had endured (and which would pester him throughout his life), but those didn't hold him back. He had designs on flying his own plane, just like his big brother. He just had to get through basic first.

With the emphasis on physical and field training, he reduced the unfiltered cigarettes—"gaspers," he called them—that he had started smoking in Panama. He also had to moderate his growing fondness for whiskey, another indulgence procured in the rough and tumble of the Canal Zone. Poker, on the other hand, was entirely permissible, and he was good at it. He proved even more adept at filling his dance card at the USO, where he met a young woman named Anne Nichols, to whom he would write throughout the war.[1] After a successful eight weeks with the 526th Army Air Forces Base Unit, Baggs received orders to report for preflight school at Ellington Field, set on the fertile coastal prairie near Houston, Texas.

The eager student soared to the rank of group commander at Ellington. According to his final grade sheet, reported on June 21, 1943, Baggs excelled in communication, interpretation, and recognition exercises—the more strategic tasks—and was a solid B in math and physics.[2] After a battery of "written and psychomotor skills screening tests" to determine crew position, Cadet Major Baggs exhibited the fine hand-eye coordination and steely resolve the U.S. Army Air Forces desperately sought in a "new breed" of aviator, the bombardier—and the USAAF needed tens of thousands of them.[3] Baggs would not be in the pilot's seat, but he would be close, encased in the glassed-in nose of the plane.

After Ellington, Baggs made a six-week detour to Laredo, on the U.S.-Mexico border, for instruction on how to assemble, disassemble, and operate a .50-caliber aerial machine gun while flying in a B-17 Flying Fortress. Then he was on to the arid, oil-rich plains of West Texas at Midland Army Air Field for eighteen weeks' immersion in the new curriculum for bombardiers, whose crew position was to master the technical choreography required to drop bombs on targets big and small while the plane flew 265 miles per hour.[4]

Ground school comprised the first ten weeks of training and involved daily exams on the theoretical and practical aspects of bombing, which was a relatively new and evolving science spurred by the military's belief that the practice was more precise with the latest in bombsight technology and, therefore, would result in fewer civilian casualties. Baggs studied maps (pilotage) and aerial photography to understand how to identify strategic military targets. He and his fellow cadets learned how to dead-reckon their positions and worked on becoming proficient in operating both the Sperry s-1 and Norden M-Series bombsights—although the Norden, declared so accurate that bombardiers could "drop a bomb into a pickle barrel from 20,000 feet"—was the preferred instrument of destruction.[5]

According to its operating manual, two units made up the Norden, a stabilizer with a balanced gyroscope and a sight head with telescope and analog computer. Together, the components weighed nearly seventy-five pounds. To operate it involved a complicated sequence of flipping switches, turning knobs, pulling clutches, calibrating crosshairs to site the target, evaluating wind and plane speeds, assessing altitude and weather impacts—all the latter being information that Baggs and his fellow bombardiers then fed into an analog computer that triggered an autopilot mechanism to lead the plane over rail yards and factories, presumably dropping bomb loads at just the right angle and moment for maximum disruption of the Axis war effort. In battle, the sights were set to automatically self-destruct through an incendiary device should crews have to ditch their aircraft. Use of the top-secret Norden required Baggs to take a second oath to never divulge to anyone how the sight worked, even though it was later learned that the Germans already had access to this technology.[6]

While buckling down in ground school to avoid "washing out," like a good number of his classmates did, the journalist in Baggs was revived. He assumed the editor's position of the "Bombs Away, 44-1" yearbook, overseeing a staff of ten cadets working as photographers, reporters, and cartoonists. The yearbook extolled the promise of bombardier technology as "a most modern tool of offense." Within the yearbook's pages, the staff paid homage to cadet life on base, from pickup basketball games and the mess hall to a goodwill tour by singer-actress Dale Evans.[7] It was a life Baggs took full advantage of, filling every moment as if he had no time to waste. Between editing, training, and carousing at the Midland Country Club, where Baggs hustled several officers and a few oil-and-gas men out of folding money, he subsisted on a diet of black coffee, bourbon, and Camels, and stayed up well past lights-out to write short stories that he hoped to turn into a novel one day.[8]

In the "Hell from Heaven" detachment at Midland, away from the cultural confines and familial expectations of Colquitt and Panama, Baggs settled into the persona that would come to characterize him as he grew further into adulthood. He made friends easily and relished meeting people from across the geographic, religious, ethnic, and economic divides. Well read and deeply rooted, he could gab with the guys on the ground crew as well as the men with stars and bars on their shoulders. Yet he grew out of the agreeable persona of his youth, during which his high school principal described him as "very cooperative, ingenious, and endeavor[ing], at all times, to please his supervisors." Instead, Baggs balanced the charming attributes of good humor, dependability, and street smarts with the brash mischievousness of a court jester. He played the latter most earnestly when he sought either to entertain his peers with a great story—usually embellished for a bit more flavor—or to take the air out of someone's bloated arrogance, especially a college boy's, a desk jockey's, or his own.

One oft-shared anecdote: Whether fueled by tequila or the desire to test the limits of the military regulations that had begun to chafe against his penchant for both challenging questions and practical jokes, Baggs once swam across the Rio Grande River into Mexico to buy an authentic sombrero. Ranked a cadet colonel at the time, he wore the ornate wide-brimmed shade-maker while leading a battalion for review. In return, he was grounded for two weeks and placed on guard duty.[9]

In early December 1943, during the eight weeks that followed ground school, Baggs put in more than 120 hours flying both day and night and practicing bomb runs under various conditions and at different heights to improve his accuracy. However, no amount of rehearsal could recreate the conditions of hundreds of planes flying in formation over dense cloud cover with black puffs of flak erupting nearby, or of fighting against an aerial assault of German Me 109s (officially, the Messerschmitt Bf 109) with machine guns blazing. Yet as practical information was gathered daily from the front and aircraft designs were updated at assembly plants, the cadets' training regimen was adapted to prepare them as much as possible for the realities of battle.

At Midland, Baggs trained on an early version of the Consolidated B-24 Liberator, the U.S. Army Air Forces' latest weapon in the Mediterranean and Pacific theaters. A chunky four-engine behemoth with an inimitable twin-tail design, the "Lib" flew faster and further and carried heavier bomb loads than its sleeker, slightly older sister, the Boeing B-17—the paragon of the Mighty Eighth Air Force. The B-24 became the backbone of the Fifteenth Air Force, which had not even been founded when Baggs arrived in Midland that summer but would trouble the Axis powers by the following spring when Baggs shipped out to Venosa, Italy.[10]

CHAPTER 5

1944

One thing is a certainty—war must be stopped. Our posterity must not so suffer. Insofar as I can see—there is only one good forthcoming from this conflict: a fuller appreciation of peace.—To Anne Nichols, July 28, 1944

In October 1943, British forces captured the Foggia plain, a strategically desirable agricultural area in the spur of Italy's boot. With existing airstrips and plateaus conducive to adaptive reuse, the Foggia Air Complex allowed Allied forces to expand the Mediterranean theater of operations beyond North Africa, where German and Italian forces had surrendered earlier that year.

The United States formed the Fifteenth Air Force in November with the clear purpose of engaging the Germans on multiple southern fronts and drawing the Luftwaffe away from England and France. This vantage point gave the United States and Great Britain much easier access to German support systems, such as railroads and marshalling yards, oil refineries, and manufacturing plants scattered across the Balkans and Eastern Europe. With German attentions dispersed and reserves diminished, the Allied invasion at Normandy, France, would have a greater chance for success.

As the Fifteenth geared up for operations that fall and winter, Second Lieutenant William C. Baggs graduated from bombardier school in January 1944. He then chalked up more air time in advanced training at Westover Field, Massachusetts, where he was assigned to Captain Herman G. Davis's ten-man Liberator crew. While they awaited overseas orders, the Davis crew flew anti-submarine patrols along the eastern seaboard of the United States. They finally received their orders on May 26, 1944. Transferred to the 485th Heavy Bombardment Group, the crew was bound for Venosa, an ancient village along the Appian Way that served as a critical garrison for the Roman Empire and where the lyrical poet Horace was born. Baggs and crew were the first replacements for the 830th Squadron, which had flown its first mission only two weeks before.[1]

The temporary base where they were stationed sat five miles outside of the village, where the stone Aragonese Castle, built by a line of the powerful Orsini family during the 1400s, rose like a swan out of the horizon. The Church of the Santissima Trinità (Church of the Holy Trinity) welcomed the few hundred remaining villagers, many of them elderly or children, who were, by this time, impoverished and starving because the war had stripped them of their livelihoods. Venosians would cut the airmen's hair for fifty cents, and wash and mend uniforms for whatever the Americans could spare. Sometimes the local women offered their bodies because it was the only currency they had left.[2]

The bomb group's headquarters were set up in an old farmhouse on the edge of the camp. Two neat rows of tents housed each of the four squadrons assigned to the 485th, with enlisted men to one side and commissioned officers like Baggs on the other. At the far end of the tents, cooks in the mess hall served up powdered eggs and milk, Spam dipped in pancake batter, then fried, and a dish of chipped beef on toast called "shit on a shingle." Hot coffee was readily available, and on scorching summer days relief was ladled from fifty-gallon drums filled with iced tea.

The men dug trenches for latrines and crafted makeshift lavatories from wooden planks. Their helmets served as sinks. Officers and enlisted men all slept on folding canvas cots with wool blankets. The floors were dirt, which mucked up their boots on rainy days, and the only light at night shined from a single bulb that hung from the center of each tent.[3]

Despite all the good-natured trash talk between the Eighth and the Fifteenth about whose conditions were better (the Eighth's) as well as who was braver—the boys in the sky or the ones on the ground—there was little glamor found in the practice of war. Other than letters from home, one of the few perks arrived every two weeks in the form of rations of chocolate bars, cartons of cigarettes, cans of beer, and sticks of gum, the final staple a necessity to keep ears clear in the unpressurized cabins of the B-24s.[4]

If Baggs were flying that day, one of the commanders would wake him at 3:30 a.m., followed by breakfast and assembly. There, commanders briefed the crews on the details of the day's targets, including the route, the weather forecast, fighter positions, and flak potential. Once leads and coleads were assigned, the chaplain offered a blessing.

No matter the weather on the ground, Baggs and crew suited up as if they were trekking to the North Pole: wire-heated coveralls and "booties," fleece-lined leather bomber jacket and flying pants, sheepskin boots, flak jacket, helmet, goggles, and an oxygen mask. Even though they resembled spacemen, they at least were protected from extreme conditions once they were sailing through the skies. At twenty thousand feet, the temperature could drop to seventy degrees below zero. Frostbite was just one of their concerns. They carried their parachutes separately, because the bulk could catch as they crawled into their positions in the nose and the gun turrets.[5]

To calm their nerves before a mission, the flyboys often smoked around the planes as they were prepping for flight. B-24s were notorious for emitting gas fumes and a few planes were lost in the early days because of carelessness. But once the payloads were installed by the ground crews (often done the night before) and the pilots completed their flight checks, the controllers in the wooden hut in the middle of the airfield gave the thumbs-up for takeoff. Whichever squadron was taking lead that day would line up first.

The U.S. Army Corps of Engineers laid nearly four thousand linear feet of interlocking pierced-steel planking over former wheat fields for the runway. Balanced on tricycle-like wheels, the Libs had to accelerate in short order to reach the 120 miles per hour necessary to take off uphill into a shallow valley—all while carrying thousands of pounds of demolition, fragmentation, and incendiary bombs. The plane's long, narrow, high-mounted wings helped the Libs get airborne in a hurry.

Because it was too dangerous to remain in the vulnerable glassed-in nose during takeoffs and landings, Baggs and his navigator and nose gunner would hold on for dear life, seated unbuckled on the bulkhead behind the pilots on the flight deck. As long as they and the other crew avoided unsecured gear shifting around the uninsulated fuselage, they could escape injury. Once they reached a relatively safe altitude, Baggs would crawl through a narrow tunnel underneath the flight deck and take his position in the "Monster." If he were in the lead plane, he would make the complex calculations demanded for accurate hits. If he were in the second or further back, he would wait for the lead plane to drop its load to cue him into action. Always on the crew members' minds were the possibilities up ahead: flak bursts that could leave their plane looking like a boxed cheese grater, getting shot down by a much more agile German Me 109, parachuting behind enemy lines, or a dreaded water ditching in the Adriatic Sea.

If they could not make it back to the base, they prayed for a friendly field within reach, like the one at Bari or on the island of Vis.

Within a week after arriving at Venosa, the Davis crew with Baggs as bombardier tallied mission one, a round trip to the Turin marshalling yards in the still German-occupied northern part of Italy.[6]

Crews typically flew two to three times a week. So, two days later on June 6, 1944, the Davis crew suited up again and flew in tight formation toward the Dacia Romana oil refinery in Ploesti, Romania. Ploesti alone provided nearly 30 percent of all the Axis oil supply and was protected by more than two hundred heavy flak guns. For the Allies, the industrial hub represented one of the key targets for disruption.[7] With the improved proximity of Venosa, the bombers still had to cross the Adriatic Sea, German-occupied Yugoslavia where a civil war raged, and a sliver of Bulgaria to reach Ploesti. With P-51 Mustangs and P-38 Lightning fighters as escorts, the thirty-five Libs that flew that day pushed through a fertile garden of black flak puffs blooming all around, causing their planes to bounce like spring coils. Once the crew saw the bright-red centers burst, they braced for the onslaught of metal bits flying through the sky—bits that had the capacity to rip through wings, rotors, and fuselages and bring down B-24s, which were neither well armored nor nimble enough to make defensive maneuvers within their formations.[8]

Flak riddled Baggs's plane, severing oxygen lines. Two of the crew passed out from anoxia. As Baggs readied the bomb hatch, he encountered a heavy smoke screen that made it near impossible for him to know whether or not he actually hit his target. He let the eggs go, a few thousand pounds of the more than fifty-two tons of bombs dropped that day. Then, using the tape and knife from his bombardier's toolkit, he spliced the lines together to get the oxygen flowing again to revive his two crew members. He moved them out of the nose to a safer part of the plane until they could land. For his steadiness, Baggs received the Distinguished Flying Cross.[9]

Throughout the rest of June 1944, Baggs and his crew hit a variety of targets, including the Milbertshofen ordnance depot in Munich, Germany, and the Florisdorf oil refinery in Vienna, Austria. During the June 26 attack on Florisdorf, the bombers came under aggressive attack from more than thirty-five enemy aircraft. Two crews were lost that day, among multiple casualties. The flyers, including Baggs's crew, earned a Distinguished Unit Citation.[10]

According to newspaper clippings and family lore, Baggs's crew bailed out of their Liberator over Yugoslavia on one (possibly two) bombing runs.

Even with little training in how to jump, all ten made it safely to the ground. They were recovered, according to Baggs, by Partisan forces, one of the two factions—the Chetniks were the other—willing to provide cover for Allied troops in the war-torn nation. The Partisans spirited Baggs from one farm-house to the next until he could safely make it back to base.[11]

In July 1944, the USO raised the morale of the airmen at a series of shows featuring a Middle Eastern belly dancer. The Isle of Capri opened up as a five-day rest camp. The Corps dedicated a group chapel for religious services and a new officers' club, which Baggs and the men dubbed the "Flak Shak." Pickup basketball, baseball, and poker games helped fill downtime between missions to the German submarine pens in Toulon, France, and back again to Vienna.[12] When not tossing a ball or calling a card game, Baggs could be found reading or writing letters to Anne Nichols, the young lady he had met at a USO dance during basic training. Nichols remained his steadfast "girl" throughout his time in Italy.

"If only we could get an accurate account of the past, we might better shape the future," he wrote her on July 4, 1944, after he'd flown sixteen missions. He almost always wrote with a fountain pen on stationery he had lifted from headquarters. His trademark script possessed both a Jeffersonian flourish and a hurried bit of shorthand.

He was reading a pocket-sized softcover Armed Services Edition of Walter Lippmann's *U.S. Foreign Policy: Shield of the Republic*.[13] "A thorough study if I've ever read one," he offered in review. "It is written somewhat akin to Ralph Waldo Emerson's essays—built on logic and reason, with the most highly constructed form of subtle sarcasm."

He told her about himself, more than he had had a chance to the night of the dance back in Nashville. After assuring her he had come from good breeding, he clarified his modest ambitions.

> Summed up—I am not a very intelligent boy—carry no titles and consider myself very uneducated. The only thing I have to advantage is knowing so. But I am constantly reminded I must go to college when I go home. Being free, white and just 21—I think not. Will wind up in a newspaper office. . . . I will probably never amount to much, will write a book that will never be published—essays and such. But am sure I am going to continue to be happy and contented. Just another boy from the country who wants a small newspaper in a small town, so he can write as he pleases.

He tended to keep his letters light, just giving Nichols a glimpse of life on base. On rare occasions he let slip a hint of longing. He dreamt of home at Christmastime and of walking through the woods around Colquitt. He missed turnip greens and desperately wanted a hamburger with "crushed potato chips between two griddle-browned buns . . . and a Coca-Cola, tingling in a thousand small bubbles that rise to the surface through near-liquid ice. Of course—with a juke box playing 'Imagine' by Ella Fitzgerald—#17. I can't stand it—let's talk of something else."

After a run to the Unirea Sperantza oil refinery in Ploesti on July 15, he captured the strange mixture of awe and fear he'd felt while suspended in the nose of his bomber: "It was one of the most beautiful days I have ever seen. We go up to 20 or 25 thousand and make the run. Now Ploesti has a great deal of 'clumps' and it gets pretty black. Few men say they're not bothered—but you can easily see 'lie in the eye.' So, down the run we go. Watch flak pop all around the Monster and keep wondering when those darn Me 109s are coming in."[14]

His quarters became a gathering place for the men to unwind and listen to music on his portable hand-cranked phonograph. Somewhere along the way he and the crew had adopted a mutt, which Baggs named the Mongrel, who had a habit of chewing his slippers and sleeping curled up beside him on the cot.

Through July, Baggs helped take out a bridge at the Luftschiffbau Zeppelin works in Friedrichshafen, damaged the Hermann Goering tank works in Linz, then hit Ploesti again. By July 28, 1944, he was lamenting the war's effect on the children—"Kids are blameless of war, completely innocent of it. Yet . . . they are unable to escape its fortunes."

By August, Ploesti had been reduced to less than 10 percent of its operating capacity. Romania surrendered later that month and the Red Army moved in, pushing the Third Reich further west and closer to its final days. Still, for all the successes of the Fifteenth Air Force, more than two thousand airmen lost their lives in the Mediterranean theater.

Of the eighty-six total missions flown by his unit between May and September 1944, Baggs served on thirty of them, receiving double credit for ten of those because of the length and hazard involved.[15] By the time he received his leave orders on October 10, Baggs had been promoted to first lieutenant and was awarded an Air Medal with three oak leaf clusters.[16] Once he got stateside again, he wrote Nichols, he was "planning to fill up on good coffee, white bread toast, put a handful of U.S. dirt in each pocket and head for the nearest turnip field."

CHAPTER 6

1944–1945

If we're going to have those few principles, we've got to give up quite a bit for them.... Give [our future children] a better opportunity than we had ... that's the meat and strength of World civilization—giving the next generation an easier lane to trod—if that isn't the idea, then I've missed the point again.—To Joan "Frec" Orr, May 18, 1945

Baggs's first stop back on U.S. soil was Pa and Aunt Grace's house, and the reentry proved bumpy. He was hardly the obedient and jolly boy who had left for Panama three and a half years earlier. There, he had lived among people who did not look or talk like him, and they had accepted him just the same. He had then trained and fought with men from all corners of his own country. They had saved each other's lives and some had died. He had experienced a world beyond the narrow confines of religion and southern propriety that defined the Dancer household and had learned there were just as many good and bad Catholics and atheists as there were Methodists. And he had dropped bombs that most certainly had mangled and destroyed as many people as they did machinery. War had given him muscle, sharpened his edge.

Instead of trying to please everybody, he went through the motions as Aunt Grace trotted the war hero around town. Half the people, he claimed in a letter to Nichols, he did not even remember. Some of the other half he called "odd works of nature and environment." With indignance, he wrote, "Don't give a damn if they do regard me as anti-social"—a reputation he had never been saddled with before.

Baggs spent the better part of several days lost in boxes of scrapbooks and old letters, where he found a book he had written for his mother when he was just ten years old and a tintype of her at the age of sixteen. "It has been so long ago—suppose I should forget," he seemed to sigh in print. "Don't believe any of us can very well say (with exacting truth) that we are either Realists or Romantists [*sic*]. Everyone must have a soft sentimental spot for the past."[1]

The past could not hold him for long, however. Baggs made plans to visit Nichols around Christmas, then left for Miami Beach, where thousands of flyboys were holding steady before the USAAF reassigned them to further duty. Nichols never heard from Baggs again.

When he arrived in Miami in the autumn of 1944, Baggs encountered a subtropical port city transformed by war, not unlike Panama. The former frontier town had become "a combination of Casablanca and Grand Central Station" through a series of booms and busts, up-and-down cycles resulting from the aftershocks of both hurricanes and failed schemes.[2] The narrow mainland and barrier islands between the Everglades and the Atlantic Ocean had been stitched into a crazy quilt of grand waterfront abodes and Florida cracker cottages, crowded slum areas housing immigrants from Haiti and the Bahamas, hotels, motels, and tourist traps, all interwoven with a massive military presence. The Richmond Naval Air Station housed the blimp force. The extravagant Biltmore Hotel in Coral Gables served as a hospital; the grand Royal Palm hosted the Coast Guard. Winding through the middle, the Miami River was the hub of PT boat–building and repair. Individual owners retrofitted their boats for civilian patrols on the lookout for German U-boats, which had sunk no fewer than twenty-four ships off the Florida coast. Miami Beach's hotels and clubs no longer lit up the night sky with neon, because the glow could be seen from thirty-five miles out to sea.[3]

Baggs would have witnessed a magical city in motion as he drove across the MacArthur Causeway. He most certainly would have driven past an ornate seventeen-story Mediterranean Revival tower painted the shade of a Tropicana rose, where reporters for the *Miami Daily News* churned out the afternoon's stories while overlooking Biscayne Bay. Once at the beach, he landed at the Caribbean Hotel on 37th Street and Collins Avenue along with other bachelor airmen resting and recouping before heading back into the wild blue yonder.

When his time in the sun and sand neared its end that November, Baggs attended one of many Red Cross–sponsored dances in the hotel's ballroom. On duty for the first time as a recreational assistant that night was a petite brunette named Joan (pronounced "Jo-Ann") Orr who spoke with a honeyed drawl. She noticed him first by the way he strode across the ballroom, "one foot slapping almost across the other one," then by how all the other ladies sang out "Billy" as he walked past. She also noticed that he knew them all by name. Another recreational assistant introduced her to Baggs, and once he learned that she hailed from Athens, Georgia, he asked her to dance. Although she was impressed with his footwork, she grew less so with how much he talked about himself.

"I thought him to be the most egotistical young man I had ever encountered," she said. "Later, I realized he was the loneliest."[4]

He took a breath long enough to learn that Joan had earned a degree in English from the University of Georgia and a master's degree in romance languages from Northwestern University in Illinois. She had grown up in Athens on Carr's Hill, where her father's family had lived since the 1700s and where her father Craig Orr had made a name for himself as a landscape designer noted for his penchant for ornamental plants.[5] That very evening Baggs christened Joan "Freckles," for the constellation of dots across her nose and cheeks. By the end of the evening her nickname grew even shorter. From then on, throughout her long life, Joan was called "Frec."

Despite her wary first impression, Red Cross recreational assistant Joan Orr and First Lieutenant Bill Baggs spent every possible moment together over the next twelve days, before he had to leave for Midland, Texas, for a new assignment and training. He hung around after socials and helped clean, even removing his bars when they were in the company of enlisted men. Some days he and Frec would take a drive up to Haulover Beach, where German prisoners of war were held. Often, they simply walked along the shore near 41st Street and studied the stars. By the end of those two weeks in November 1944, Baggs was talking about the house he would one day build for Frec in Panama.[6] But first, he had duties to attend to.

He hopped a B-17 to Tampa, where he spent an evening with his uncle Billy Bush, his mother's older brother and an attorney, whom he called "the Colonel." While there, he purchased a used black Mercury Eight and christened her "Lenore," after the "rare and radiant maiden" in Edgar Allen Poe's "The Raven." He filled the back seat with nearly a dozen books, mainly ones on politics, history, and philosophy, with a few satires thrown in, covered them with a claret dressing robe given to him by his uncle, and took the long way to West Texas.[7]

On the way, he paused in southern Georgia at Aunt Grace's home once again and was in a much better state of mind than a few months earlier. "Spent three hours walking through woods I ran through before. Was awfully good to get alone, entertain thoughts prompted by the infecting presence of Mother Nature." He drank eggnog with Sis Charlie and they reminisced all night.

In nearly every city along the backroads and byways to Midland, Baggs stopped for coffee and conversation with a friend. He took a detour to Anniston, Alabama, to meet his nephew, the son of the older brother he had not seen in nearly six years. He picked up hitchhikers and followed the wrong road on occasion and tried to stay sober. And he sent letters and telegrams to keep himself ever-present in Frec's thoughts, as she took returning servicemen on fishing trips to Key Biscayne when she wasn't planning cookouts, horseback riding, listening to their stories, or staffing information booths at the Easter basket of Art Deco hotels along Collins Avenue. "Have thought of you . . . and the Beach quite often and pleasantly over those many coffees since leaving. Am so very glad all are pleasantly indexed in memory."[8]

In each dispatch, he revealed a little more of himself—clues to how he navigated life. Neither West Texas nor commanding officers were high on his list of favorites, but flying, black coffee, Camels, whiskey, writing a novel or a letter, and books were worth making time for.

His general life philosophy was to "take it all with a grin," but he was restless as he awaited orders on what would come next. "Combat theater on B-29s or as an air support officer" in California, New Mexico, Massachusetts, or New York—who knew? (He eventually signed papers volunteering for combat duty.)

When the war finished, he wanted to get back to newspapering, but wondered what the future held for someone like him. "I don't fit in too well into regular, prescribed work. Rather hard to me, but there's reason behind it all and as long as I think I'm doing the right thing, to hell with the rest."[9]

That lack of appreciation for order and hierarchy finally nipped him in the behind, not one month after he returned to Midland. "Have again become too individualistic and a bit recalcitrant to Army patterns, conventions, customs, procedure and dress," Baggs confessed in a letter to Frec dated January 17, 1945. He readily admitted to sarcasm and to wearing golf socks and green ties, all while scribbling on stationery he had pilfered from the commanding officer while he awaited disciplinary action. The CO eventually "gave me my last (and 497th) chance."

By February, he was headed back east for radar training. First to Tampa, then to Monroe, Louisiana, and finally to Boca Raton, Florida, near Palm

Beach—just a couple hours' drive north of Frec. Baggs begged her not to have too much fun until he could see her again. "No better time than now for the true confession that I miss you very much this evening. Be good, Love, and eat lots of ice cream, cream puffs, and fattenings. The woman-to-man ratio isn't near bad enough."[10]

He drove Lenore south out of Boca Raton on the Old Dixie Highway every chance he got, usually on enough siphoned airplane gas to make it there and back. When duty required that he stay put, he threatened to "tie his body to the flag pole."[11]

One afternoon in late April 1945, Baggs phoned Frec and told her he'd be down early: he had something he wanted to ask her. "He was very serious," she recalled.

When she walked back to her apartment at the Atwater Hotel that afternoon, her first lieutenant was already waiting across the street, chatting with a fellow airman. Baggs drove Frec across the camel-back bridge on 41st Street to the Old Forge, the swankiest restaurant on Miami Beach, then and now. Housed in a repurposed blacksmith shop bedecked with opulent, high-ceilinged mahogany interiors, the Forge drew A-list celebrities, crime bosses, and politicians who made deals and smoked cigars while they dined on thick-cut steaks and sipped pricey vintages. Baggs flashed a twenty-dollar bill like a regular swell, and the headwaiter in black tie and vest led the couple to a small table in the center of the grand salon.

After drinks arrived, Baggs reached into the pocket of his dress uniform to pull out the ring box. Unbeknownst to Frec, Baggs had already called her dad, "Big Craig" Orr, up on Carr's Hill in Athens, whom he had yet to meet, to ask for his blessing.

Frec's eyes were trained elsewhere, however, drawn by three tall men making their way through the crowded dining room. Even with Ward Bond on one side and another actor on the other, John Wayne could barely walk upright.[12] By the time they reached the middle of the room, the two men had lost their grip on Wayne, who fell across the table. Nonplussed, Baggs reached over Wayne and blurted, "Frec, will you marry me?" while holding out a yellow gold ring.

Wayne mumbled something unintelligible—perhaps congratulations—as Bond hoisted him up, apologized, and carried on like a soldier dragging his buddy off the battlefield. Amidst the spilled wine and scattered silver, Frec snapped back to attention and cried, "Yes."[13]

PART II

From Reporter to Editor

CHAPTER 7

1945–1946

All over this town today. Nothing that we want. Finding most newspapers tied
to politics—owned by some Senator or mealy-mouth public grafter. They want
men, but I wouldn't even look at a typewriter for wage scale they've got.
—To Frec Baggs, October 15, 1945

For the first time in his life, Baggs felt anchored—maybe not to place or to
purpose just yet, with all the uncertainty surrounding the final days of the
war, but most certainly to Frec.

"More and more it strikes, home is with you," he wrote to her.[1]

But he gave her a shock when he told her to never expect him to attend
church. "I am an atheist," Baggs declared, recounting for her that morning at Colquitt Methodist Church when he took the offering plate from a
murderer.

His pronouncement surprised her, as poetic and idealistic as his letters
to her had been. She, a devout Presbyterian, held out hope that he would
come around, and he did. But it would be years, after they had children,
before Baggs could comfortably sit in a church again. Even then, he was
known to turn a gimlet eye on matters of the spirit, interrogating and de-
bating the pastor after the service, often to Frec's great mortification.[2]

Still, so young and in love, with no clear plans for what would come next,
Baggs and Frec married on Saturday, July 7, 1945, in the sunbathed courtyard of the Greenbriar Hotel on Miami Beach. The groom wore his dress
uniform; the bride looked angelic in a formal satin and organza gown she
purchased with money wired by her father. Baggs's uncle Billy Bush drove
over from Tampa to serve as best man. Frec's mother Sally Orr and sister
Ann took the train down from Athens. Frec's father, Craig, stayed home,
still waiting to meet Baggs face-to-face for the first time.[3]

With two weeks' leave, Baggs and Frec honeymooned for several days at
the Green Heron Hotel, a midcentury-modern resort right up the Atlantic

coast in the then-sleepy hamlet of Sunny Isles. Baggs spent the afternoons typing stories on his portable and reading them to Frec, as they envisioned leading a literary life in some coastal town, doing as they pleased, and living off the earnings of his bestselling novels.[4] They drove up to Athens, where Baggs visited Frec's beloved Carr's Hill home. His debut before the court of "Big Craig" went swimmingly. In Frec's own words, they became "fast friends." After the honeymoon, Baggs reported to MacDill Field in Tampa, Florida, and the newlyweds would stay there for the duration of the war.[5]

When Baggs separated from the USAAF in October 1945, he and Frec moved back to Carr's Hill for what they believed would be a few days until Baggs found a job and a place to live. With big ideas and a portfolio full of confidence, he jumped into the roiling sea of returning GIs seeking jobs in a flourishing postwar economy that had not quite made room for the millions of men coming home from the battlefield. While Frec stayed put in Athens awaiting the good word, Baggs contacted buddies throughout the South and followed up on leads and rumors for weeks, traversing the roads between Atlanta and Brunswick, Georgia; Richmond, Alexandria, and Charlottesville, Virginia; Raleigh and Greensboro, North Carolina; and Washington, D.C.

Despite early losses in life, for Baggs most things—school, friends, jobs, opportunities, love—had come easily. Looking for gainful employment among the many, however, proved equalizing. As he sized up the competition, a good portion of whom held college degrees, Baggs was humbled. He seemed cast straight from *The Best Years of Our Lives*, a Fred Derry type, wanting and knowing he was capable of something more than the soda jerk job he had left behind.[6] If it were just him, Baggs might have accepted some of the lower-level newspaper jobs he had been offered thus far, including one at the *Washington Post*, which at the time operated more as a local newspaper than a national publication. He had to consider Frec, the life she had imagined, and the family they wanted to build together, despite her protestations otherwise.

She tried to buoy his spirits. "I don't worry one minute about the job. I know that suddenly you'll get the right one. . . . Please don't make any snap judgment. I reserve that as my prerogative, and a very bad habit it is."[7]

But Baggs, lovesick and missing Frec, grew so discouraged about finding a job and housing that he wondered if they should go to Central or South America. "Hablo?" he asked.[8]

"Is it hard, Billie, is it anything like what you expected?" Frec asked in one letter. Every day they were apart, she grew more antsy on the Hill, realizing how after having lived away and returned married, her own definition of home was altered irrevocably.

To fund the interminable job search, Baggs sold Lenore and hopped on busses and trains to get to the next city. From one day to the next, growing ever more frustrated, he waffled between writing a book—"Think perhaps our talent lies in the literary end of writing"—and trying to get his old job back at the *Star and Herald*.

After nearly two months had passed with Baggs on the road, Frec pondered a different course.

Did you ever consider that perhaps you might have to take something you didn't like so well, just to get started? But with that goes the consolation, that no matter what we do at first, if it's too depressing, we can, in after years, do something entirely different. 'Cause, after all, aren't we somewhere in the ninety and nine going to publish a magazine, write the atomic (excuse the already hackneyed adjective) novel, build a pink cottage in Florida, and live in a shack on the Brunswick coast, drive Mercury's with little boys who look like you hanging out the back, philosophize to one another and maybe the rest of the world on human nature, buy me a pale blue cashmere sweater, eat scrambled eggs at 1 a.m. nightly. 'Cose [*sic*] the thing you like best is the best thing and that ugly old word "stable" lurks around to soft-pedal the idea of job-thumping, but we're surely going to progress—only before we can start progressing, we've got to start.[9]

By late November 1945, Baggs did just that. He settled into a rented room in Raleigh and sat for and aced an insurance exam. On his first trip into the field, he sold a farmer with thirty acres and seven children an insurance policy, one that Baggs promptly tore up because he knew the man could not afford it.[10]

Frec still held out hope for Baggs's journalism career. She encouraged him to keep writing and to show his stories to any editor whose door opened. "You're such an intelligent newspaper man. . . . I expect that in five years you could easily be managing editor of the *Post* or something equally impressive along those lines."[11]

Baggs journeyed back to Carr's Hill for the Thanksgiving holiday. Before he left Raleigh, he had quit the insurance business and, on the way to Athens, stopped in to see an old friend at the *Greensboro Daily News*, the city's morning paper. He was offered—and accepted—a cub reporter's job for forty-five dollars a week. He shared the news with Frec and her family after he arrived for dinner. Three days later, Baggs and his wife were on a Greyhound headed to North Carolina with not much more than a boxed lunch packed by Frec's mother. They found a room for rent in a Victorian-era boarding house and settled into a routine where Baggs headed to work around five every evening and returned after two in the morning, walking the eight blocks in between office and home no matter the weather. Frec found occupation at the nearby Red Cross office for thirty-five dollars per week.[12]

As a young bride with not a lot of caretaking experience, Frec did not know what to do when Baggs got a serious kidney infection around Christmastime. They had no money for a doctor or medicine, but the landlord's husband, who worked at a chemical company, came through with an experimental sulfa drug that got Baggs right again. It would be an early indication of the kidney problems that began after the war and would worsen in years to come.[13]

After the fits and starts of 1945, Baggs presented his wife a letter on New Year's Day 1946 that stipulated he would "make sincere effort towards being a better man, a better husband" by focusing on his literary writing, settling into his job, and making sure his actions were making the world a better place. By February, however, Baggs had grown restless with the cold weather and small-town reporting. Every week, he scoured *Editor and Publisher* for newspaper jobs in an ever-narrowing geography: Florida.[14] He was drawn to the coast and craved warmth, feeling that anything below seventy degrees Fahrenheit was a cold snap.[15]

He dreamed of Miami, where he had encountered a city coming to life in the nine months he spent between Boca Raton and Miami Beach during the war. It was diverse, like Panama, and reflected his broadening interests. He could come of age along with a city that was just fifty years old.

And it was where he and Frec had fallen in love.

On February 20, 1946, Baggs wrote *Miami Daily News* managing editor Hoke Welch and sent him clippings of his work in Greensboro and Panama. He preferred the afternoon *Miami Daily News*, he said, because of the more agreeable hours, but when it came to selling himself, he seemed to fall back on Aunt Grace's admonitions to never boast or be too proud.

Neither my experience nor my talents are extraordinary. I have approximately six and a half years of newspapering behind me, accomplishing everything from the menial job of post office runner to the often-mental position of editorial writer. The majority of my experience has been accumulated in Central America in the Banana Republics. . . . If you have a vacancy or an anticipation of such, from spot and feature reporting to the other jobs I have mentioned [drama, editorials, editing], I would appreciate your consideration. I do not regard myself as a spectacular news reporter, but do think I am steady, stable and capable.[16]

Welch returned Baggs's clippings five days later with a short note that he would keep his information on file should they have an opening in the future.[17]

A few weeks later, Baggs received an answer to one of his *Editor and Publisher* queries. There was an opening for a publisher of a small paper in Key West. He handed in his resignation, dropped Frec off at Carr's Hill so that he could get settled, then trekked to the southernmost point in the continental United States, just ninety miles across the Florida Straits from Cuba.

On his way down, he made a slight detour off U.S. 1 to 600 Biscayne Boulevard. The octagonal tower modeled after one in Seville, Spain, had housed the *Miami Daily News* since 1925. Baggs wanted to introduce himself and put a face with his name—just in case an opening had appeared since he wrote to Welch.

That stop turned out to be a smart move. When Baggs reached Key West, he learned within a few days the publishing job was not as promised. He turned around and headed straight back to the *News*. He and Welch, two Georgia boys, cut a deal.[18] Welch dug into the tight budget and found room for a reporter who could speak Spanish and who knew something about aviation, a burgeoning Miami industry. Welch could not have found a hungrier reporter with better credentials for the beat than Baggs.

Baggs called Frec and told her there had been a change of plans. She should take the train to Miami instead.

CHAPTER 8

1946–1949

To get serious in the last paragraph, a Democracy depends more on an enlightened citizenry than it does on streamlined governmental machinery. After all, the reasoned public opinion which keeps our type of government running can't be formed when the public doesn't know even a few facts of the case. This is like putting too many unknowns in an algebraic problem.
—In the Bag by Bill Baggs, *Miami Daily News*, March 5, 1950

Baggs was not alone among the thousands of servicemen who returned to the shores of Biscayne Bay after having been trained in or rehabilitated by its salt-scented breezes. Miami's population had nearly doubled since the beginning of World War II, bringing rapid urbanization, industrialization, and immigration to a community just barely old enough to absorb and anticipate the changes.[1] Tourism, construction, and agriculture spread as fast as the invasive melaleuca trees in the Everglades, and once again Baggs had shown up on the scene at a propitious point. He may have dreamed of working at a small newspaper in a small city somewhere along the coast, but his adopted home could not be contained. As his editors later learned, neither could he.

If news is, indeed, "the first rough draft of history," the *News* was most definitely present for the dawn of the city.[2] The newspaper itself was born on the banks of the Miami River in May 1896, two months before the city of Miami was incorporated. Standard Oil cofounder and Florida East Coast Railway developer Henry M. Flagler bestowed on this southern-most newspaper its original moniker, the *Miami Metropolis*, in keeping with his vision for the swampy outpost. In fact, the first issue of the paper was planned to coincide with the arrival of Flagler's first train into Miami, but a storm and a sunken ship delayed delivery of the press.[3]

In 1923, two-term Ohio governor and former Democratic presiden-tial candidate James M. Cox bought land on Miami Beach for a winter residence.[4] While in town, he dropped a cool million dollars to purchase the *Metropolis*, adding it to his growing media empire, which included at the time the *Dayton (Ohio) Daily News* and the *Atlanta Journal*, plus a trio of radio stations. He changed the paper's name to the *Miami Daily News* and added the tagline, "Today's News Today." Two years later, he built the Spanish tower on the bay.[5]

By the time Baggs walked through the ornate-as-a-wedding-cake entrance and passed the mezzanine's mural-sized map of sixteenth-century Florida, the crusading *News* had already won a Pulitzer Prize, the first paper in Florida to do so. After the *News* had exposed corruption in city government in 1938, nearly half the council was recalled. The paper was also the first in the state to use wire-photo transfers, bringing images from the larger world right onto its pages and into the homes of its readers.[6]

Hoke Welch, the spark plug of a managing editor who hired Baggs, could have passed easily for one of the mob bosses he chased in print. With slicked-back hair and an ever-present cigar clenched between his teeth, he had been in the newspaper business since the age of eighteen, starting out in the sports department of the old *Atlanta Georgian*. After Cox purchased the *Georgian* and combined it with the *Atlanta Journal*, Welch rose quickly in the ranks of the organization, and took over the *News*' managing editor position at the start of the war.[7] Just shy of forty years old, he confronted communists, the KKK, and the underworld in equal measure, all of which earned the *News* a reputation for righteousness, red-baiting, and sensationalism. His tough, unflinching public demeanor, however, belied a gentle facility with managing people, playing the piano, and letting his reporters shine.[8]

Into Welch's newsroom strode the eager, baby-faced Baggs, still sporting a military crew cut and rotating his wardrobe between the only two suits he owned. Baggs joined a team of sixty-six reporters and editors, nearly all white men who had been with the *News* an average of twenty years. There were a few women on staff who oversaw the society column and lifestyle pages or worked as secretaries and sales managers. A housewife, "a Mrs. Fred Mergen," moonlighted as the *News*' award-winning editorial cartoonist.[9] Baggs settled in among them, becoming versed in all things mobile, whether it had wings or wheels or spoke with an accent.

The aviation sector had grown up alongside the city, which often played host to its daredevil pioneers. Miami Beach became a hub for exhibition flyers and barnstormers as the chamber of commerce sought to entertain and awe winter residents and tourists. Glenn H. Curtiss established the country's first flying school at Miami Beach. In 1937 Amelia Earhart took off from the municipal airport for her ill-fated around-the-world voyage. After the war, former military airstrips were transformed into airports to accommodate the more than four hundred privately owned aircraft in the community.

Eastern Airlines, Pan American World Airways, and Chalk's International Airlines all established headquarters in the city. Eastern, founded by World War I flying ace Eddie Rickenbacker, flew the main connector between New York and South Florida, launching a leg to Puerto Rico in 1947. Pan Am's Juan Trippe had cornered the market on Cuba and Central and South America, on routes mapped, in part, by Charles Lindbergh. Chalk's fleet of seaplanes covered the Bahamas. Miami was the first city in the United States to hire an aviation director. By the time Baggs sat down to write his first article for the *News*, more than four thousand commercial passengers were already passing daily through the newly christened Miami International Airport and the former Miami Army Airfield.[10]

A start-up cargo and passenger carrier scored Baggs his first byline in July 1946. He covered two veterans who had purchased a four-engine c-54 plane as surplus from the War Assets Administration. Within two years as Peninsular Air Transport, their business had doubled and they had a shiny new plane to show off. During the reporting for the story, Baggs met a young up-and-comer in Democratic politics named George A. Smathers, the future congressman and senator from Key Biscayne who often entertained his close friend, Massachusetts representative John F. Kennedy, on the waters off South Florida.[11]

Baggs wrote his second bylined story about a Pennsylvania transplant who still drove a "horseless carriage" built by Henry Ford in 1904, when he still operated a bicycle shop in Detroit. "Gets 35 miles to the gallon of gas and will run along at 25 miles an hour," Baggs quoted the man. The car was an earlier version of the ones Baggs's own father sold when he opened his first dealership in Georgia back in the early 1900s.

During those first few months, Baggs tried out variations of his name for his byline—Bill, William, William C.—finally settling on the older-sounding William. In short order, he racked up an ever-growing range of articles, from profiles of Bolivian and Nicaraguan revolutionaries to transit strikes as bus drivers considered unionizing. In August, Welch sent Baggs to Ohio to follow a couple of Miami pilots competing in the Bendix National Air

Race. By September, Baggs was penning a standing Sunday column, Flying in Miami, and was covering labor and transportation issues during the weekdays.

In the ten months since he and Frec had married, moved to Tampa, then to Georgia, then to North Carolina and back, Miami's housing shortage had grown all the more fraught with the influx of veterans, immigrants, and fortune hunters. With little time to search, and slim pickings in both inventory and finances, Baggs signed a lease to share a house with a pilot and his flight attendant wife. After Frec arrived from Athens, delighted to finally be with her husband once again, she grew none too pleased with the arrangement. Baggs worked long hours, and when the mile-high couple blew into town between flights, they threw raucous parties that may have involved swinging. And even though Frec carried with her two degrees, she had the sense that the cosmopolitan couple considered her a country bumpkin.[12] Frustrated, Frec returned to Athens until Sally, Frec's mother, called Baggs to come get his wife. He drove north to fetch her and promised Frec that he would stop being a fool.[13]

On her return, Frec promptly found an apartment, just slightly beyond their budget, in the leafy enclave of Belle Meade on Miami's Upper East Side. After a few fits and starts in secretarial jobs, she landed a position teaching first grade at Morningside Elementary School.

Early in his career at the *News*, Baggs gained a reputation for seeking out the people and stories on the margins—the shoeshine guy, a lady bullfighter, blimp pilots, migrating birds. As he grew more confident, his wit emerged on the page and in the newsroom. Columnist Grace Wing overheard an exchange between Baggs and the city editor one day and included it in her daily social report.[14] While covering the All-American Air Maneuvers air show in January 1947, Baggs described a female pilot as an "aviatricks." The frustrated city editor, working to meet a looming deadline, asked why Baggs wrote it like that. Baggs quipped, "She's a stunt flier, Boss."

Baggs's reporting and travels placed him in conversation with heads of state, military and business leaders, local politicians, and criminals. He scored one of his first front-page stories when he was tipped off about a ring of bellboys and travel agents who were scalping tickets for Eastern and National Airlines. The piece led to an FBI investigation.[15] Baggs ended that first year at the *News* with a two-page spread on the boom in air cargo, which, he predicted, would be "the next great growth of aviation and Miami, nearby to the great cities of Latin America." He talked with the folks in the trenches instead of the people at the top—orchid suppliers, cattle and poultry shippers, inspectors—and backed up his insights with testimony from experts in science, technology, and developing economies—a process that became his trademark.[16]

By mid-1947, at age twenty-four, Baggs was one of the most requested presenters from the *News'* speakers' bureau. He was a natural-born raconteur who wrapped discussions about airport expansion, labor disputes, or housing needs in a resonant baritone burnished by a languid drawl that disguised a whirring intellect. As one woman later commented, "You wouldn't think he knew so much. But when he starts to talk, you know that boy has studied the subject!"[17]

Baggs's evolving profile garnered the attention of publisher Daniel J. Mahoney, owner James Cox's son-in-law. "Big Irish," as he was called, had a personality as bold and brash as his height and girth. He was a high school dropout who sought adventure on the Mexican border, first as a railroad surveyor, then as a tracker of Pancho Villa under General John J. Pershing. He fought in France during World War I, then prospered as the general manager for Cox's enterprises after he married the boss's daughter. When he moved to Miami Beach to oversee the business side of the *Miami Daily News*, he showed little fear in taking on mobsters and syndicates in front-page editorials, even the likes of Al Capone, who had relocated to Palm Island from Chicago in 1930. When he received a series of phone calls asking whether he would like to be measured for a coffin, Big Irish reportedly countered, "I would like to meet at any hour at any place the man who thinks he's big enough to put me in it."[18]

Mahoney became a kingmaker for local and state politicians. He ordered his editors to endorse certain candidates for office, even a man who made his fortune under the table as a bookie, whom the *News'* reporters covered (as well as the police who protected him). But if those same people griped to Mahoney about showing up unfavorably in the *News*, he stood by his writers. That support maintained their loyalty, even if they were only paid peanuts.

Baggs seemed to relish being in the thick of things. By mid-1947 he had started digging into more human-interest stories, where his humor shined. One article, in which he covered a group of local magicians, carried the byline William "Presto" Baggs. In another, he recounted an evening with two Florida crackers on a rattlesnake and water-moccasin hunt in the Everglades. "Caesar's Ghost, but there's two belts and a wallet crawling on the right side of the road," he reported—but he was none too happy when the men threw a bag filled with fourteen poisonous slitherers in the back seat where he sat perched with pen and notepad.[19]

For the twentieth anniversary of Pan Am Airways, Baggs flew with national aeronautical officials, state legislators, and Cuban dignitaries on a junket from Miami to Key West, then on to Havana. Although very much in the background while Welch and Mahoney hobnobbed with the powerbrokers, Baggs developed a friendship with the airline's public relations people that would bear fruit over time.[20] Soon, he was a regular guest on the Pan Am yacht for fishing trips on Biscayne Bay, and he and Frec dressed in borrowed black-tie and cocktail attire for the inaugural Miami-to-Havana Flight Club.

Although Baggs's star rose within the community, his paycheck had not improved much under the parsimonious Cox leadership. He and Frec had moved into a less expensive unfurnished apartment nearby, but they longed to buy a house and start a family—both goals out of reach without some additional funds. So, during the summer of 1948, Frec returned to Athens for six weeks to earn teaching credits so that she could get a raise when the new school year started in the fall.

Baggs wrote her nearly every day that summer in lieu of calling because they had to juggle paying the phone bill against rent, utilities, and car repairs on an old Pontiac they had named "Gratitude."[21] He presented a record of every dime he spent, including for two dressers he had purchased for $17 each and hand-lacquered for their bedroom—a strong hint that financial management was not his forte, even though he was known around the office to overcome writer's block and keep his mind sharp by solving complicated math and physics problems.[22]

In his letters, he shared with Frec what he was absorbing from another read of War and Peace, the latest issue of Time magazine, or the slew of newspapers he gathered every morning. He discussed his concerns about war in the atomic age, with Russia's power now countering the United States', heightened by the Communist takeover of Czechoslovakia earlier that year. More than anything, though, he was lovesick for his wife and counted the days until he could bring her home.

"I miss you as if you were a lost hand or foot," he wrote after he had returned from delivering her to Carr's Hill. It was their third anniversary and he was alone. "I don't have vivid memories of my life without you. . . . When Mother died [when Baggs was twelve], I didn't think I ever again would be very happy."[23]

As the summer and pain of distance wore on, Baggs started showing that same restlessness he experienced just after they had married and he had gone job hunting. He wrote about leaving the newspaper, waffling between going into corporate or government work, if it meant they could pay off the car and he could focus spare hours on writing the novel he kept promising her.[24] It was clear in his letters, though, that he was wired for newspapering. "I better get on my horse and start out for the windmills."[25]

While substituting that summer for vacationing political reporters, Baggs got a front seat to a fistfight that broke out between a city council member and the editor of a Miami Beach gossip rag. Then he snagged an exclusive for a sweeping three-part series about communist infiltration in local and national politics.

With the help of an unnamed source, Baggs covered in detail how communist leaders abroad and at home were seeking to sow discord among labor groups throughout the United States that would lead to class and racial animosity. One thread focused on the housecleaning at the main union for Pan American Airways, the Transport Workers Union, "where 16 of the 26 top leaders reportedly are communists, party-liners or sympathizers, and there are between 35 and 40 other communists, party-liners or sympathizers, in key positions throughout the organization's nationwide system."[26]

Another thread highlighted the clandestine role communists played in the formation of the Progressive Party, helmed by former vice president Henry A. Wallace, who was forced by President Harry S. Truman to resign after Wallace gave a speech conciliatory to the Soviet Union. Because the Progressive Party promoted desegregation, free trade, and gender equality, it proved attractive to labor unions and liberal democrats who were not fully in Truman's camp. In his reporting, Baggs exhibited a future hallmark of his writing style on controversial subjects, whereby he made his point not with a broadax, but with a scalpel nick.[27] "The third-party promotion of Henry A. Wallace as a presidential candidate is a ticklish matter inasmuch as there are so many completely honest citizens in this political organization."

A year later, the identity of Baggs's primary source became clear. Paul Crouch, referred to obliquely as "a Miami newsman" in testimony, had served the Communist Party in the United States for more than seventeen years before severing ties in 1942 and agreeing to testify before the House Un-American Activities Committee. He had been employed by the *Miami Herald*, but was let go once he turned state's witness. The *News* offered him a place to land, possibly as a paid informant.

Crouch had joined the party after a hardscrabble childhood on a North Carolina farm, where he grew up hating just about everybody from Jews and Catholics to Blacks. He was indoctrinated in Moscow at the Lenin School, alongside Josip Broz Tito from Yugoslavia, and returned to the United States with the idea that he would help laborers in his own country combat the poor working conditions and even poorer pay in textile mills, coal mines, and factories. Along with other communists in the United States, he grew increasingly disillusioned when he became aware that the true intention of the U.S. Communist Party was to exploit workers and create enough friction among the people for the ultimate overthrow of the U.S. government.

After Crouch testified in a closed-door session before the House Un-American Activities Committee in May 1949, Baggs was assigned the task of editing Crouch's testimony for the *News*. Crouch's statements offered several revelations that illuminated the extent to which Soviet tactics undermined democracies within the Western Hemisphere.

- Starting as far back as 1929, "Miami has become, and is today, the base from which international communism is spread over South and Central America and all the major islands of the Caribbean Sea."
- Miami Local 500 of the Transport Workers Union served as the communications center for the Communist Party in Latin America and members used Pan Am flights to carry directives from Moscow to all points south.
- Havana was considered the second most important city in the Latin American network. "A large underprivileged class offers a fertile field for spreading the party doctrines."
- Control of the Panama Canal for political and military purposes was the ultimate goal; therefore, building ties with "fascist cliques" in Argentina and Nicaragua was paramount.[28]

Cox copyrighted the eleven-part series and syndicated it to more than thirty national newspapers, putting "Edited by William C. Baggs" before hundreds of thousands of readers across the country.

CHAPTER 9

1949–1957

> He's a gentleman and scholar and his column packs a punch. He's Bill Baggs, Southern gentleman from the deep south—and he's no mean hand at the typewriter. To see him, you'd guess him to be a rugged individualist—and you'd be right. To talk to him, you'd pigeonhole him as a wit—a philosopher—and a keen observer of human nature . . . and you'd be right again.—*Miami Daily News* advertisement, September 28, 1954

Whatever doubts Baggs had expressed to Frec about his future as a newspaperman were allayed when Welch promoted Baggs to daily columnist. His column In the Bag debuted on December 20, 1949, and for the next seven and a half years, Monday through Friday of every week, Baggs picked any topic that fascinated him and ran with it. Because he had reported on everything from air shows to Soviet spies, he had developed a vast community from which to draw fodder. The time and place in which he wrote, too, proved a bottomless well of inspiration.

Baggs had big shoes to fill. The popular writer of the Miami Diary column, Charles Leydon, had passed away, and the *News'* most provocative columnist, author-activist Philip Wylie, had moved on to bigger projects. On and off since December 1943, Wylie had written the Off My Chest column. He was an agitator of the first order and had already caused quite the scandal in 1942 with his book of essays, *Generation of Vipers*, in which he confronted the hypocrisy of American values, including fake Christian civility and the growing cult of motherhood. He was well known nationally for the Crunch and Des column he penned for the *Saturday Evening Post*, which established him as the poet laureate of game fishing and put the deepwater sport on the map. Yet his also was one of the earliest voices sounding the alarm on the environmental degradation of Florida's waters from the influx of residents and tourists, as well as the horrors brought on by the atomic age.[1]

Wylie believed the columnist's job was to serve a dose of reality to the reader, to make the reader think. "The reader could take it and needed it," Wylie advised his young colleague.

In a guest column Wylie penned while Baggs was abroad on assignment, he recounted a conversation the two men had shared. Baggs worried that, after a hard day's work, the reader needed a laugh and some warmth when he or she opened the afternoon paper. Wylie thought there was already "too much candy" in newspapers, what with the sports, comic strips, movie and club listings, gossip columns, and crossword puzzles filling most of the paper's pages. "I don't believe you have to be handed a sugar-bun before you'll allow anybody to break the bad news that your clothing is on fire." Wylie rightly predicted Baggs would grow "grimmer" and would serve up "dishes even more worth chewing."[2]

In those early columns, Baggs tried to balance both substance and absurdity as he auditioned a number of voices while settling into his own. There were hints of H. L. Mencken's unrepentant tweaking of cultural pretensions and George Bernard Shaw's social criticism mixed with Mark Twain's folk wisdom and satire. There was even the romance of Emerson. Running through them all was a vein of humor, like a wink or an elbow to the rib of the reader, signaling that he, too, was in on the joke. In that first year, Baggs often began his columns with a cheeky couplet to set the scene.

A good intent
Can't pay the rent.

Santa Claus suits
Instead of grass roots.

He was garbed in blue
And seemed so, too.

Yet beneath the jovial persona, Baggs dealt with real issues. He mercilessly needled Dade County Sheriff Jim Sullivan for looking the other way on illegal gambling and organized crime. Time and again he shined a white-hot spotlight on the slum owners and developers who were bilking the city's poor Black residents by overcharging for substandard housing without electricity, privies, or running water. He capitalized *Negro* out of respect at a time when most of the nation's newspapers, including the competing *Miami Herald*, used a lowercase *n*. He championed slum clearance programs, taking the air out of conservative claims that social programs were just a form of communism. He called for better urban planning so that the city and county would not always be playing catch-up with unmanaged growth. He marveled at the wealth of the ocean and the value of trees. Beginning in the early 1950s, he developed a lasting friendship with Bernard Baruch, the financier and presidential advisor, interviewing him on economics and war. He tweaked the noses of pure market-driven capitalists while cautioning passionate young intellectuals against embracing immature Marxist theories written at the dawn of the Industrial Revolution.

> In the land which claims to be the motherland of Communism, the working man has no protection from the management. Quotas for production are set, and the workers labor until these quotas are met. There are no strikes in Russia. Arbitration consists of a state order, with no prior consultation with the workers.
>
> Have you ever wondered why the American trade unions fight the betrayer Communism harder than anyone else in this country?[3]

Early on, Baggs lamented that he was a man of no party, because he was neither industrial tycoon nor a benefactor of the welfare state. "The Communists wouldn't have me if I tossed a bomb into a National Manufacturers' Association convention, and my forehead isn't high enough to join the Socialists. Liking red meat, I am not a likely prospect for the Vegetarian movement, and I don't think there is a future in the Dixiecrat party. Perhaps there is a minority I could join, but I haven't seen any soul sponsoring the cause of Georgia-born Irishmen."[4]

This independence afforded Baggs a free-range mind led by his singular curiosity and apparent humanism. Even a two-part series on UFO sightings in early 1950 turned into a thoughtful investigation that had him trekking more than twenty-five hundred miles to interview a doctor in Pennsylvania, two pilots in Arkansas, a mother and son in New Jersey, and photographic experts. "I don't know what to think," he wrote, "but a strong case certainly can be made out for the saucer."[5]

It did not take long for Baggs to become a local character himself. His language and his manners seemed to evoke another era, even if the ideas he put forth to readers were progressive and often in conflict with the Old South of his youth. One colleague described the way he walked the streets of Miami as having "the flair and air of a river-boat gambler."[6] Often loud, ever ready with a joke and a deep belly laugh, he drew people, especially children, into his orbit.[7]

He adopted a uniform of sorts: striped seersucker suits. The look, which he had picked up from an attorney in town, had an "elegant slouchiness"

akin to pajamas that Baggs admired and perfected.[8] After Baggs had hum-
bly excluded himself from a tongue-in-cheek Worst Dressed column, former Florida governor Fuller Warren, an avid reader of Baggs's, wrote a letter to the editor of the *News* wherein he described the columnist as being
in a sartorial class all by himself: "He has peculiar qualifications ... [includ-
ing] the unsymmetrical angularity of his body. . . . His iridescent ties flash
in solitary splendor amid the barren wastes of his neck and shoulders. His
loping side-wise gait gives his garments a certain aspect easier seen than
described."[9]

Other than in the length of his hair, the expanding-contracting size of
his waistband, and the type of "cigaret" he smoked, Baggs rarely veered
from this regalia. It was simply one less thing for him to think about in the
mornings.

The relationships Baggs formed as a columnist had a profound impact on
his future in journalism, granting him access not only to the lives of everyday Miamians and their struggles, but also to the corridors of power. He
never knew who would show up at Hoke Welch's weekly poker games—a
city attorney, a commissioner, a businessman—but sports writer Morris
McLemore was a sure bet. At the office, publisher Dan Mahoney included
Baggs on the general council, the group of managers and editors setting
policy, because of Baggs's unique view "on the town plat observing events
and those playing a part in them."[10]

A publisher from New Jersey who had read his columns while visiting Miami approached Baggs to write a weekly article for his magazine.
"National level, straight or humor," Baggs told Frec. And, as he had promised since their wedding day, he had finished a second draft of a World War
II novel and had sent it to a friend for feedback. Baggs wondered if, with
the Korean conflict looming, it was already dated.[11]

Yet the friendship that would change his life the most took root because
Governor James Cox went on a buying spree.

In early 1950, Cox decided to purchase the *Atlanta Constitution* and con-
solidate all of his Georgia media holdings under Atlanta Newspapers, Inc.
Along with the newspaper he procured radio and television stations, the
Constitution's whip-smart then–general manager Jack Tarver, and Ralph
Emerson McGill, one of the region's most revered and reviled editor-
columnists for his moderating stance on racial equality. The change in own-
ership made both Tarver and McGill nervous, so Cox sent the company

plane to Atlanta and flew the pair to Miami to assuage their fears. Cox liked them both—Tarver for his acumen in turning the *Constitution* into a moneymaker and McGill for his liberal conscience—and he wanted to keep them.[12]

McGill's daily columns began to appear in all the Cox properties. In the *News*, it moved around until settling on 1B, directly across the page from Baggs's column, which by September 1950 needed only his name in bold to draw attention.

McGill was generous with advice and encouragement for young reporters and often provided a refuge for fellow journalists coming through Atlanta, especially those who shared his more progressive sensibilities, because there were so few of them in the South. His Atlanta office became an outpost for the likes of Harry Ashmore, editor of the *Arkansas Gazette*, and *New York Times* correspondents John Popham and, later on, Claude Sitton. They all called McGill, the elder statesman, "Pappy." Sensing a kindred spirit in Baggs, McGill would soon welcome the young columnist into the small but powerful fraternity.

The initial idea behind Baggs's promotion to columnist was that he would comment on local happenings of his choosing. However, it became clear to Welch and Mahoney that Baggs possessed an uncanny facility for distilling national and international issues into relatable, and sometimes urgent, topics for the "people walking down Flagler Street," the city's main commercial corridor. So, in February 1951 they sent Baggs on a three-month, eleven-nation tour through Europe to report on the thoughts and concerns of the "man in the middle." After a weeklong vacation with Frec in Washington, D.C., and New York, Baggs boarded a plane to Oslo, Norway, with a portable typewriter in his luggage.

Over the next twelve weeks he traveled by train, plane, car, and bicycle through Sweden, Denmark, Holland, West Germany, Belgium, France, Spain, Italy, Trieste, Yugoslavia, and Great Britain, talking with students, factory workers, poets, flower vendors, farmers, and housewives about how their lives had improved (or not) in the aftermath of the war and the growing threat of Soviet aggression. He took their temperature on the effects of reconstruction efforts funded by the U.S.-led Marshall Plan and explored the challenges of rebuilding economies, disarmament, and defense. It was his first time back in Europe since the war, and although he found much had improved, some things had remained the same or worsened.

In Naples, Baggs reconnected with a man named "Luige," whom he had befriended while stationed in Venosa. Back in 1944, Luige had denounced Mussolini. Seven years later, he appeared wistful for a powerful leader. "Mussolini was a symbol, a strong symbol, and he reminded us we were Italians. We were proud of being Italians and we had national spirit."

When Baggs reminded Luige of how he had once felt, when the dictator had stripped the people of their personal freedoms, Luige sighed, "I would submit some of my freedom for order today. . . . People have no faith in anything but bread."[13]

In Communist Yugoslavia, Baggs found bread even harder to come by without a ration coupon. A seven-month drought had destroyed the country's crops, and its economy had been devastated since the split with Russia in 1948. The nation's plans to industrialize had been delayed years because of a lack of skilled workers and an inefficient bureaucracy. A $100 million infusion from America had saved the people from starving.

The shops in Belgrade carried imported goods, but the one-third of the population that held ration coupons still had no purchasing power. "But what is the difference," Baggs asked, "between 20 dollars and 100 dollars in the cost of an item to a person who probably hasn't got 50 cents?"[14]

While in Belgrade, Baggs talked with the editor of the largest newspaper in Yugoslavia, who insisted that they were free to criticize the leaders but never communism itself.[15] A loose-lipped guy in a bar, sloshed on slivovitz, a golden brandy made from plums, declared that elections were, of course, free, but you could not vote against the communist leaders.[16]

The conditions of the people in Yugoslavia contrasted sharply with how Baggs found his hotel room when he arrived. Filled with flowers, fruit baskets, and liquor bottles, it had been festooned at the request of the chief of the Yugoslav air force, a man he had met during the war. The former Partisan pilot had helped Baggs and his crew evade German forces after their plane had been shot down behind enemy lines after a bombing run to Romania. They had a lot of catching up to do.

In the meantime, as McGill relayed the story years later, "the colonel, wishing his old friend to be content, asked him if he would also like the company of a young lady while there. Bill informed him he had a young lady at home, but he would make love to the slivovitz and would appreciate it if no shortage developed."[17]

Cox heavily promoted the Man in the Middle series and printed it in all six of his newspapers throughout the country. The articles showcased

Baggs's ability to chew the fat with regular citizens, intellectuals, and leaders, and they afforded him a gravitas he had not known before. On his return, he was interviewed on Miami radio station WIOD and spoke to various professional organizations and clubs around the greater Miami community about his impressions of "life in the shadow of the Iron Curtain."

Because of the double-whammy of his folksy style and broad intellect, Baggs evolved into the de facto spokesperson for the *News*, not just on the speakers' circuit but also as an emcee at public events and on the new medium of television.

Back in 1949, before he was made the local columnist, Baggs led off a special section of the Sunday *News* that heralded the debut of WTVJ Channel 4, Miami's (and Florida's) first independent television station, established by Col. Mitchell Wolfson Sr., cofounder of the Wometco chain of movie theaters.

"In this edition," Baggs wrote, "the reader will find articles covering what kinds of programs TV offers or plans to offer, the costs of sets, how to get the best reception on a set and many other matters which will be of real concern to the average American, who, in view of his taking to radios, automobiles and telephones, will one day own a television set."

At the time, fewer than thirty-five hundred of Miami's half a million households owned television sets. Baggs predicted color television would dawn within the decade and that TV would bring back the "ham" in politics, influencing votes based on a candidate's smile and twinkle in the eye.[18] He did not imagine then his own capacity for hamming it up on the little screen.

A University of Miami graduate named Ralph Renick, who modeled the modern announcer's voice with his chest-deep monotones, was named WTVJ's first news director. He debuted South Florida's first evening news broadcast in 1950, then launched *What's the Story?*, a weekly panel discussion program, a year later. Baggs and UM government professor Donald Larson were the regular panelists. With Renick moderating, they would discuss the local, state, and national news of the day. When Renick needed a night off, Baggs often substituted for him.

In June 1953, Baggs received the Award of Merit and Honorary Fellowship from the George Washington Carver Memorial Institute for his "outstanding efforts on behalf of inter-racial understanding and human welfare." As part of the awards program, he participated in what was believed to be the first interracial panel discussion ever telecast on WTVJ. On the panel with him were Garth Reeves, editor of the *Miami Times*, the city's Black weekly, and G. E. Graves, the attorney for the Miami chapter of the National Association for the Advancement of Colored People.[19] These three men would become allies in the tough fight for the dignity of Miami's Black population in the years ahead.

Later, as other channels joined the landscape, Baggs became as ubiquitous a television personality as one in print. Jack Lloyd hosted a segment on WCKT Channel 7, the NBC affiliate, called Meet the News, a program to introduce members of the local press to the viewing public and feature discussion of timely topics. Baggs was a frequent contributor, calling in from political conventions or sitting for a behind-the-scenes interview on the big story of the week. The program became part and parcel of Lawrence Spivak's national program *Meet the Press* in 1956, and Baggs was named host of the local segment, conducting informal interviews with the newspaper's writing staff.[20] He often irritated advertisers because he ran into their allotted times by not only asking reporters to talk about what they were investigating but also explaining how those stories affected the daily lives of viewers.[21]

By 1952, Baggs and Frec had saved up enough money and moved into their own home, not far from the Belle Meade neighborhood where they had been renting for six years. Their modest Mission-style abode was in the same neighborhood as several of Baggs's *News* colleagues. Governor Cox's winter home sat just across the 79th Street Causeway. Cox had been taking an increased interest in Baggs, sending story ideas, recommending readings such as Hans Zinsser's *Rats, Lice and History*, and inviting him to parties and on fishing trips.

Later that summer, Baggs covered his first national political conventions, both held in Chicago two weeks apart. There to capture the quirks of humanity amid the chaos of horse-trading, Baggs was the rookie member of an all-hands-on-deck team involving four different wire services, plus McGill. McGill, who thrived on the energy surrounding the conventions, showed Baggs the political ropes, which also involved initiation into the small cadre of reporters who called themselves the Southern War Correspondents and Camp Followers. This loose association was founded by the stout, bespectacled McGill and the long-winded, apparently always behatted Popham, a Virginia-born correspondent who traveled back roads from Washington, D.C., to Galveston, Texas, reporting for the *New York Times* on race, education, poverty, politics, and the intersection of all of the above.

The group's numbers swelled and shrank as people moved among jobs, but the core members remained loyal to one another throughout their lives, even when politics got in the way. In addition to Popham, there were among the group's dedicated acolytes Ashmore; Harry Golden, publisher and editor of the *Carolina Israelite*; Hodding Carter Jr., the editor of the Greenville, Mississippi, *Delta Democrat-Times*; John Griffin of the Southern Regional Council; Bill Emerson of *Newsweek*'s Southern Bureau; and Mark Etheridge, editor of the *Louisville (Kentucky) Courier*. The group met when they could, most often at the annual meetings of the American Society of Newspaper Editors, but the political conventions held a special fascination.

Baggs proved his mettle at the Democratic convention that year. As Popham reminisced to writer John Egerton, his "gifted, earthy, irreverent" brother Baggs—"the most cracker-looking man who ever lived"—grabbed a chaplain's badge that the press gallery passed around to gain access to the convention floor.

"At one point, there was a commotion in the Pennsylvania delegation, and Baggs pinned on the badge and went down to see what it was all about. He looked like a Southern W. C. Fields, hung over from the previous evening, his eyes red-rimmed, his seersucker suit badly rumpled. He pressed his way into the midst of the roiling throng, and a woman there spied his badge and said, 'Well, chaplain, I suppose you've come to pray for us?' And Baggs replied, 'Yes ma'am, you're goddam right, and it's gonna be a pisscutter!'"[22]

Baggs had stumbled on that party of belonging he had been searching for and found his brothers-in-arms—an often bawdy, always tall-tale-telling band of political news junkies with a penchant for hard work and hard brown liquors (except for Popham, who abstained). They shared a near-unbreakable bond, tethered by the shared scars of being white southern newspapermen trying to shepherd their homeland into embracing the end of segregation. They had less interest in maintaining a white hierarchy than in realizing an economically and socially vibrant region. They hoped their words would change their region, if not the world.

And in McGill, Baggs found a substitute for the father he never knew. Like C. C. Baggs, McGill proved an affable and determined mover and shaker, an astute politician one moment and a glad-hander among Atlanta's businessmen the next. He commanded attention because of his position and made friends and enemies alike for his honestly held opinions. And, like C. C., McGill was prone to drink.

Frec had stopped teaching in fall 1952 so that she could prepare for the birth of their baby that winter. As the date of impending parenthood grew close, Baggs provided his wife with a detailed itinerary of where he would be each day and checked in with her often to see if the first labor pains had begun. When she finally did call on the afternoon of February 16, Baggs left in the middle of a meeting and sped home.[23]

"I had mapped carefully the quick route to Jackson Memorial Hospital," he shared with his readers, "and took the wrong turn and found myself very much confused and about that time, a labor pain struck the wife and my heart lodged right up in the throat."[24]

They made it to the hospital in time, and Craig Calhoun Baggs came into the world just after midnight. One of the first calls Baggs made was to McGill, whom he had asked to be Craig's godfather. He told him, "It's a boy, the finest looking reddest, squallingest boy you ever saw. I had to let you know ... I wish you were here."[25]

McGill dedicated his next day's column to the blessed event.

News soon came that the Korean conflict would end. Although Baggs had to report for a physical as a reservist, he was never called up. His kidneys were already showing early signs of chronic disease, but his bigger concern had been the precarious stability of détente in the atomic age.

Governor Cox cabled Baggs with a thought: "A message comes with promise of peace; thousands of lives saved that would otherwise have been lost; billions and billions of property destroyed, increasing our public debt billions and billions. All these things have the meaning of disaster. Now with the promise of peace and joy, the stock market goes down two billion dollars in one day. If all this doesn't indicate a cockeyed world then I don't know the meaning of things. You might like to make something of it."[26]

He did, turning his next day's column into a case for diplomacy through tractors, food production, and the end of illiteracy. "I think it was Lord Boyd-Orr, the man who spent years trying to teach backward people how to produce more food from their land, who said: 'Ninety percent of the problems in this world can be traced to empty bellies.'"[27]

Baggs's ambitions flourished along with the popularity of his column, and he asked McGill in the fall of 1953 to share a sample of his more humorous columns with McGill's syndicate. McGill wrote back to Baggs that October with mixed reviews.

> I have delayed writing you until now because I have been passing your pieces around to various persons whose judgment I, myself, rely on.
>
> Without exception, the lead paragraph is fresh, bright and very, very good, but after that, the columns seem to fade off into good, sound stuff but just about what you would expect a humorist to say.
>
> You may be sure I am in your corner rooting hard for Hall [Robert Hall of the Post-Hall Syndicate] to give you an enthusiastic yes, but on the basis of two or three friends of mine, don't be discouraged if it takes a while.[28]

McGill knew something of patience. He was in his late fifties before Tarver had helped him strike a syndication deal and gain a national audience. McGill encouraged his young colleague to tackle tougher national and international issues more regularly and position himself for bigger things.

Baggs followed his mentor's advice, increasing his focus on transforming Florida, pushing for civil rights, lifting up Latin America, fighting for education, conservation, peace, and an end to poverty. He so stirred the case for a two-party system and reapportionment of Florida's electorate based on population distribution that he helped break the stranglehold the Dixiecrats had on the state legislature. Charley Johns, the acting governor in 1954, so despised Baggs that he had his backers block the journalist from serving as a panelist on WTVJ's televised debate during the second primary. The backlash from viewers and newspapers around the state caused Johns to retreat. During the debate, Baggs hammered away on the fact that 50 percent of the state's population resided in Dade, Broward, and Palm Beach Counties, yet they only held 3 percent of the seats in the state legislature. Johns's vague responses about upholding state law gave his opponent LeRoy Collins an opportunity to push for a massive overhaul of the state's constitution to meet the needs of a changing Florida. When Collins was elected governor, "experts estimated the show cost Charley 35,000 votes."[29]

The 1950s were a heady time for Baggs as he came into his own, yet there would be losses that reminded him of the capricious nature of life, as if he had not learned that lesson already. Just months apart in 1955, his older brother Charles Crawford, estranged for unknown reasons, died in Houston, Texas, and Frec gave birth to a stillborn child, another son.

McGill and his wife, Mary Elizabeth, had lost two daughters and were of some comfort to Baggs and Frec, but Governor Cox was the one who gave voice to the unbearable sadness. "I have been thinking much for many days of the mother of your little child and you. I happen to have had an experience quite the same. I was 23 years old, in Washington. Our first born was what they called a blue child. The valves of the heart had not closed with the first gasp of breath and he lived just a few days.... My mind often runs back to him, wondering what might have been."[30]

Baggs struggled to understand but settled into acceptance. "We have developed in the past few weeks the dogma that our little boy did not live because the Creator of all this, for reasons we do not know, did not intend for him to grow up to be a man. I am told by people who have known similar circumstances that time is the surgeon in these affairs.... You would know more about that than we, for we are only now beginning this forced journey."

As she did nearly every summer, Frec escaped Miami's heat for the lush serenity of Athens. She and Baggs celebrated their tenth anniversary apart, but he planned to meet her and son Craig in August and spend two weeks in what he called the "Carr's Hill state of mind." It was still a tree-canopied refuge where he could relax and distance himself from the growing demands of being a news columnist. While she was gone, Baggs took on additional speaking assignments and freelance work for *Field and Stream* to bring in extra money. He accepted invitations to dinner with friends and colleagues but turned down several so that he could write. By late June, he had sent a completed draft of his World War II novel to the southern editor for MacMillan Company, Norman Berg, who became a lifelong friend and mentor. Berg seemed enthusiastic about the novel and offered to share it with the editor-in-chief at Putnam if MacMillan passed. The novel never surfaced again in the letters and visits they shared over the next decade, leaving one to wonder if Baggs gave up on the dream of literary greatness or if he was swept away by the riptide of history that overwhelmed his adopted city.

CHAPTER 10

1957–1969

> But such odds have only inspired the News to act as if it were the first, best, biggest and only paper in town. Its self-confidence is very much the image of its deceptively easygoing editor.... He keeps a brass cuspidor within reachable trajectory of his desk, shows visitors the bullet hole that some disgruntled subscriber drilled through his office window, and lets his staffers strut their stuff. "Hell, I don't have much to do," he says.—The Press, *Time*, November 16, 1962

With readership plateauing in 1956, in no small part due to televisions and automobiles, and his media company showing its age, Governor Cox let loose the purse strings and invested millions in modernizing facilities for his papers and radio stations in Dayton, Atlanta, and Miami. He attended the dedications of the new plants in Ohio and Georgia and anticipated being there for the opening of the sleek new concrete building on the banks of the Miami River when he returned to the city the following winter. That summer, though, would mark his final season. The big, gregarious Midwesterner, who had started his career as a newsboy and rose to become a power player in Democratic politics, fell in the foyer of the *Dayton Daily News* offices on July 11, 1957. His doctors believed he had suffered a mild stroke and ordered him on bed rest. Four days later, at the age of eighty-seven, the former governor succumbed to a massive stroke at his home.[1]

He had written in his will "that his newspapers should remain devoted to the working people."[2] To that end, he made specific requests of his son, James M. Cox Jr., who took his father's place as the company's chief executive. Two weeks later, Cox fulfilled one of those wishes and named Baggs editor of the *Miami Daily News*. The appointment had been driven by the need to meet the promise and challenges of the second half of the twentieth century "in America's most rapidly growing metropolitan community," said the junior Cox in his announcement.[3]

Baggs had never served in a management capacity, so it is a wonder that the governor passed over men who were more qualified, at least on paper, and who had served the *News* for decades. It is possible the governor saw some of his younger self in Baggs, an extension of his by-the-bootstraps legacy. Both men were self-taught scholars with a bottomless affection for history and literature, often swapping books with one another. They both enjoyed the solace of fishing and the contemplative benefits of nature. Each possessed the capacity to move in circles both erudite and ordinary without changing their strides or manners. Because of the governor's admiration, Baggs, not yet thirty-four years old, became the youngest editor of any major daily in the country at that time.

Baggs wasted no time settling into the editor's desk and reshaping the *Daily News'* content. Even before he accepted the promotion, Baggs had insisted on a complete separation between the business and editorial sides of the paper. The editorial page would regain its independence and publisher Dan Mahoney would no longer have a say in which candidates or issues to endorse.[4] Instead, Baggs recruited a team of six editors and reporters to serve on an editorial board that grilled candidates in off-the-record sessions. After the interviews, the board would take a vote. There definitely were instances when the count went against him, and Baggs would grouse "that being editor gave him no advantage."[5]

In October 1957 the *News* moved from the faded and chipping tower on Biscayne Boulevard to a midcentury-modern marvel on Northwest Seventh Street, replete with loading docks on the Miami River. The sleek windowed foyer gave those walking or driving along the street a view through to the water. From their offices, management could see on one side the rising skyline of downtown, and into the glass-partitioned bullpen of the newsroom on the other. Production and the presses were combined and nearer to the bays where the trucks would pick up and load the home, metropolitan, and blue-streak editions for afternoon deliveries. Following a visit to the new offices, syndicated society columnist Earl Wilson gushed, "It's so big you need a tour conductor to get you to the composing room."[6]

Despite the shiny new digs, Baggs knew the *News* could not overtake its better-funded, larger-staffed rival, the *Miami Herald*. Nor did he want to. He was comfortable as the underdog, and he was a ferocious advocate for two-paper towns. Hovering around 140,000, the *News'* circulation was less than half of the *Herald's*. So, Baggs set about creating a "writers' paper"—a *New York Times* for the South—that would take a literary approach to local issues and those national and international topics of import to Miami's diverse population.[7]

By January 1958, Baggs had dropped the "Daily" from the paper's title and changed its tagline to "The Best Newspaper Under the Sun." Then he spent the next several months strategically culling 15 percent of the newsroom staff, dispensing with, among others, the red-baiting writers like Damon Runyon Jr.[8] He homed in on the spot and investigative reporting skills of Milt Sosin and Bella Kelly, and tapped into the ability of rewrite man William Tucker to put a local twist on wire reports. He hired veteran journalists Clarke Ash, as his associate editor to manage the editorial page, and Agnes Ash, Clarke's wife, to lead the business section—one of the first female business editors in the nation.[9] Later, Baggs brought humor columnist John Keasler down from Tampa. He talked photo editor Don Wright out of quitting after an argument with a colleague and cajoled Wright into drawing editorial cartoons. It was a canny move that paid off beautifully in the years ahead.[10] Baggs equated running a staff to "volunteering to be locked in a boxcar full of stallions."[11]

Welch, who had been passed over for the top job after sixteen years as the managing editor, left by mutual agreement for an assistant county manager's position in the newly formed metro government, where he remained until his retirement in 1975. He often provided scoops to the *Herald*—in an effort to avoid accusations of bias, he assured those who asked.[12]

On the recommendation of Eugene Patterson, the editor of the *Atlanta Constitution*, Baggs interviewed a hungry young reporter anxious to break into management. Jim Bellows, another Georgia boy, had cut his reporting teeth in Columbus and Atlanta before heading north to the *Detroit Free Press*. Bellows and Baggs hit it off, and Bellows was working in Miami within a few weeks of his visit.

Tall and lanky, Bellows rarely spoke above a whisper, according to former *News* staffers, but he flashed around a newsroom like a bolt of lightning. Jack Tarver, who counseled the *News* on business affairs and had grown close to Baggs, had bestowed on Bellows the nickname "the Blue Darter" when Bellows worked in Atlanta. The moniker traveled with him to Miami.[13]

"Bellows was the greatest managing editor the *News* ever had," says Howard Kleinberg, who steadily rose in the ranks from being a seventeen-year-old high school sports writer in 1950 to news editor in 1960, then to managing editor in 1966. "Bellows was the guy [who] made all of the section fronts in full-page pictures. He started that at the *Miami News*. Every story went on his spike, and he saw every story before it went to copy so he could judge his reporters. He was famous for that."[14]

Mel Frishman, who started in the newsroom as a copy boy while still in high school, recalls how Bellows would fact-check his reporters not just by verifying quotes but also by sending copy out to a few in-the-know people outside the newsroom to get a sense of whether it read true, especially during those first years of plane hijackings to Cuba and Israel. "He had a strong sense of the community and for accuracy," Frishman says.[15]

In his memoir, *The Last Editor*, Bellows gives Baggs the credit for teaching him how to deal with people, keep tabs on what was happening, and navigate two-martini lunches. Bellows called Baggs a "sidewalk editor," the kind of fellow who came from the streets, valued face-to-face conversations, and championed the powerless—not unlike a fighter Bellows would later hire as his local columnist at the *New York Herald-Tribune*, a guy out of the sports beat named Jimmy Breslin.[16]

Of their vision for the paper, Bellows wrote, "We went after the best people, paid them more, encouraged them more, and pared our staff to fit new people at the same overall cost. We didn't try to match the giant story for story. We did try to find the best editors who would exercise the best judgment on what stories to cover."

If they could only send one reporter versus the *Herald*'s three, then they would get the story the *Herald* missed by talking with people on the fringes and behind the scenes. Baggs never told his editors and reporters how to cover the news, just that they had to get it right.

One time, when Frishman had been running late on sports stories, Baggs called him into the office.

"Well, let me explain . . . ," Frishman began.

"Don't explain. Just don't [be late]," Baggs responded, matter of fact.

Frishman swears he never missed another deadline. "You didn't want to disappoint him. He engendered that loyalty without being a tyrant."

"Feel free," was Baggs's answer to editors when asked if they could approach a story from a different angle or try a new layout, as in the time Bellows and team retraced the human toll of Hurricane Donna from the moment it struck the Leeward Islands to its final stop off the coast of Maine.[17] He said "feel free" so often that his executive secretary and loyal gatekeeper, Myrtle Rathner, "Miss Myrt" to all, cross-stitched those words and framed them for his office wall. It hung near another embroidered decoration that read, "A Nervous Man Shouldn't Be Here in the First Place," a saying that Keasler called Baggs's "editorial creed."

Anytime the paper scored an exclusive because of Baggs's connections—an interview with former President Harry S. Truman, an account of rehiring of a county manager unjustly fired—they "promoted the hell out of it," most often by taking ads out in the *Herald*.[18]

Every morning after oatmeal, coffee, and a perusal of the *Times* and the *Post*, Baggs arrived at the office by six, before almost anyone else. His hair, if not in a crew cut, would be as askew as his seersucker suit, which was "wrinkled the moment it came off the hanger." When the newsroom was filled, he stood in his office doorway and yelled, "Ain't newspaperin' fun?" Then, according to one of Bellows's reporters, "he'd rip a mad cackle and dart into his burrow."[19] By seven, he was already penning one of the six columns he wrote each week.

When he became editor, Baggs renamed his column View of the News and moved it to the top-right corner of the editorial page. There, he started playing around with satire, introducing characters like a talking raccoon and wild turkey that hung out on the "low shoulder of a hammock in the Everglades," where alligators and water moccasins lurked just off the page and "civilization ain't so civilized." Walt Kelly, the syndicated cartoonist most famous for the comic strip *Pogo* and a close friend of Baggs's, drew the two characters to accompany these columns. With the two creatures conversing, Baggs tackled multiple sides of controversial issues. Raccoon was a deep digger full of intellectual curiosity, and Turkey an easily flustered tenderfoot. Over the years, they discussed nuclear disarmament, quiz show scandals, rising pharmaceutical costs, and the growing reliance on "mother's little helpers" in the modern era. On one occasion, they lamented that the theory of evolution was an insult to monkeys because monkeys never did so much harm to "this old green earth." One of Raccoon's diatribes about the false rationality of austerity and balanced budgets confirmed for many a reader that the striped-tail bandit was Baggs's alter ego.

Some of his more popular columns appeared as imaginary letters, memos, and telegrams between heads of state, legislators, or CIA operatives, mocking group-think, missed connections, and bureaucratic legalese. In one example, he presented "cablegrams intercepted from our far-flung correspondents in the basement of the CIA," running on March 27, 1965.

Dear Fidel,

I saw a newspaper story quoting an American doctor as saying everything is hunky-dory in Cuba. Good economy. Plenty of food. But you told me something different.

Alexei Kosygin

Moscow

Dear Alexei,

The spirit of the free people of Cuba soars to heights far greater than an astronaut. But we could use some rice and Polish hams.

Castro

Yet no matter the form a column took, Baggs would take progressive stands rather than court the milquetoast middle ground on topics such as school desegregation, Cuban refugee resettlement, and environmental degradation.[20]

In 1959, the Florida regional chapter of the Anti-Defamation League of B'nai B'rith honored Baggs with the Leonard Abess Human Relations Award for bringing about "better understanding among the peoples of Florida." At the same time, however, he received so much hate mail he could not answer it all, as much as he tried to use those opportunities to open a dialogue or convince a reader not to cancel their subscription. He resorted to picking and choosing which ones demanded a longer response, based on the recommendation of his circulation manager or news editor. For all the others, he commissioned a rubber stamp with the words, "This is not a simple life, my friend, and there are no simple answers." He stamped those words on postcards and mailed them to his detractors.[21]

Even if Baggs encountered challenges with the complicated nature of adults, he possessed an effortless ability to connect with kids. Children were welcome in his office, at his home, and at any party—business or celebratory. Although Miss Myrt proved a stern guardian of her boss's time, she rarely stopped a staff member's child from visiting the editor to get a hug and a story or a treat from the gumball machine Baggs kept on his desk to raise money for UNICEF.[22] Baggs's son Craig remembers "dashing through the city newsroom in my Sir Lancelot cape and sword to meet my father on the other side, only to feel somehow part of the crusade."[23]

Don Stinson, whose father started at the *News* the same day as Baggs in 1946, recalls Baggs's impressions of Huckleberry Hound and his vivid stories of the Seminole attack on the Cape Florida lighthouse on Key Biscayne. Baggs's passion for reading made such an impression on the young Stinson that he has remained a voracious reader throughout his life.[24]

Baggs felt a deep need to preserve the wonder of childhood, perhaps because his own had been cut so short. In 1951, Baggs penned a Christmas Eve column that grew into an annual tradition for the *News* over the next twenty years. He wrote the original one directly to children around the age of five or six who might be beginning to disbelieve in Santa Claus, wanting them to hold onto the enchantment of the season just as he had.

"I'll never forget the day when the older boys told me there was no Santa Claus," he began the column. He was calling on the memory of when his neighborhood hero, the best football player he knew, laughed at him and said it was just "make-believe." But Judge Alexander Stephens, the man who had served as Baggs's guardian after his mother's death, told him the story of the real St. Nicholas, a wealthy fourth-century merchant who left a poor family a bag of gold and committed other good deeds each year until his death.

"Nicholas was a giver, who loved little children. He was as real as anybody alive today," Baggs wrote. "The older boys were wrong. There is a Santa Claus."[25]

Early in their courtship and marriage, Baggs and Frec had envisioned a rambling house full of kids. But after their second son was stillborn, they had not been blessed with another pregnancy. Baggs had spoken with Frec about adopting, but not in any great detail, she admitted in her memoir. As an orphan himself, Baggs held a special affinity for men like Pa, Judge Stephens, and Ralph McGill—all surrogates for C. C. It was only natural, then, that when he received a call in 1961 from the Children's Service Bureau about a four-year-old boy named Bobby, he made a visit to the LeJeune House, the foster home where the CSB children lived.

For nearly a decade, Baggs had served on the board of the CSB, originally an offshoot of the Junior League that provided shelter, clothing, and food to children without parents or who had been removed from unsafe, unstable homes. Baggs talked it over with Craig and Frec, then he and Frec went to meet Bobby. When they got there, Bobby was backed into a corner by three older boys and he was loaded for bear.

"When I was introduced by the foster home matron, all four children changed immediately. . . . They all knew, instantly, why I was there and hoped the 'nice lady' would choose one of them," recalled Frec. She was impressed by Bobby's independence and forthrightness after they spoke for a while. He always looked her in the eye. Bobby came home with them for dinner, and then he stayed for good. Later, when the adoption was finalized, Bobby and Baggs discussed a name change, and Robert Mahoney Baggs officially became part of the family. From that day onward, Bobby was called Mahoney.[26]

By then, the Baggs family had moved to French City Village in Coral Gables, an enclave (at the time) of nine spacious French Regency townhomes built in the 1920s and set behind a series of high interconnected walls and courtyard gardens. Their two-story home at 1029 Hardee Road sat next door to the Allen home, where son Charles became a playmate of Craig and Mahoney's. The Allen matriarch served on the board of Belcher Oil, which Baggs eventually would confront over the fight for Biscayne Bay.[27] To the south at the far end of the block lived Alec, Lacy, and Brian Jones. Their father, Beverly, was a renowned physician at Jackson Memorial Hospital and Doctor's Hospital and became a close friend of Baggs's despite their opposing politics. Their mother Rosemary, who hailed from Savannah, Georgia, was one of the rare female judges in town, and her prickly personality often rubbed Frec, the belle from Athens, the wrong way.[28]

The block, home also to pilots, professors, and their growing broods, all sent their kids to the same schools—Sunset Elementary, then the Cushman School, where Frec taught English, or Ransom and Everglades. They belonged to the same country club, where Baggs was known to golf with a single telescoping club that turned into a putter, a driver, an iron, or a wedge based on which way the head was twisted.[29] With these connected couples and their passel of kids, nearly seventeen among them and counting, the French City Village became "cocktail central," where nearly every weekend the families gathered in the backyards and around pools to sip and savor. When Bill and Frec hosted, Baggs would play Leonard Bernstein or mambo music on his hi-fi.[30] Every Christmas Eve, the Baggses held a party for the *News* families and their ever-widening circle of friends. Jolly St. Nick—played with relish by Al Daniels, the head of Burdine's Department Store—delivered gifts. Alec Jones says he realized Baggs was a big deal and not just any ordinary dad when he walked into one of the holiday parties and NBC correspondent Sander Vanocur was there clinking glasses.[31]

Baggs's cache of contacts had grown considerably by the late 1950s. McGill had sponsored Baggs's election to the American Society of

Newspaper Editors (ASNE), which put Baggs in the company of the *Times*' James "Scotty" Reston and the *Post*'s Philip Graham, among others. Ashmore, who had taken a brief leave from the *Arkansas Gazette* to support Illinois governor Adlai Stevenson's 1956 bid for the U.S. presidency, opened many doors for his fellow Camp Followers. Baggs's longstanding friendship with Bernard Baruch led to a cordial acquaintance and correspondence with former president Harry S. Truman.[32] Most significantly, Baggs's continued coverage of political conventions led to friendships with governors, senators, and congressmen on both sides of the aisle, particularly Senator John F. Kennedy and Vice President Richard M. Nixon, which led to an amusing confrontation in the fall of 1960.

Watching the third Nixon-Kennedy debate on television, a seven-year-old Craig looked over at his father and said, "Daddy, I like that man." He was referring to Nixon. When a stunned Baggs asked why, his son replied, "Because he is trying so hard."

Baggs relayed the story to the vice president in a lightly teasing letter. "I tried all the arguments I knew to convince my son that although he is not quite eight years old and cannot vote, he should talk up the candidacy of John Kennedy."

"I've got a right to believe in what I believe in and I believe this," Baggs reported Craig as saying, as his son marched off to his room.

"And you probably think you've got troubles," Baggs ended the letter.

Nixon replied directly to Craig: "You may be sure that support such as yours is giving me inspiration during these closing weeks of our drive to victory on November 8 and I greatly appreciate it. Incidentally, I hope that you will not be too disappointed with my good friend, your Dad, as even the finest of fathers sometimes get on the wrong side of the political fence! Perhaps you can persuade him as to the rightness of our cause."[33]

When Baggs responded to Nixon a few days later, he asked if Nixon had had anything to do with the lightning bolt that had ripped a hole in the roof and knocked Baggs out of bed while he was reading to Craig on Halloween evening.[34] That jolt would hardly be the first or last time Baggs's world was shaken.

Childhood

Crawford Collins Baggs, circa 1923. *Courtesy Mahoney and Valerie Baggs*

The only known image of Kate Bush Baggs, holding newborn daughter, Billie, with ten-year-old son, Charles Crawford Baggs, circa 1920. *Courtesy Mahoney and Valerie Baggs*

Aunt Grace Bush and
Uncle William "Pa"
Dancer. *Courtesy Craig
and Mary Baggs*

Cousins Felix Bush (left)
and "Calhoun" Baggs, in
Colquitt, Georgia, circa
1926. *Courtesy of Craig
and Mary Baggs*

"Calhoun" Baggs as a toddler in Colquitt, Georgia, circa 1926. *Courtesy of Craig and Mary Baggs*

"Calhoun" Baggs, aged 12 or 13, playing ball. He lettered in multiple sports in high school and was a lifelong tennis player. *Courtesy Craig and Mary Baggs*

Bill Grow's SS Class Colquitt ME Church in 1938: Front Row L to R: Barbara Bell and Jessie Ann Drake: Second row L to R: Mary Jean Bailey, Laura Jim Rawlings, Joyce Newberry, Ann Johnson: Third row L to R: Buck Bell, Jr., and Ruth Jinks: Fourth row L to R: Dorothy Wilkin, Lynwood Jinks, Billy Spencer and Felix Bush, Jr.; Fifth row L to R: Clyde Jinks, Jr., Harold Long, Wiley Bird; Sixth row L to R: Ray Cross, Gordon Wilkin, Bill Grow, teacher, and Calhoun Baggs.

Courtesy of Mrs. R. N. Bell

Colquitt resident Laverne Kimbrel Shaw, now 93, held onto this clipping from the *Miller County Liberal* since 1972. It is a picture of Bill Grow's Sunday school class from Colquitt Methodist Church, circa 1938. "Calhoun" Baggs is pictured in the upper right corner. *Courtesy of Laverne Kimbrel Shaw*

"Calhoun" Baggs (fourth from left, top row), aged 17, played receiver
for Miller County High School's championship six-man football team
in 1940–41. *Courtesy of Harold Moore*

Cadet William C. Baggs, seated in the middle at the desk, helmed the *Bombs Away, 44-1* yearbook staff as editor. Here, he is pictured with fellow bombardier candidates and yearbook staff from the Hell from Heaven detachment at Midland Army Air Field in Midland, Texas. *Courtesy Craig and Mary Baggs*

Baggs flew with the Davis crew, the first replacement crew for the 830th squadron of the 485th Heavy Bomb Group. The entire crew completed all fifty missions from May through September 1944. Pictured from left to right, back row: Herman G. Davis, pilot; Charles Parker, copilot; Baggs, bombardier; Jesse Hartley, navigator; front row, left to right: Albert G. Dupuis, ball gunner; Isadore Kozatch, engineer/waist gunner; Tony M. Gallegos, tail gunner; Edward Gunn, radio operator/top turret gunner; Harold P. Dupuy, nose gunner; Andrew Dougherty, waist gunner. "The Mongrel," front and center, slept with Baggs. *Photography courtesy of Craig and Mary Baggs. Crew names and information courtesy of Jerry Whiting, historian, 485th Bomb Group, Fifteenth Air Force.*

From Baggs's service scrapbook, an image of B-24s on a bombing run over Ploesti, Romania. *Courtesy Craig and Mary Baggs*

B-24s in a field of flak bursts. *Courtesy Craig and Mary Baggs*

2nd Lt. William C. Baggs, 1944. *Courtesy Craig and Mary Baggs*

Baggs and Joan "Frec" Orr met at a Red Cross dance in Miami Beach in November 1944 and were married on June 7, 1945, in the courtyard of the Greenbriar Hotel. *Courtesy Craig and Mary Baggs*

Reporting

Baggs as the new aviation reporter for the *Miami Daily News*
in 1946. *Courtesy Craig and Mary Baggs*

A practical joker, Baggs captured the attention of his fellow reporters and publishers with his wit. *Courtesy Craig and Mary Baggs*

First hired as an aviation reporter, Baggs developed friendships with many in the burgeoning industry, including Juan Trippe, founder of Pan Am Airways. Notice Baggs's wrinkled suit—his look. *Courtesy Craig and Mary Baggs*

All decked out, Baggs and Frec (at the bottom of the stairs) await the inaugural flight of Pan Am's Flight Club to Havana, Cuba. *Courtesy Craig and Mary Baggs*

One of the many test headshots taken of Baggs for his new column, In the Bag with Bill Baggs, 1949. *Courtesy Craig and Mary Baggs*

In 1951, Baggs traveled throughout Europe for the Man in the Middle series. He interviewed everyday factory workers, farmers, shopkeepers, vendors, newspapermen, and people he had met during the war to discern the economic and social improvements under the Marshall Plan as well as what it was like "living in the shadow of the Iron Curtain." This series introduced Baggs to a national audience when his columns were carried across all of the Cox newspapers. *Courtesy Craig and Mary Baggs*

When Baggs was home, Frec would often find him wrapped up in a book or a magazine. He was known to devour up to three books a week and was an avid reader of *Harper's* and *Time* magazines. *Courtesy Craig and Mary Baggs*

The proud papa with newborn son Craig, February 1953. *Courtesy Craig and Mary Baggs*

An early adopter of the new medium of television, Baggs (far right) served as a regular contributor to *What's the Story?*, hosted by wJCL Miami's longtime news director, Ralph Renick (far left). *Courtesy Craig and Mary Baggs*

Larry King (center) launched his broadcast career in 1957 on Miami's
AM radio stations. By the 1960s, he also hosted a roundtable interview
show on WTVJ, where Baggs visited to talk about his visit to North
Vietnam. *Courtesy Craig and Mary Baggs*

PART III

From Cuba to Vietnam

CHAPTER 11

1958–1962

Lordy, it is hard to be on the good side in this world, isn't it?—To governor of
Puerto Rico Luis Muñoz Marín, October 10, 1961

Even as Baggs charged his news team to maintain a hyperlocal focus, he
understood that "local" was relative, given Miami's geopolitical vantage
point. Baggs's own interest in the Caribbean and Latin America was tethered to his years living and working in Panama. Reporting on people and
events throughout the region, he grew finely attuned to how persistent
poverty, hunger, and illiteracy in developing nations, as well as in America's
ignored inner cities, fomented revolution. By putting down roots in Miami,
he became acquainted and empathized with the exile and immigrant communities that had settled in South Florida. Because he experienced first-
hand a Yugoslavia diminished by communism and dictatorship, his ears
were constantly to the ground, listening for the sounds of boots marching
northward from Argentina, Guatemala, and Mexico.

Beginning in 1949, Baggs had begun traveling to Puerto Rico, where
he struck up a warm and trusting friendship with Governor Luis Muñoz
Marín that lasted throughout Baggs's life. Baggs followed the evolution of
the island's redevelopment program, known as Operation Bootstrap. He
returned nearly every year, reporting the territory's progress through news
articles and columns, and, within a decade, he saw marked improvement
in slum eradication and increased participation in education and industrial investment.[1] It was clear evidence to Baggs that a U.S.-style economy
and democracy could thrive throughout the region if it were accompanied
by patience and public-private partnerships in housing, schools, infra-
structure, and business.[2]

"I submit the stronger we build our New World, from Cape Horn to
Canada, and beyond," Baggs wrote in a column during the summer of 1954,

"the better chance we have of surviving the assaults and traps of the Old World."[3]

After he was named editor, Baggs hosted a forum in 1958 with a small group of Latin American newspapermen touring the United States at the invitation of the U.S. State Department. The group warned of growing resentment in countries throughout the Western Hemisphere, where the United States had propped up totalitarian regimes and dictatorships, such as in the Dominican Republic and Venezuela, rather than take the "bootstrap" approach of tax incentives and industrial development in Puerto Rico. They also predicted that with its succor of trade agreements, military assistance, and financial aid, the Soviet Union would gain an advantage among the developing nations of the Western Hemisphere.[4]

Both his columns and his letters to business and political leaders took on a tone of caution against America's "appropriating to Europe and to Asia more than their appropriate importance," because it left the country blind to the problems bubbling up in its own back yard.[5] He expressed this worry to then–vice president Richard Nixon, a frequent visitor to Key Biscayne, with whom Baggs had dined on Thursday, April 16, 1959, while in Washington attending his first ASNE meeting.

"I think that there is a tremendous need for the United States to try to restore itself to the position of a friendly papa in the hemisphere," wrote Baggs in a follow-up letter. "It worries me that with such a tremendous economic system, so explosive and detonating as it expands, that we have been unable to export the principle of our economy to so many countries in this world."[6]

On that same trip to Washington, Baggs interviewed Cuba's new leader Fidel Castro, who spoke by invitation to the ASNE membership in gratitude for a largely supportive and often effusive American press, which had been captivated by Castro's youthful machismo as he, his brother Raul, and their friend Ernesto "Che" Guevara led their rebel forces from the Sierra Maestra into Havana only four months earlier.[7] It was Castro's first visit to the United States since the *Revolución Cubana*, and he was on a two-week goodwill tour, seeking financial support for his new government.

Baggs felt no nostalgia for the repressive and corrupt Fulgencio Batista, Cuba's deposed dictator. For nearly two decades, he and the *News* team sat ringside as the regime's ties to the Mafia's gambling and illegal drug trade spilled onto Miami's soil. The *News'* Havana correspondent, Jay Mallin, was forced to find alternative means of conveying his reports off the island and to his editors, through Mexico or the Bahamas, because of Batista's scissor-wielding censors.[8] Mallin had found himself on the business end of a revolver more than once and had to flee to the Swedish embassy in Havana to avoid jail. Yet he managed to report Batista's secret flight out of Cuba less than an hour after it occurred, giving the *News* an edge over its bigger and better-funded rivals.[9]

During the three months since the revolution, Baggs had put off meeting with Castro, who had invited Baggs to Cuba more than once.[10] Given the island's troubled history before independence, Baggs exhibited cautious hope for the inexperienced leader.[11] However, he held little romance for revolutionaries, simply because he had witnessed throughout the world how punch-drunk with power they became soon after winning. Now, with a private audience arranged to take place during Castro's visit to the States, Baggs would finally get to judge for himself.

Their confab was delayed by four hours and began at midnight in Castro's Washington, D.C., hotel room. They drank beer and talked for more than two hours, so at ease in one another's presence that Castro removed his signature cap and Baggs kicked off his size-twelve brogans. Castro exhibited a "scholarly" aptitude regarding revolutions, often invoking the words of Lincoln, Jefferson, and Washington. He lamented that Americans had lost their rebellious spirit.

Baggs asked Castro point blank if he were a communist, which Castro flatly denied, going so far as to say he hoped to hold an election within a year and return to the countryside. Although Baggs was impressed by Castro's "enormous sincerity," he walked away with one part hope and two parts doubt that Castro had the sagacity "to translate the revolution into a democratic government."[12]

In a follow-up letter to Castro, Baggs implored the new Cuban leader to set aside his own ambitions in order to stabilize the island nation, which had been ravaged by one corrupt dictatorship after another since Cuba had gained its independence from Spain in 1898. "One more word from a friend of the Cuban people," he offered. "With all respect to you and to your associates, I do not think that the revolution has been organized well enough to invest its philosophy into government. And, in all candor, I must say I am very worried about this."[13]

Baggs alerted Nixon to misgivings Castro had shared with him that reaffirmed the warnings of the pressmen from the year before. "Dr. Castro has gained the impression that animosity towards the United States is much more widespread than many of us would have believed. This animosity is generated by people of all economic groups and of [all] political faiths."[14] Nixon responded that he believed Castro would be "a man to reckon with in the Americas in the years to come," but, as he told Baggs, he thought it possible Castro would change his attitude toward America if public opinion shifted away from him.[15]

Baggs made his own shift in short order. Within a few months, and more so over time, Castro had assumed the role of dictator, seizing private lands, expropriating U.S. and other foreign businesses, implementing communist indoctrination into the educational system, and growing ever closer to the Soviet Union for military and economic support. He freely, often, and openly criticized the United States, the "Yanqui imperialists," in long-winded addresses. And, instead of allowing space for dissent or free elections, Castro's detractors were either imprisoned or executed by firing squad.[16]

That summer of 1959, the massive migration of Cubans off the island into South Florida began, altering forever the political, social, and economic landscape of Miami, and ensuring its transformation from beach resort town and retirement community to global city. The first wave of immigrants comprised wealthy landowners who often made it across the Florida Straits with only a portion of their riches intact. In the second wave came the professional class—the doctors, lawyers, engineers, and architects. In the third, farmers, teachers, and laborers.[17] Between December 1960 and October 1962, more than fourteen thousand unaccompanied minors, aided by the Catholic Welfare Bureau, fled Cuba through Operation Pedro Pan. Throughout Miami and surrounding areas, children were placed with relatives or in homes and camps run by church and refugee organizations.[18] Beginning in the spring of 1961, Pan American World Airways sent up to two empty planes daily from Miami to ferry more than 19,600 refugees over an eighteen-month period.[19] More than 280,000 Cuban refugees poured into Miami from 1959 to 1962, almost all of them processed through the old and empty *Miami Daily News* building on Biscayne Bay, which became known locally as the Freedom Tower.

"Caught up in a little eddy of the Cold War, Miami has become a sort of modern Ellis Island, renewing the old promise of our country to receive all who come to seek freedom, and it is as necessary a work as it is often a difficult one," Baggs wrote in a letter to a student several years later. "I must say that I am very proud of this city for the intelligence and adult manner it has displayed in handling this role which circumstances have thrust upon it."[20]

Within a few short years, one in every ten Miamians was a Cuban refugee. Baggs listened to their stories and worked toward their assimilation as he served on the county's resettlement committee and fought for federal funding to help with the efforts.

Howard Kleinberg, the *News'* sports editor at the time, offers a slightly different take on the tectonic shift the Cuban Revolution exerted on his home. "It dominated us. I wrote a column about feeling like a stranger in my own town. It changed Miami from a middle-sized Southern town, which I loved and really enjoyed, into a madhouse."[21]

Few of the refugees, however, thought they would live in the United States for long. Hundreds of anti-Castro organizations were formed to plot and prepare for Castro's eventual overthrow.

All through 1960, the Eisenhower administration ramped up its efforts to quell the growing influence of the hemisphere's newest dictator. President Eisenhower, under the guidance of Nixon and Allen Dulles, director of the Central Intelligence Agency, authorized the CIA to secretly train and equip paramilitary forces made up of exiles, many of whom had no previous combat experience, for an eventual invasion. Later, the president signed off on a State Department proposal to back a predicted uprising of Cubans who remained on the island.[22] These two directives brought veteran operatives, such as future White House "plumbers" E. Howard Hunt and Bernard Barker, to Miami, which became host to a series of spy games that would tether the city forever to some of the twentieth century's most seismic political events: the Bay of Pigs Invasion, the Cuban Missile Crisis, the assassination of President John F. Kennedy, and Watergate. The administration had also set in motion a plot to hire Mafia hit men, smarting from the loss of Havana's gambling and prostitution revenue, to assassinate Castro.[23]

This new chapter in the Cold War also ushered in a change in the relationship between the CIA and the American press. Baggs, the *Miami News*, and its rival the *Miami Herald* found themselves smack in the center.

As Kleinberg recalls, *Miami Herald* reporter David Kraslow "got a tip that there was a lot of rifle practice going on in South Dade, and he investigated to get a story that Cuban exiles were rehearsing in the Everglades, and the *Herald* rejected [his article]. Why?"[24]

Up until this point, this agency devoted to secrecy had used precision in leaking information in order to garner public support for missions that most often took place on foreign soil. With Miami now a hub of operations, the local press got an up-close-and-personal account of CIA activities and began to question its intentions and often overpromised outcomes.[25]

Kleinberg says that if he were to get Kraslow's story today, it would be all over the front page.

During the political season leading up to the 1960 presidential election, Baggs appealed to both the Democratic and Republican National Committees to recognize the economic disparity in Latin America as part of their platforms. As he elucidated, the United States was in a unique position: with just 6 percent of the world's population, it generated nearly 38 percent of its income, while Latin American represented almost 8 percent of the world's population and only 5 percent of its income. Baggs envisioned a sort-of modified Marshall Plan to help bring economic strength and political unity, more than military might, to the Western Hemisphere. He advocated for education, technical assistance, and an ease of trade tariffs more than thirty years before the North American Free Trade Agreement was signed. He recruited his widely respected Puerto Rican friend, Governor Marín, to write articles for the *Miami News* proposing as much, which were circulated in newspapers throughout the country.[26]

The fate of the CIA's clandestine plans, however, hung in the balance after Senator John F. Kennedy was elected president that November. Eight days after Kennedy took office in January 1961, he got his first briefing on the CIA's collaboration with exiles to spark a quick and decisive civil war in Cuba.[27] In the time between his election victory and the inauguration, Kennedy summoned Baggs to the family compound in Palm Beach and solicited his advice on issues of concern in South Florida—civil rights and Cuba, among them—tapping Baggs as an unofficial and sporadic member of the Kennedy kitchen cabinet.[28]

While Baggs believed the journalist's role in society was to inform and enlighten the citizenry and hold the powerful accountable, his actions after he became editor show that he also believed he had a personal responsibility to inform decision makers, within reason, of his impressions and findings. The facts and opinions Baggs gathered through on-the-ground research, observation, and reporting he shared generously with local, state, and national business and political leaders, in the hope that he could help add to or even shape the strategic conversations taking place in board and conference rooms.

On April 15, 1961, the *News* reported that Kennedy was honoring the seventy-first anniversary of the Organization of American States by pledging "to assist free men and free governments in casting off the chains of poverty." Under another banner headline that day, the *News* announced that four planes manned by defecting Cuban Air Force pilots had bombed the island. (The world would later learn that the planes, repainted American b-26 bombers, had been flown out of Nicaragua by exiles and that Castro had already moved his air force to another location, circumventing the attack.)

The next day, the *News'* Latin American editor Hal Hendrix posted a story about counterrevolutionary unity among Miami's exile community, while the not-so-secret CIA recruiting center on S.W. 4th Street was slammed with more than six hundred refugees ready to enlist in efforts to overthrow Castro. On April 17, 1961, the Bay of Pigs Invasion began in full force, but Castro and his army awaited the aggressors at Playa Giron, overwhelming the ill-prepared invaders, who found themselves mired in the swampy landing. The CIA's forecasted uprising by the Cuban people never materialized, because of both Castro's strong hold on the population as well as the number of sympathizers who had welcomed the revolution. After the failed first air strike on April 15, Kennedy scuttled a second one, which left the invading exiles vulnerable and exposed. Within two days, the *News'* coverage had turned grim, reporting that two Americans and seven exiles had been executed, 114 others had died, and hundreds had been captured.

Despite Baggs's relationship with Kennedy, little information flowed from Washington to enliven the paper's reporting. His editor's column on the day of the invasion, "A Single Issue," heralded the men who sought to "regain a revolution which was kidnapped from them," while also looking halfway across the world at the communist incursion in Laos with the weary realization that the Cold War was a different animal than the world had ever known. He had no patience for the Soviets' hypocrisy in criticizing United States training of anti-Castro groups while the Russians were supplying Castro with jets, tanks, and antiaircraft guns.

On April 20, Castro claimed victory over the invasion with more than eleven hundred exiles locked away in Cuba's prisons. That same day, Baggs traveled to Washington for the annual meeting of newspaper editors. Kennedy, stung by the Bay of Pigs failure and his misplaced faith in his military and intelligence advisors, addressed the crowd.

According to Baggs, the consensus among those in the room was that the young president had declared "war" on the Soviet Union by defining a new kind of struggle requiring "discipline." The battles in this new war, Baggs wrote days later, were drawn along political, economic, and psychological lines. "These are the battles in the new 'war,' and unless we win them, we lose the 'war,' no matter how many atomic weapons are stored in the national barn."[29]

Not one month after the Bay of Pigs, the military dictator of the Dominican Republic, Rafael Trujillo, was assassinated following a bloody thirty-one-year reign. With Castro's growing influence and calls for independence coming from colonial states throughout the Caribbean Basin, Baggs urged the Kennedy administration to seize the opportunity to nurture democracy.[30]

In a private conversation with his old pal Adlai Stevenson, now the ambassador to the United Nations, Baggs shared his opinion on a way forward, then followed up with Kennedy with advice on where to turn within his own administration for support. "[Deputy Assistant Secretary of State for Inter-American Affairs] Arturo Morales Carrión knows a great deal about the trouble in the Dominican Republic, and I think he can explain, as well as any man, why this trouble is urgent. At the expense of being considered rude, and certainly impolitic, I might add that Morales Carrión knows a great deal more than some of his associates in Washington think he knows."[31]

That September, Secretary of State Dean Rusk appointed Baggs to serve as observer to the Caribbean Organization, a newly formed moderating body of island nations allied with Britain, France, the Netherlands, and the United States.[32] The president tasked Baggs with delivering a message on his behalf at the establishing assembly. Crossing over from journalist to unofficial diplomat, Baggs obliged, donning his trademark seersucker suit.

"A new kind of 'Yanqui' is emerging," he read. "He is one who wants to see in the twentieth century that every human in the Americas shall acquire learning, to read and write . . . and that all families live under roofs which do not leak. When we accomplish this, we believe the Americas will become a community of achieving people who will achieve a better life."[33]

Later, in describing the moment to Harry Ashmore, Baggs wrote, "at the end of the message, I advised the several hundred spectators they had just witnessed history. This was the first time Mr. Kennedy ever had delivered an address in a Southern accent."[34]

These duties were not typical of a daily newspaper editor, then or now. But then, as a U.S. senator Kennedy had developed cordial friendships and confidences with a number of journalists, including his old Georgetown neighbor Ben Bradlee of the *Washington Post* and Scotty Reston of the *New York Times*, which he carried with him into the White House.

Before being drawn further into international politics and the day-to-day work of the Caribbean Organization, Baggs resigned his observer post four months later in January 1962. In his letter to Secretary Rusk, he recommended that the United States provide planning experts, engineers, and other technical and economic guidance to the Caribbean nations. He added that the United States should do everything to "make as much noise as possible in the press" about this type of developmental diplomacy, even if it peeved the country's allies. "The pinch should be small," he wrote. "Our reward should be a warmer friendship with the people down there."[35]

Attorney General Robert Kennedy apparently did not get that memo. Even with the civil rights struggle growing more violent throughout the South and his Justice Department opening another front with a war on organized crime—a rich irony, considering—the attorney general was fixated on bringing Castro down by whatever means necessary, even if it involved outright murder. In tandem with the CIA and the National Security Administration, Robert launched Operation Mongoose, the largest peacetime spy operation in U.S. history. The CIA's Miami office, once a small outpost, mushroomed into the agency's biggest.[36]

Baggs had little knowledge of Robert's relationship with Operation Mongoose, however. In fact, he was concerned enough about the tenor and scope of CIA activities in South Florida to file a claim of "improper conduct," which was submitted to the Department of Justice and went all the way up to the attorney general.[37]

Miami churned in those days with what Clarke Ash, the *News'* associate editor, later described as a "frenzied level of anti-Castro activity—rallies, parades, radio broadcasts, demonstrations of all sorts." He believed, along with most of the *News'* editorial staff, that the CIA was taking advantage of and stoking the anti-Castro fervor with significant investments in propaganda. Ash recalled that "Baggs used to tease the CIA in his columns and CIA replies would appear mysteriously in his home mailbox."[38]

But that didn't stop *News* reporters from pulling whatever leads they could from CIA operatives. The secretive Hendrix, who spoke as if he had a permanent case of laryngitis because of a childhood accident, was nick-named "the spook" because of his ability to gather details long before the Kennedy administration would confirm or deny them.[39] Mary Louise Wilkinson, a former reporter for the *Havana Times*, often listed her husband's profession as "advertising." In reality, he led the CIA field office on the Swan Islands just off the coast of Honduras, where anti-Castro radio messages were broadcast daily. Another reporter, Dennis Berend, left the paper to become an official spokesman for the agency, eventually landing in Panama.[40]

It is possible that the CIA viewed Baggs and his team as "assets," as Gil Cranberg, editor of the *Des Moines Register and Tribune*, claimed years later in an opinion piece. (Hendrix eventually parlayed his CIA connections into more lucrative jobs after he left the *News*.) However, according to Dr. David Hadley, who conducted extensive research into the ties between the CIA and the press for his book *The Rising Clamor*, it is more likely that Baggs saw the CIA as just one of many valuable sources of information.

"It was a strange paper in those days," says Kleinberg. "I would think Bill knew these guys were affiliated with the CIA, but it was going along with the U.S. government on foreign policy, which is not something we do anymore."[41]

CHAPTER 12

1962–1964

Very seldom is there anything moral in war or the prelude to war. You must tell this boy this truth.—"The Children," *Miami News*, October 23, 1962

At some point after the Bay of Pigs fiasco in 1961 and before the Cuban Missile Crisis in 1962, President Kennedy installed a secure phone line in Baggs's home study that connected directly to the Oval Office. Baggs instructed Frec and their sons never to answer the phone, no matter how many times it rang, even if he were away. Craig, however, did one time under the watchful eye of his father, and got a kick when the man with the Boston Brahmin accent on the other end said, "Well, hello, Craig, how are you?"[1]

Looking back, Craig surmises that Kennedy needed someone in South Florida who would tell him the truth about what was happening on the ground. He also suspects that his father had no qualms telling the president when he or someone in his administration had it wrong. His dad, Craig says, lived by the creed, "Don't ever let anybody have something on you."

Baggs seemed able to strike a balance between his friendship with Kennedy and his ethical responsibility as a journalist. A review of his columns shows he rarely soft-pedaled his criticism of the president or the federal government, when necessary, even owning up to not pushing hard enough for information on the Bay of Pigs Invasion when he had the opportunity.[2] He also grew frustrated with Kennedy's press secretary, Pierre Salinger, who tightly managed information. Baggs even went so far as to criticize the administration at a speech to the Chicago Headline Club in the winter of 1963. "Newspapers should gain new precision, new accuracy, and perspective," he told the roomful of journalists, whom he also indicted for publishing stories based on gossip and innuendo without confirmation from verifiable sources. "If there is any meaning in America, truth is the vital part of our weaponry, and not managed news."[3]

Kleinberg affirms that the newspaper's honor remained intact. "We had a reputation, even among the Cuban exiles, of telling it right, telling it straight. People respected us for that."

On the morning of October 6, 1962, before he left for work, Baggs received a call on the secure line at home. No one knows if the call came directly from the president or one of his aides, but whoever called provided Baggs with intelligence on Cuba—a list of possible missile launch sites on the island. Baggs immediately contacted Hendrix, who for weeks had been running down rumors that the Soviets were building half a dozen, maybe more, ground-to-ground intermediate-range missile launch sites throughout Cuba, capable of blasting missiles with nuclear warheads as far south as the Panama Canal and as far north as the interior of the United States. The list provided by Baggs confirmed Hendrix's leads.

As his reporter worked quietly to verify the information through other channels, Baggs performed a little gumshoe reporting himself. He tapped into the network of Cuban exiles who had provided him with verifiable leads in the past. He met with a young fixer at the English Pub at the Jamaica Inn on Key Biscayne—one of Baggs's favorite haunts. There, the young man, who had just returned from Cuba by way of Mexico, revealed that an increasing number of Russians were living on the island and had almost completed a launch site near the village of San Cristobal. Baggs passed on the information to Hendrix, who wrote the lead story for the next day's paper.[4]

"Soviets Build 6 Cuban Missile Bases" screamed the seventy-two-point headline on October 7, 1962. The *News* was the only paper with the story. The White House officially denied the intelligence reports. Undersecretary of State George Ball had even said the week before that Cuba was "still not a military threat."

News editor John O'Neil challenged Baggs and refused to publish any further reports by Hendrix until the White House, State Department, or Defense Department went on the record. Baggs, of course, would not and could not reveal his source, and so relented, keeping to his pledge to not direct his editors how to cover the news. Instead, he created a work-around by pushing Hendrix's evolving Cuba story to the editorial pages.[5]

Even as the administration overtly pushed for restraint from the news media for purposes of "national security," Baggs's obligation came first to his family, his staff, his readers, and his community, who were all quite aware something dire was afoot and that they were at ground zero for either the attack, the response, or both. Military convoys carrying as many as eleven thousand troops, eighteen thousand tons of equipment, and more than five thousand Marines clogged U.S. 1 heading south to Opa-locka, Homestead Air Force Base, and Key West. Four hundred Navy ships filled the waters around the peninsula, and pleasure boaters were warned to keep close to shore and to avoid the Windward Passage. The noise of jet engines pierced the quiet at all hours.[6]

Meanwhile, seven Pan Am planes awaited the go-ahead to fly to Cuba and transport eleven hundred Bay of Pigs prisoners to safety if negotiations succeeded between the Cuban government and New York lawyer James Donovan, who had brokered the release from a Soviet prison of U-2 pilot Francis Gary Powers two years earlier. With increasing tensions among the United States, Russia, and Cuba percolating among the U.N. Security Council members, the talks, so close to being completed, appeared likely to break down.[7]

Four days after Hendrix's first story appeared, the Kennedy administration remained publicly silent, even as Havana claimed the United States was violating its airspace and a group of exiled commandos known as Alpha 66 raided the Cuban village of Isabella de Sagua—a badly timed maneuver.[8] In an editorial on October 13, Baggs speculated that the Soviets were using Cuba as a testing ground for America's potential response to any aggressive move on West Berlin.[9]

Despite the imminent threat of war, Baggs kept an appointment to cover the seventeenth anniversary of the United Nations. Secretary Adlai Stevenson had invited him along with McGill and Ashmore. It also got Baggs closer to the chess game between Kennedy and Khrushchev.[10] On the way back to Miami, he stopped in Washington for a round of meetings, perhaps to help Kennedy polish the televised speech the president was to give the next day, Monday, October 22, in which he finally confirmed for the American public what Hendrix had reported two weeks earlier.[11]

On hearing Kennedy's address, Frec's father, Big Craig, summoned her and the boys up to Athens, but Baggs would not hear of it. "Rather bluntly," according to Frec, Baggs informed her that "the bombs would pass over Miami and land in Georgia." Still, with jets roaring over Miami constantly, there would be no calming their fears.[12]

At two o'clock on Wednesday, October 24, Baggs received a phone call at the office. He walked out into the newsroom, where reporters were working to put out the final edition of the day's paper, and announced, "The Russians have backed down."

The writers and production crew went into overtime remaking page one of the day's final edition. They celebrated the exclusive with a three-line, all-caps, 120-point headline—"SOVIET SHIPS TURN BACK; NIKITA WANTS TO TALK; ARMS POUR INTO FLORIDA"—and a collective sigh of relief.[13]

The crisis didn't fully resolve for another four days. Before it was over, it would include Stevenson's scathing takedown of Russian ambassador Valeria Zorin at the U.N., the shooting down of U.S. Air Force pilot Rudolph Anderson's U-2 plane, and backdoor diplomacy between attorney general Robert Kennedy and Soviet ambassador Anatoly Dobrynin.

"On one level, it was scary and intimidating," says Frishman, who was working as the chief copy editor at the time. "But with Baggs in charge, you had no reason to be afraid. If he said don't worry, you didn't worry."

Time magazine profiled Baggs and the *Miami News* in its November 16, 1962, issue. Marveling how the *News* had scooped the *New York Times*, the piece wrongly assumed that it was done "without any handouts or help from Washington." Whenever he was asked how he knew, Baggs answered, "A little roseate spoonbill told us."[14] He protected his source publicly until his dying day.

Baggs did confess to one person, though, who kept his confidence for the next forty-five years. Frec wrote in her memoir, "When I asked later how he knew the Russians had turned back, Bill grinned and said, 'Jack Kennedy said *The Miami News* can be the first to have the story.'"[15]

A year later, on the evening of November 18, 1963, President Kennedy addressed the annual meeting of the Inter American Press Association, a group of Latin American newspapermen, at the Americana Hotel in Bal Harbor (just north of Miami Beach). In the twenty-five-minute speech, the president reaffirmed his commitment to nations fighting against communist takeovers. To those politicians and press people in the audience, it sounded as if he were launching his reelection campaign. "I'll come back here next year and make a longer speech," he promised before heading back to Washington to prepare for a whirlwind trip through Texas that week.[16]

Four days later, President Kennedy was dead.

Frec was watching Craig in the play *Alice in Wonderland* at the Cushman School, where she also taught first grade, when Baggs called her with the news that Kennedy had been shot in Dallas. She sat crying through the rest of the play, desperate to tend to her husband, who was in "shock."[17] Craig recalls that when his father finally made it home that evening, Baggs sat in the dark in his study for hours without saying a word.

The next morning, Baggs and columnist John Keasler flew to Washington, while reporter Milt Sosin headed to Dallas. The rest of the staff worked straight through the next seventy-two hours, rewriting wire copy and transcribing field stories.[18]

Setting aside his own grief, Baggs wrote on the plane, penning a column to honor the slain president. In the piece, which ran next to a haunting portrait of Kennedy taken by a *News* photographer in Miami only five days before, Baggs noted that the "soaring optimism of bold young men cannot quickly batter down the ramparts of bold prejudices." Yet rather than wallowing, Baggs transformed the tribute into a call to action to finish the hard work of emancipation and peace—what "the man" had only just begun.[19]

While in Washington for the funeral, he did what he did best. He conferred and commiserated with everyone—there was not a person in power, Democrat or Republican, that he did not know, said Keasler—and then he looked for the people lingering around the margins.

In one column Baggs focused on an old woman in a tattered orange coat who clung to the iron fence around the White House with quivering hands. "She did not seem to notice the rain."

The woman became the symbol of a nation suspended in mourning while political dealmaking continued to roil behind the scenes. It was possible, Baggs wrote without cynicism, that the bill for civil rights, which had been languishing, might now have a chance to pass.

After the services, he and Keasler retired to a bar. "This seems like a waste of good liquor," said Baggs, and they finished their drinks in silence.[20]

According to Ashmore, the assassination wounded Baggs gravely. Those closest to him witnessed a little less puckishness and saw a lot more drive and activism emerge after that November.

How an orphaned, self-educated editor from the best second paper in the country became such a good friend and close advisor to the most powerful man in the world remains a mystery. Perhaps the secret lay in Kennedy's affinity for writers. After all, he had considered journalism as a career and toured Europe as a reporter in 1945 after recovering from his war injuries.[21]

Perhaps Baggs's quick wit, street smarts, and courage to stand alone on tough issues provided a refreshing balm to a man surrounded by ideologues, hardliners, and strategists. Or maybe he recognized in Baggs that same alchemy of dogged purpose and open-mindedness that he appreciated in his brother Robert, and so Kennedy trusted him. Baggs also knew how to make the president laugh.

On one occasion when Baggs was waiting to meet with the president, Kennedy ran late and Baggs had to leave to catch a flight back to Miami. The editor had grown quite skilled at forging his hero Abraham Lincoln's signature and would pen pretend cables to friends. He left a note for the president that read something along the lines of "Sorry, but I had to leave, Mr. President. I'll come back another day if I can. Keep up the good work, young man. You might make something of yourself one day. Sincerely, A. Lincoln."[22]

On another visit, relays his son Craig as "one of those stories I don't know whether to believe or not," his father and President Kennedy snuck into the Library of Congress late at night, "probably after having a nip or two," and made a copy of the mock epitaph Benjamin Franklin had written for himself in 1728: "The Body of B. Franklin, Printer; like the Cover of an old Book, Its Contents torn out, And stript of its Lettering and Gilding, Lies here, Food for Worms. But the Work shall not be wholly lost; For it will, as he believ'd, appear once more, In a new & more perfect Edition, Corrected and amended By the Author."[23]

Baggs had the copy framed and hung it in his study, and now it hangs on his son Craig's wall.[24] The story may be embellished. Baggs, for sure, possessed the grand romance of southern yarn-spinners, but it is not out of the realm of possibility for it to be wholly true, as many people found out over time that Baggs's network ran higher and wider than they could have imagined. Plus, he and Kennedy knew where all of D.C.'s tunnels led.

Early in January 1964, Baggs wrote Jacqueline Kennedy, assuring her that her husband's flame would burn eternally for those left behind.

> That you should mention the eve of the New Year prompts me to tell you that I sneaked out of a supper several minutes before 1964 began. I felt a necessity to be alone, and out in the yard, I had whatever pleasure a person could find in personally kicking the old year over a coral rock wall and beyond my vision. I agree with you that what we must salvage from the assassination is the growing of the seeds which John Kennedy put down into

the ground.... And please know that many of us are not about to concede to any plowing under of what the late president planted in the hopes of ending racial injustice in our country, of sparing the human family from nuclear war and the whole noble enterprise of elevating the discretion of the American people in order that they could make better choices in the changing world.[25]

Baggs asked for a pen or some small memento of the president. The former First Lady sent him a gold button that had come from one of her late husband's favorite jackets.[26] Preserved in a block of Lucite, Baggs kept it on the desk in his home study—a reminder "of moments past and duties present."

CHAPTER 13

1949–1960

For Bill, it was a question of equality—not equality ritualized, but equality assumed, bolstered by simple courtesy and applied in the ordinary affairs of daily life.—Harry Ashmore, August 10, 1969

After Baggs and Frec settled in Miami in 1946, he learned Black citizens fared no better in a growing postwar metropolis than in the rural Georgia of his childhood. In the years immediately after World War II, African American war veterans and more than thirty-two thousand Bahamian and Caribbean immigrants poured into South Florida, hoping that some of that newfound Magic City prosperity would rub off on them. No matter their education, income, or abilities, however, their job and housing prospects were few and they were relegated to the back of the bus.[1]

The same extralegal practices enacted throughout the Deep South and industrial North of race-restrictive zoning, gentlemen's agreements, and racial violence pervaded South Florida. Real estate developers and brokers worked in concert with city and county officials to draw a bold red line around only a handful of neighborhoods, keeping Black residents away from tourist-heavy areas like Miami Beach and confining them to slums where people were packed cheek-by-jowl at nearly 150 people per acre.[2]

The Central Negro District (CND), a one-and-a-half-square-mile neighborhood west of the FEC Railway tracks near downtown, held more than 40 percent of all available dwelling units for Black families in Dade County. In the 1930s and 1940s, the area was home to a thriving Black middle class. The eastern edge of the district along Northwest Second Street garnered acclaim as a Black entertainment destination, anchored by the grand Lyric Theater where Count Basie and Ella Fitzgerald performed after shows on Miami Beach, where they were not permitted to stay in the hotels. But after the war and as highways bisected the community, the CND, called

Overtown by then, began to decline as businesses were bought out, closed, or moved and housing grew scarce.

The people relegated to the segregated Black area of Coconut Grove (Black Grove) lived in squalor, sometimes seven in a one-bedroom apartment or a single, narrow shotgun shack.[3] Building codes of the time did not require running water, indoor toilets, or tubs, so instead builders provided communal water pumps and outhouses that served dozens of people. "Honey wagons" patrolled these neighborhoods regularly to carry away human waste. Health problems abounded.[4] It was worse than Aunt Grace Estates, the shanties for the lumber mill workers back in Colquitt.

Once Baggs had the bully pulpit of his column in 1949, he spotlighted the slumlords at least once a week, often more, to get the ghettos cleaned up. City residents had overwhelmingly supported slum clearance measures in 1948 and again in 1950, which would have made available millions of federal dollars for land purchases and new houses and apartment buildings, but city leaders would not budge.

Slums were big business for speculators and developers—the same people who also made some of the largest campaign contributions. The speculators bought up the undeveloped parcels in the CND and Coconut Grove as well as in Liberty Square and Brownsville, which had been designated by the county planning department for future Black residential development, far away from jobs and public transportation. Then the speculators increased land prices three times over the cost of vacant property in white areas, forcing developers to build clusters of small, zero-lot-line apartment buildings with no amenities and no community assets such as parks or safety measures such as sidewalks. The developers charged rents that took nearly 50 percent of the prevailing salaries Miami's Black population earned at the time. When they could no longer make a profit, the owners offloaded the properties back on the city and county.[5]

As Baggs admonished, "The city of Miami has the finest slums that money can buy. Or maintain."[6] He squared off against these interests, who operated under the guise of the Committee Against Socialized Housing— or as Baggs referred to them, the "Committee Against Reason Plus Other Things."

"I refer the slum owners to two matters," he wrote in May 1950. "One is the fact that socialism and communism are born of the desperation found in the social dungeons of the slums. Two is the national housing bill. . . . If you slum owners and your friends are going to spend large sums of money, like the almost $3,000 you spent on radio advertisements alone . . . then why not learn what the facts of the matter are and pursue an honest argument."[7]

Baggs made those arguments both in print and on the speaking circuit. He talked of the high cost of fire insurance, not just for the slums but also for the neighboring areas, because the buildings were made of the cheapest possible materials and were built an eyelash-width apart. He feared that children would be hurt playing on narrow sidewalks a breath away from speeding cars—a fear sadly realized in Coconut Grove.[8] He decried the poor health bred by these conditions and the lack of access to decent medical care because of prejudice. Most of all, he lamented the loss of hope and dignity that led to a cycle of crime and despair.

When an unidentified Black man (unnamed, to protect him against reprisal) visited Baggs at the newspaper's office, Baggs gave voice to the man's concerns through a column while making the case that slum clearance was not simply a Negro problem. "The frame jungles of the downtown Negro district are a disgrace, and they mock any suggestion that this is truly a progressive city. . . . If that Negro man has to move from his home, or is forced to sell it, so the public housing can be constructed there, then none of us are really safe from our local governments. Unless, of course, we have special influence."[9]

With their designated communities bursting, Blacks with some upward mobility began to encroach into white residential neighborhoods. This started a rash of protests, cross burnings, and bombings, not just against Blacks but also Dade County's Jewish population, as religious and racial bigotry often danced side by side. Coupled with the 1954 and 1955 Supreme Court school desegregation decisions effectively dismantling the separate-but-equal doctrine, the White Citizens' Council grew to more than fifteen thousand members and the local KKK made known its presence.[10] Miami's police tended to attribute the violence not to the actual culprits but to a "communist plot to incite racial hatred."[11] It was not the first time Baggs had heard that tired old refrain. It certainly would not be the last.

Baggs had traveled enough of the world and witnessed how caste and class systems dubbed one group worthy and another less than, but those societies were not created under the ideals of personal liberty espoused in the U.S. Constitution—ideals he cherished, even when his country hardly lived up to them. He recognized, too, that no matter where he went, birds of a feather flocked together, and people remained in communities where they felt most comfortable.[12] Enforced and state-sponsored segregation erased any pretense of fairness and negated any national aspirations of real equality. So how, he wondered, could anyone expect people enslaved less than a hundred years before and diminished daily by Jim Crow to become full participants in a representative democracy when shut out of a good education, decent housing, economic opportunity, reliable transportation, voting rights, and medical care? The circular logic that multitudes of whites used to justify racial intolerance mystified him, and the revisionist history and scriptural manipulation used to promote segregationist policies infuriated him.

When an anonymous flyer circulated throughout Miami asserted that one of his heroes, Abraham Lincoln, was really an ardent segregationist, Baggs used his five hundred words to counter that, in fact, Lincoln had been against slavery from the first message he delivered in office. "He said: 'This is essentially a people's contest. On the side of the Union, it is a struggle for maintaining in the world that form and substance of government whose leading object is to elevate the condition of men; to lift artificial weights from all shoulders; to clear the paths of laudable pursuit for all; to afford all an unfettered start and a fair chance in the race of life.'"[13]

Baggs believed that literacy was the clearest pathway to that fair chance. He never shook the image from his mind of old Alec, ashamed and unfulfilled as a young Baggs read stories to him, and he resurrected those memories in a 1961 column to support federal investment in reading programs.

"What chance has the system of self-determination, which we call democracy, got among men who are unable to read or write? Moreover, how much more could keen men like Alec, truly smart men, give to the world if their minds were honed by books, newspapers, and words which explain and reveal the currents of human life? Certainly the campaign to open minds in knowledge, beginning with reading and writing, is as important to the notions of human freedom as the Polaris submarine which patrols silently beneath the seas or the 13-megaton atomic device fastened in a guarding bomber."[14]

Unlike Alec, Dade County's Black students had schools available to them, but they still fell one to four grade levels below their white peers.[15] The reasons then were as complex as they are today, but at the nexus of the achievement gap was, and remains, the disparity between the resources available to and the conditions of schools for white and Black as well as rich and poor students.

So, when the Supreme Court ruled in 1954 that the doctrine of separate but equal had no place in public education, Baggs understood the necessity of federal intervention, but he earnestly hoped the South could get out of its own way and gradually integrate. That December after the decision, Baggs traveled to Tallahassee to take the temperature of Florida's leaders as other states in the region were planning to oppose any and all directives to desegregate, with some even considering closing or abolishing public schools altogether. When he interviewed the state's attorney general, Richard Ervin, he found a man accepting the inevitable: "Don't kid yourself about this thing. The highest court in the land has ruled. It was a unanimous decision."

Baggs learned that Ervin had already proposed a plan to the federal courts that would allow Florida to give the responsibility of desegregation to the counties, which would be guided in their efforts by committee and with citizens having the right to petition the court for redress. "The people in each county know their problem better than does a man sitting in Tallahassee," Baggs quoted Ervin as saying.[16]

The state's superintendent of schools would not even consider closing or abolishing the school system, Baggs reported. "He said there were 630,285 children in the public schools of Florida. For a century, men and women have put their courage and talents in the classroom to make a school system which would give these children of today a fine opportunity to learn. [Thomas D.] Bailey cannot conceive of destroying this noble construction."[17]

But three years later when Baggs became editor, little in the way of access to schools, housing, jobs, and other opportunities had opened up for Blacks in Dade County, and patience was growing thin—including his. For every small advance, a backlash followed, and he was there to shine a light on it.

Baggs took note when L. E. Thomas was the first Negro judge appointed in the South since Reconstruction. Thomas had built a near-unassailable record in the five years he served the city of Miami, but when a block of newly elected commissioners was sworn into office in 1955, Thomas was fired. "They decided to let four of the city judges go, and in their places, the new commissioners appointed political aides and friends," Baggs lamented.[18]

When one of Dade County's more progressive representatives, John B. Orr, was up for reelection in 1958, Baggs put Orr's plan for desegregation forward as a positive move, mainly because Dade County had made no progress in the four years since the Supreme Court ruling. Orr recommended that high school students elect their own legislature, comprised of both Black and white students, which would then work out a plan of gradual enrollment of Negro students in the schools most closely tied to their residences.

"Wherever desegregation has been successfully begun it has had the acceptance of the students themselves," Baggs wrote, drawing on lessons shared by his colleague Harry Ashmore at the *Arkansas Gazette*. "There is good reason to believe that had the parents not interfered, the gradual desegregation of the Little Rock high school could have succeeded."[19]

Orr lost his seat in a runoff by nearly 23,000 votes to a candidate who favored keeping intact Florida's pupil assignment procedure, which limited transfers of Negro children to white schools to no more than a handful annually, if that.[20]

While Ashmore fought for the Central High Nine in Little Rock and McGill took up his mighty pen against Georgia's KKK—both men winning Pulitzer Prizes for their work—Baggs kept pushing for moderate steps forward. Even then, he drew the ire of readers and advertisers and a flood of canceled subscriptions. Baggs's philosophy never wavered, however. He believed a newspaper's responsibility was to present all sides of an issue as truthfully as possible and that a paper was not worth printing if it sought popularity over being right or moral.[21]

"It is with no little regret that I have received your request to cancel your subscription to the *Miami News* because you disagreed with an editorial which appeared in our newspaper on September 29," Baggs wrote to a Mr. C. Grady Mixon, who had called him "smug and complacent."[22] Hundreds of letters throughout his early years as editor began this same way, always followed by Baggs's efforts to clarify where he stood personally. To Mr. Mixon, he offered:

> The raising of economic and all other standards of living must be accomplished for the Negro of the South and this, I think, is the most important thing to consider in this moment. Perhaps, along with raising the living standards . . . there will begin a trickle of integration. We are dealing with a very complex problem here and it is not going to be solved by bullies and loud voices. Nor, is it going to be solved by over-simplified statements, for these tend to hoodwink people. These are not the sentiments of a smug and complacent fellow. Frankly, they are the sentiments of a worried man.

As the years dragged on and little progress for Dade County's Black students had been achieved, Baggs's editorials and responses took on a more pointed tone. By the end of the 1950s he had transformed from a moderate to a more ardent integrationist, paving the way for his activism in the years ahead and leaving him, in many ways, alone.

There is nothing much but anguish when you feud with so many of your readers and friends. Perhaps most of your readers and friends. But there are times when you have no other choice. Which brings us quickly to the practice of enforced segregation in the public schools of Florida.

It is wrong.[23]

CHAPTER 14

1960–1968

We have arrived when we can get mad at each other for reasons that have nothing to do with the color of our skins.—To a protestor after the Liberty City riots, 1968

When Rev. Theodore Roosevelt Gibson, the head of Miami's NAACP chapter, walked into Baggs's office in December 1960, he said, "I want to know you." Baggs offered up his signature lopsided grin and a handshake. "There's not much about me to know. Why don't you sit down and tell me what you think this civil rights business is all about?"

Over coffee, the editor and activist talked for hours, sharing their frustration with the slow pace of desegregation. Before the meeting was over, they made a pact that they kept secret even from their families.

"We both had opportunities to leave the South, but we decided if the South was to be saved, Southerners would have to save it," recalled Gibson.

The two men made another promise to each other that day. They would be in the fight together for as long as it took.[1]

For nearly fifteen years, their worlds had brushed up against one another but had never fully intersected. Wielding his typewriter, Baggs used his words to push for change. Gibson raised his voice from his pulpit and in the streets.

Gibson was that rare bird, a native Miamian, born in the CND in 1915. When he was still a toddler, his mother, who worked as a domestic for the founding family of Miami, the Brickells, sent her son to George Town on Great Exuma Island in the Bahamas to live with his grandfather so that he could escape the poverty, the crime, and the poor schools that plagued Miami. There, Gibson said, the leaders all looked like him.

As a teen, he returned to Miami and graduated from Booker T. Washington High School in 1934.[2] Miami's school officials had promised running water and a gymnasium while he was still a student, but by the time he had graduated from the seminary in 1945 and taken over the leadership of the historic Christ Episcopal Church in Coconut Grove, the promises remained unfulfilled.

Gibson had considered becoming a lawyer but chose the cloth not because he felt particularly called, he confessed, but because he believed his ministry was in making a difference for his people. He noticed that having the power of God behind him seemed to capture white people's attention far more than the weight of the law.[3]

His street ministry began almost immediately. In 1948, he met Elizabeth Virrick, the petite, well-to-do wife of an architect who lived in the more affluent—and white—part of Coconut Grove, and together they created the Coconut Grove Citizens Committee for Slum Clearance. With her connections and his community organization skills, they were able to get an emergency city ordinance passed in 1950 that required every residential unit to have a flush toilet and sink. (They would fight another decade to get the minimum housing code rewritten and passed to include indoor bathrooms.)[4] "Plumbing has cost this country a fortune," Gibson said.[5]

Gibson also helped found the South Dade community of Richmond Heights. This was designed to give middle-class Blacks a safe and affordable neighborhood in which to purchase single-family homes.[6]

He was elected president of Miami's chapter of the NAACP in 1954 and led the bus integration fight with NAACP attorney G. E. Graves, the lawyer who appeared with Baggs on the first interracial television panel. Their lawsuit led to the state supreme court decision in January 1957 that segregation on public transit was unconstitutional. When the ruling was upheld by an appeals court in April 1958, Gibson and Graves took their seats at the front of the bus in a moment captured by the *News*. In 1959, they celebrated the opening of the city and county's park and recreation facilities, including the beaches, to Negroes.

"People don't realize that in the civil rights movement you can go crazy. Every so often you need some semblance of success," Gibson told a *News* reporter a decade later.[7]

In spite of gaining some agency for Miami's Black community, Gibson faced a crisis of both freedom and faith beginning in 1955. In a Florida-sized reenactment of the Army-McCarthy hearings, Senator Charley Johns formed a legislative investigating committee to ferret out communist infiltration of the state's NAACP organization.[8] The committee targeted only the

Miami chapter, and only after Gibson had filed the state's first school integration lawsuit on behalf of his son to attend Coral Gables Junior High.[9]

The Johns Committee demanded that Gibson turn over the local chapter's membership list, comprised of nearly fifteen hundred names. Gibson refused time and time again, knowing that if he capitulated his members would lose their jobs, their houses, and maybe their lives.[10] When he refused to submit the lists once again in 1959, he leaned on the words his grandfather had drilled into him—"give less of a damn about other considerations than what is good for the community"—and faced the consequences, which could have cost him the priesthood. He was sentenced to six months in jail and a $1,200 fine. He appealed, and the case went all the way to the U.S. Supreme Court.[11]

Just before he walked into Baggs's office, Gibson received word that the Florida Supreme Court had upheld Gibson's sentence and conviction because he had refused to "respect two branches of government in Florida." He had, by his own admission, lost faith in his fellow man and had begun to hate so strongly that it ate away like acid, until he felt he had no right to wear the cloth.[12] The head of the Florida chapter of the Anti-Defamation League suggested he give Baggs a call. Gibson protested because he did not believe it would do him any good, but he relented and picked up the phone.[13]

Baggs had gone through his own transformation during the 1960 presidential election, moving from observer to participant, a role he had been inching closer to as more city, state, and national leaders asked him to weigh in on issues affecting the domestic and international politics that swirled in and around South Florida. From where Baggs stood, as both a son of the segregated South and a public figure in the trenches of Miami's civil rights struggle, the Kennedy ticket offered the best hope for real progress on civil rights—although the young candidate's efforts had been hesitant and plodding.

Kennedy had been lukewarm early on about desegregating public places, such as schools, lunch counters, and interstate public transportation, because he needed the southern Democratic governors not only in order to secure the party's nomination but also to propel him to electoral victory in 1960. The great majority of those governors were either ardent segregationists such as Mississippi's Ross Barnett, who stuck to the populist message of a state's right to oppose actions of the federal government (interposition), or moderates such as Georgia's Ernest Vandiver, who considered the Supreme Court's 1954 *Brown v. Board of Education* decision judicial overreach into state affairs. As an Irish Catholic, the president certainly had felt the sting of prejudice, yet his religion, buffered by wealth, never kept him from the corridors of power and privilege nor legally prescribed him to a lower class.

But in October 1960, Jack and Bobby Kennedy intervened to help secure the release of Rev. Dr. Martin Luther King Jr. from Georgia's Reidsville State Prison following his arrest during a lunch counter sit-in at Atlanta's Rich's Department Store. This act helped push an ambivalent Black vote toward Kennedy over Nixon, who had remained silent when DeKalb County judge J. Oscar Mitchell sentenced King to four months hard labor for violation of his probation on a traffic citation. The conventional wisdom among King's supporters and Kennedy's civil rights advisors was that King would have been killed after he was transferred from his county jail cell in the middle of the night.[14]

Among the multitude of calls the brothers and their campaign staffers made while strategizing King's release, one, at least, was made to Baggs. Baggs had long fought for the "black man's human dignity" while possessing an uncanny ability to command the grudging respect of even the most ardent racists.[15] He thus lent value in the process of thinking through how different camps would respond, should Kennedy step into the fray. Ashmore and Kleinberg confirmed that Baggs had some hand in the behind-the-scenes mechanisms by which Robert Kennedy assessed southern leaders regarding intervention on King's behalf, but to what extent, Kleinberg is unsure.[16] Did Baggs provide a sounding board for Robert Kennedy or did he offer counsel? Did he use his Georgia connections to make a smoother road for Kennedy's subsequent calls?

We will never know. Baggs was the soul of discretion. Besides, true to the lessons of his aunts regarding pride, he often downplayed his own profound influence.

The meeting with Gibson gave Baggs renewed energy in the civil rights fight in Miami. Not long after they vowed to work together, Baggs stopped at his secretary's desk and declared, "Miss Myrt, the time is coming when any Negro child will be able to walk into any school in this county."[17]

Still, the two men feared Miami could sink to the level of violence in Arkansas, Mississippi, Alabama, and Georgia. They also knew that nothing but deeper resentment would come if change was not realized more immediately than at the slow pace of the law of the land. Baggs and Gibson both supported civil disobedience and peaceful demonstration, when needed. In a column on July 24, 1963, Baggs made the case for the social value of demonstrations: "Talk, for instance, to a young man on a picket line for civil rights or nuclear disarmament. He likely is not the fellow talented to make a speech. He cannot write messages which burn with the passion he feels. He is a single person, the individual, without a party he can lead. The picket is a blessing for this person. It is a way he can involve himself."

But Baggs never approved of violence. On the day after the Liberty City riots during the 1968 Republican Convention, Baggs acknowledged the mounting frustrations of young Black men who had waited too long for the full measure of equality, but he admonished them for their methods and their dismissiveness toward the veterans of struggle. "The wreckers who spawned an evening of violence last night did not one whit to advance the legitimate ambitions of the Negro here."[18]

Baggs often took on the role of mediator between business and civil rights leaders in the community. Even though the Walgreens, Woolworth, Kress, and McCrory stores had integrated their lunch counters in 1960, after sit-ins coordinated by the NAACP and the Congress of Racial Equality (CORE) proved successful, the finer downtown department stores of Burdine's and Jordan Marsh had made little effort to open their eating and restroom facilities to Black patrons.[19]

Gibson and other Black leaders sensed a storm brewing for the 1961 Christmas season, as sit-ins were being proposed by activists, some of them welcoming the possibility of violence.[20] Gibson, knowing he would incur the wrath of his members, agreed to hold off the protests until after the shopping season, on the condition that Burdine's put in writing its intention to desegregate its tearoom, dressing rooms, and restrooms. Baggs in turn assured his friend and poker buddy, Al Daniels, the president of Burdine's, that he would not publicize the day of desegregation, so as not to draw gawkers or troublemakers. On November 14, 1961, Baggs received a letter from the department store's vice president, C. B. Potter, who pledged to open the store's facilities on the first working day of 1962. Handwritten by Baggs in the upper right corner of the letter: "Compromise—until after Jan. 1. Jordan Marsh concurs."[21]

All agreed, too, that Baggs would hold the letter in trust, insurance against any party that faulted on the terms of the arrangement. In that case, Baggs could write about it, but it was a story he never had to tell. "I knew that if they double-crossed me, Bill Baggs would have exposed them as traitors," Gibson declared. Garth Reeves, publisher of the local Black newspaper, the *Miami Times*, affirmed Gibson's faith. Baggs, he said, was "one of the few white men the most militant blacks could trust."

Still, Miami had work to do. Black schools remained pitifully deficient and new public housing developments were turning into second ghettos, while the old ones continued to deteriorate.

In a talk to Miami's Rotarians, Baggs cautioned business and civic leaders to not pat themselves on the back for too much progress. "You will find that every tradition as it relates to the Negro is practiced here.

"We should thank God the Negro leadership in this community is wise and responsible," he continued, surely with his friend Gibson in mind. "They have read the Emancipation Proclamation . . . and realize they still aren't free. They don't desire to go to the senior prom with white girls, but they do want an end to discrimination in housing, education, labor unions, and hospitals."

In March 1963, Gibson received word that, in a 5–4 decision, the highest court in the land had ruled in his favor and his long ordeal was over. The Supreme Court had tested and affirmed the first amendment's protection of free and private association. The headline in the *News*' Blue Streak edition that day declared, "NAACP Chief Cleared by Supreme Court Decision."

In his unsigned editorial two days after the verdict, Baggs wrote, "Moreover, the man involved is one of the most valuable members of the community, who, far from being a communist, has spent the better part of his life trying to promote a more democratic society."

Three months later, Baggs and Gibson coordinated a meeting of leaders in the county's religious community. On June 12, 1963, the day after the murder of Medgar Evers, Mississippi field secretary for the NAACP, and President Kennedy's televised civil rights address, Baggs sent a letter to the Department of Justice hailing Miami's religious community for coming together to call for "an end to racial discrimination in all matters of human activity."

> The experience of this may be instructive as we wade into what appears to be a summer of violence. . . . As you may or may not know, Miami is a southern

town. People confuse the Miami community with Miami Beach, which in population is but 5 percent of the population of Dade County. Approximately 150,000 Negroes live in Dade County. The largest number of whites came from Georgia. Then comes Tennessee. And so on. In other words, while we have New Yorkers and Pennsylvanians, they are far out-numbered, and I can remember 15 years ago when a Negro would not walk on our main streets after the sun had gone down. I say all of this to suggest that whatever will work to end discrimination in Miami should work in other places.

It was the first time in the South, according to Baggs, that Catholic bishops, Jewish rabbis, and Protestant leaders gathered together and signed a proclamation that spelled out any form of discrimination as "un-Godly."

"This proclamation did not compromise."

He admitted that it would take time to get the Baptists, Presbyterians, and Methodists to the beloved communion table. Still, he was able to point out that the local medical society and two unions had, in just the few days since the proclamation, announced they would accept qualified Negro members. The Dade County commission moved immediately to establish a community relations board, on which Gibson and Baggs would serve.

It seems that the segregationist is also a religious man, or at least he regards himself as a white Christian. When his minister removed "white" from in front of Christian, this man who is a segregationist is pretty well forced to make a choice of:

1. Abandoning an old and hard tradition of respecting his minister and viewing his church as the House of the Lord;
2. Accepting, reluctantly, an end to racial discrimination.

The fact that the southern white segregationist considers himself a Christian cannot be over-emphasized in importance. His prejudice for the Baptist church or the Presbyterian church is as old as his prejudice against the black race. . . . It would seem to me that if we could encourage this in other southern communities, we might hasten the inevitable and bypass violence on the way.[22]

Five days after Baggs sent his letter, President Kennedy met with Catholic, Protestant, Orthodox, Quaker, and Jewish leaders in the Oval Office. He held up Miami as an example of moral and religious leadership in helping to end segregation in voting rights, public accommodation, housing, and employment.[23]

However, it was clear two weeks later in Miami Beach at the annual meeting of the National Governors' Conference that hardened segregationists still had a stranglehold on the Democratic Party. Alabama governor George Wallace once again insinuated that Dr. King and other Negro leaders were in bed with communists.

Baggs's front-page column the next day challenged Wallace's dog whistle. "For at least three decades, the communists prospected the waters of Harlem and tenant farms of the South, and they did not catch many fish. It would seem that a philosophy of promises would have dazzled the Negro, down in a ditch of spiritual despondency, unable to vote or have a crack at a decent job. But the Negro declined the bait."[24]

Vice President Lyndon B. Johnson, who attended long enough to deliver the keynote address, put Wallace and all the other racists in the room on notice by predicting that a comprehensive civil rights bill would be passed before the end of Kennedy's first term. Johnson also extolled Miami as an example of how various groups had worked together to avoid some of the violence plaguing other southern cities like Birmingham, Greensboro, and Atlanta, a not-so-slight indictment of the segregationist governors seated before him.[25]

In a follow-up letter to Baggs after the conference, the vice president thanked the editor for helping with his remarks. "Only one line was missing," Johnson wrote. "We should have said 'and this progress has been made largely because of Bill Baggs.' One of the great resources we have in the South in the entire field of civil rights is the help contributed by journalists like Ralph McGill, Hodding Carter, Bill Baggs!"

Johnson closed by inviting Baggs for a burger next time he found himself in the nation's capital. "I'd like . . . to pick your brain on this whole subject."[26]

When Johnson ran for the presidency in 1964, Baggs and the *News* supported him with positive editorials and became his champions on the passage of landmark civil rights legislation in 1964 and 1965. Baggs brought Gibson and Gibson's teenaged son as guests for Johnson's inauguration.

All during his efforts to help lead Miami to at least some measure of racial harmony, Baggs found solace in the friendships he had forged with his fellow journalists, especially McGill and Ashmore. If, in print and among one another, McGill was the voice of the evangelist and Ashmore the voice of reason, then Baggs was the rapscallion whose humor belied a seriousness of intellect and cause. He was prone to call both men in the early hours before dawn, Miami time, when his kidney problems forced him out of bed. He would laugh uproariously when he awoke them, then get down to business, whether it was discussing a candidate's chances, one of their columns, or something he had gleaned from one of the three or more books he had read that week. The three men maintained a regular correspondence among themselves for more than a decade and spoke on the phone almost daily. Baggs and McGill had come to rely on one another's counsel so greatly, in fact, that Baggs hung a picture of McGill on his office wall with an inscription by McGill that read, "To Bill Baggs, who is closer to me than a brother."[27]

As for the larger network of Camp Followers, they were guaranteed a conclave every April on the fifth floor of the Jefferson Hotel in Washington, D.C., at the annual ASNE conference. Baggs, Ashmore, and McGill often took a suite that served as the central assembly after the day's events and an extensive tour through Washington's cocktail circuit. Carter, Popham, and Golden reserved rooms nearby. The *Chicago Daily News'* Larry Fanning, cartoonists Herb Block and Walt Kelly, and NBC correspondent Sander Vanocur were honorary members who would stop in and stay into the wee hours to partake in the merciless teasing, boisterous storytelling, and whiskey that flowed as liberally as did the opinions.

Just before their ASNE gathering in 1961, McGill wrote Ashmore (with a copy to Baggs) a note that chided, "I used to think that it was strenuous for you and me to get together and, in fact, it was. But I have learned by virtue of the two political conventions last summer and the inauguration, that to be with Mr. Baggs is to have permanent damage done to one's health. While we all love Mr. Baggs, we must admit that he is a menace."[28]

Even though they were few, the Camp Followers had grown into a powerful block of thought leaders. Still, they represented a minority among southern editors, accounting for "probably no more than 20 at any one time, who risked the anger of their readers as well as circulation and advertiser boycotts to urge compliance with the Supreme Court's school desegregation decisions of 1954 and 1955."[29] The American public generally proved tepid regarding the civil rights movement, even with the evident violence perpetrated on passive demonstrators trying to foster awareness and action in response to the plight of African Americans. Only 23 percent of Americans, North and South, supported the civil rights movement in 1963.[30]

Thus, "humor often proved to be the only antidote and best bond among the dissident editors."[31] Often loud and crass when together, their humor ran toward the gallows type, and much of it to an outsider might have confirmed the worst of southern stereotypes. When someone accused them of "speaking for the niggers," they welcomed what another white man would have considered an insult. To them, it was a compliment, a badge of honor.

Martin S. Ochs, whose family owned the *New York Times* and the *Chattanooga Times* (where Popham landed after he left New York), convened with the brethren at conferences and conventions. Decades later, in a review of a biography of McGill, Ochs wrote, "All of us occasionally passed along the vilest of racial jokes—something it took my wife 20 years to understand. We laughed *at* the jokes, not with them. If you did not laugh, you died."[32]

Nothing was off limits: their drinking and smoking, their egos, their weight. Even their fellow progressives were not safe from scorn. After his first foray into ASNE in 1959, Baggs wrote a personal letter to the head of the American Press Institute at Columbia University that illuminated the group's wry, jaded outlook.

> Some years ago, I wearied of attending the brotherhood suppers of the National Conference of Christians and Jews. It seemed to me that something should be done about all this goo spread by Christians and Jews, who got real gone brotherly one evening and reverted to type on 364 evenings of the year. As a matter of fact, I think it is at least safe to float the opinion that I met more prejudice and bigotry at these brotherhood suppers than anywhere else.

Baggs went on to write that he had established the National Conference of Anti-Christians and Anti-Jews "to improve the general quality of bigotry." He continued, "Our motto is: Burn the Church of Your Choice."[33]

Baggs was named pope. Walt Kelly served as bishop of New York and Herb Block as bishop-at-large. McGill was christened bishop of Georgia, Tarver of the "Southern Defamation League," and Ashmore of California. Baggs awarded the title of bishop of Cuba to Fidel Castro, who they had all just heard speak at the conference; "and there is a good man," Baggs drolly commented.[34]

In their irreverence, members of the brotherhood frequently signed off, in their copious amounts of correspondence among each other, with phrases like "Pontifically Speaking" or "Ecclesiastically Yours." When they reunited throughout the years, they addressed each other by their ecumenical titles.

Grace Lundy, McGill's long-serving secretary, later wrote to Ashmore that she sometimes failed to grasp their wit. "You had your private jokes and I did not pry. I would assume it had to do with the vilification you, [McGill] and Mr. Baggs were taking good humoredly (if there is such a word) after the Supreme Court ruling. The three of you had turned your back on your homeland and race, etc., etc."[35]

The truth was that, however brave the stances they took and however defiant they seemed, they often felt isolated, especially Baggs. He was situated southernmost, far from the most visible and violent moments of the civil rights movement, yet no less embroiled in the struggle for equality— maybe even more so, in many ways, because of South Florida's confluence of Black, Jewish, and Hispanic populations.

In April 1960, Baggs wrote to Popham, lamenting the anti-Catholic menace swirling in Miami in response to both an influx of Cuban refugees and the prospect of a Kennedy in the White House. "The trouble is that you are in Chattanooga and Mac is in Atlanta and [Ashmore] is . . . in Santa Barbara and I am here, and we should all be under the same roof somewhere. I get tired of talking to my dog."[36]

A few months later, following the political conventions in July, at which both civil rights and Latin America loomed large, a dispirited Baggs reached out to Ashmore. He could not understand how a people who could split an atom could not meet the challenge of racial inequality. "Sometimes," he wrote, "I wish my name was Giuseppe Serlo, an immigrant just off the boat who had never met a Negro, knew the South only from [Erskine] Caldwell and was not involved at all in this traumatic experience."[37]

Of course, they enjoyed privilege simply by being white and male. Their collective isolation and impatience were nothing compared to what Blacks endured daily. Nor was it lost on them that, when they looked around the room, there were few, if any, Black journalists within their professional circles or on staff at their newspapers. Yet they had some inkling of what it meant to fear for their lives because of the positions they took in print.

A veteran of the slings and arrows hurled by both friends and detractors, McGill described the pervasive tension he and others carried. "In this climate with harassing telephone calls and threats a routine part of each evening, one rarely gets a good night's sleep. . . . While you honestly don't think they are going to dynamite your house, you nonetheless know very well they may. This largely, I think, is in your subconscious. It is like flying in a plane. You don't expect it to fall, but you know it can."[38]

In 1962 Baggs was invited to deliver the commencement speech and to receive an honorary doctorate from Florida Normal and Industrial Memorial College, a private historically Black college in St. Augustine. The city was in the midst of experiencing KKK-led racial violence in response to what would later be called the St. Augustine movement within the larger civil rights struggle. Baggs was met by police on both arrival to and departure from the Jacksonville airport "because there was some fear that some virile persons who disagree with my moderate editorial policy were going to blow up the plane."[39]

At the beginning of the following year, a twenty-six-year-old avowed segregationist and anti-Semite named Donald Branch was sentenced to twenty years in prison for dynamiting the Bay Point home of the *Miami Herald's* editor Don Shoemaker. There were no injuries, but during the trial it was discovered that Baggs was on Branch's hit list.[40]

Baggs kept these events to himself so that his family would not live daily in fear. Publisher Dan Mahoney gave Baggs a revolver for personal safety that Baggs stashed beneath the bed. Frec discovered the gun, unloaded, while changing the sheets one morning. She called her husband at the office to inquire as to why it was there. He admitted to also having a pistol in the nightstand. She then learned that the unmarked car sitting at the corner was occupied by two plainclothes Coral Gables policemen, who sometimes followed their son Craig when he rode his bicycle to Sunset Elementary.[41]

Even his neighbors understood the dangers of taking a stand. During times of intense attention when Baggs himself became the news, as happened during the Cuban Missile Crisis, Dr. Beverly Jones hung a sign on his house with an arrow pointing toward the opposite end of the street that read, "Bill Baggs Lives That Way."[42]

During this time, Baggs acquired a beat-up beige Mercedes that was outfitted with an early version of a remote starter. Who or what entity equipped the car is unknown, but it was a precautionary measure, just the same. If someone had attached a bomb to the car, Baggs could start it from afar and it would blow up before he or his family opened the door.

When a home on Cotorro Street just around the corner from their Hardee residence became available, Baggs borrowed the down payment from Cox Media and purchased it, not necessarily because it was bigger but because it offered more security. The gated courtyard entrance from the street created one level of privacy; the second level was afforded by a thick wooden front door that Baggs claimed could "withstand repeated assault by a tall man on a Texas steer."[43] A bookcase in his home study doubled as a revolving door into the garage, which opened not onto the street but onto an alley behind the house.[44]

Baggs, though, never seemed deterred by the threats or even the angry readers, and he kept fighting for the fair treatment of all Floridians.

CHAPTER 15

1955–1968

What's wrong in our town? Too many otherwise intelligent men and women, who look ahead to the end of the fiscal year instead of to 1970, when their children inherit this town, and its population of 2,000,000 and all the problems their lazy and selfish parents conveniently overlooked. That's what is wrong in this town.—"What's Wrong Here?," *Miami Daily News*, May 3, 1955

More than anything, Baggs wanted his generation to be the one that solved the social and moral problems previous ones had refused to confront, and he saw the newspaper as a vehicle for enlightening the citizenry for informed debate, decision making, and action.

In 1959, after only a year and a half as editor, Baggs's "little portable paper"—as he often called it—won the Pulitzer Prize for National Reporting for a multipart series Howard Van Smith wrote throughout 1958 that revealed the inhumane conditions in "shacktowns" where migrant farm workers lived in Homestead and Immokalee, Florida. Thousands were starving and suffering from severe hypothermia and diseases after a freeze wiped out the crops on which their lives depended. The series spurred federal aid and humanitarian assistance from the American Medical Association and other groups, and it raised the issue of living and working conditions for migrant laborers all across the country.[1] It later inspired Edward R. Murrow's *Harvest of Shame* documentary, which aired the day after Thanksgiving in 1960 and on which Smith served as an advisor.[2]

Smith's Pulitzer was followed by another in 1963 for Latin American editor Hal Hendrix's breaking the Cuban Missile Crisis story.[3] This award came under scrutiny fifteen years later during a House Intelligence Committee investigation into the CIA's role in spreading propaganda through news sources. Hendrix, who left the *News* soon after the prize announcement in 1963, continued his association with the CIA while working for Scripps-Howard and, later, the International Telephone and Telegraph

Corporation (ITT). During the investigation, Hendrix pled guilty to withholding information from the committee regarding his work with ITT in Chile. ASNE, under the leadership of Eugene Patterson, McGill's former editor, subsequently established stricter guidelines for how reporters associated with anonymous governmental sources.[4]

A third Pulitzer under Baggs's leadership came in 1966 for Don Wright's editorial cartoon about the insanity of the nuclear age. It depicted two men in a postapocalyptic landscape, one saying to the other, "You mean you were bluffing?"[5]

Baggs encouraged his editors and writers to be bold, to get the story no one else would tell, to be provocative, even if it meant going up against powerful interests and advertisers. Because he was willing to do the same, they knew he had their backs.

All throughout the 1950s and 1960s as high-rises and highways sucked up more of the land and waterways around South Florida, Baggs became the local environment's most vocal champion. He took to the waters of Biscayne Bay as often as he could to fish, and he did not like what he saw in the way the county and city commissions treated the water as an infinite resource.

In February 1957, when the *News'* real estate reporter filed an article about a New York furrier offering $10 million for the last remaining undeveloped piece of land on the tip of Key Biscayne, Baggs took note. When that deal fell through the next year, only to be followed by a $13 million offer from another group of developers, Baggs started building the case for the preservation of the historic lighthouse that rose from the white sands of the pristine mile-long beach outlining 574 acres of tropical uplands. The builders promised to transform the former coconut plantation into "one of the nation's most glamorous and exciting residential communities," replete with twenty-story hotels and condominiums, sprawling tropical residences, and recreational amenities such as tennis courts and swimming pools, all within easy reach of the bay's turquoise waters. As a nod to the land's long history, the builders had included the old Cape Florida Lighthouse as a feature in their plans, but it wasn't a given. Originally built in 1827, it was the oldest structure still standing in Dade County and it was the worse for wear.[6]

The lighthouse had survived hurricanes, been burned and rebuilt during the Seminole Wars, served as a stop on the Saltwater Railroad leading escaped slaves to freedom in the Caribbean, and guided ships through the precarious and jagged reefs dotting the shallow bay until a more modern and sturdier lighthouse was built on Fowey Rock in 1878. Nature and vandals had done their best to bring it down, but there it stood still, in all its weather-beaten, ninety-five-foot-high glory.[7]

Don Stinson recalls, "I can still hear [Baggs] telling about the Seminole attack. Just enthralling. He had a way of writing and talking to a young person that made you feel very grown up. That comes from the soul."

Baggs remained relentless in his drive to save the lighthouse over the next several years, as development efforts languished and historic preservationists joined in the fight.

> If we continue to zip along at the current speed and in the same direction, the children in 2058 might get the idea that when the pioneers came to this area in the beginning, they found nothing but a concrete block and a neon tube . . . and this is what they used to build metropolitan Miami. . . . The hammocks are gone forever. Man does not know how to build them. Perhaps in time, the bay may be reclaimed as a clear and clean body of water. At this moment there is a piece of old culture around here and it can be saved. You can save it. If you want to.[8]

Baggs understood how important fresh air and green spaces were to the psyche. He took to the woods and water when he needed to set his mind right. In the aftermath of Mary Elizabeth McGill's death in 1962, Baggs invited Ralph and his son Ralph Jr. to Miami. The first place he took them to was Key Biscayne, where they walked the beach for hours each day, often with Craig Baggs by their side, trying to put the pieces of their lives back together. At one point while they walked along the beach, they passed a scowling Richard Nixon.[9]

After nearly six years of editorial prodding, the Dade County Commission requested that its planning department prepare a report to assess the possibility of purchasing the more than five hundred acres of uplands and four hundred acres of bay bottom for a state park—the first one in Dade County.[10] A year later, in May 1965, the county planning department released its report. The county's waterfront facilities were already overcrowded for the 1.1 million residents, it read, and large tracts of land available for regional parks had declined as urban sprawl consumed acre after acre. Pointing to the natural state of the Key Biscayne property and its wealth of beach access and safe coves, plus the historic lighthouse, the planning department encouraged the commission to act.

"After all, past generations provided us with the parks we enjoy today," the planners concluded. "Do we not have an obligation to do the same for generations to come?"

Baggs followed the report's release with an open letter in his front-page column to Elena Santeiro Garcia, the property's owner. In it, he spoke to the future: "The public, especially the children, should have that land, the long and sloping beaches, the old lighthouse, which is one of the few remnants of our history, the trails which wander beneath the old palms." First, he appealed to her pocketbook by laying out how the money to buy the property could be cobbled together. Then, he appealed to her heart. "This is a business proposition, but if you sell to the people, children, all the children, long after we are gone from this world, will have the freedom of that beach and the sights of the unspoiled subtropics. That idea, maybe, puts a little humanity into the business deal. So, we ask, would you answer the questions in this column?"[11]

Four days later, through her attorneys, Santeiro Garcia answered and allowed Baggs to print her letter in full the following Sunday. She confirmed that appraisals had valued the property between $13 million and $16 million dollars. "In response to your query," she continued, "I would favorably entertain an offer of $8,500,000 for all of Key Biscayne. . . . Nothing would please me more than to effect a sale of this property to a public authority to be preserved in all its natural beauty as a public park. You may be assured subject to the approval of both my banker and my attorney, I would accept municipal, county or state bonds or revenue certificates in payment of the purchase price."[12]

A month later, on June 27, 1965, Baggs took his case to the public officials who would make the decision whether or not to spend the money. "Of course, the people need roads and they need some place to work and live. But the people also need parks, room to run or recline, to listen to the soft drawl of the sea, a place to dock a small boat or simply a quiet place to walk."[13]

That same month he traveled to Washington, D.C., to gain a promise from Secretary of the Interior Stewart Udall that if Florida and Dade County did their parts, the federal government would throw in $2 million or more toward the purchase price. Baggs also used the opportunity to talk with Udall and President Johnson about the thirty-two coral reef islands dotting southern Biscayne Bay all the way to the upper Florida Keys. For a decade, this chain, known as Islandia, had been the focus of speculators who proposed building a six-lane, cross-bay bridge to carry tourists to envisioned marinas, hotels, and parks.

"If we build a causeway down the bay, please be prepared to give up fishing and acquire a new sport. The entire sea life of the bay will be thrown into confusion," Baggs admonished his readers. "It is strange that people around here do not realize the large bay out there is one of our largest natural assets. We have permitted an outrageous assault on the bay in the past, as men lined their pockets with the modern equivalent of gold, after filling up large areas of the bay and selling the new land. The mid-bay causeway is intriguing only in thinking what horror it may cause."[14] (Ultimately, the islands became the foundation for Biscayne National Monument—later Biscayne National Park—when Johnson signed the bill in 1968.)

The state purchased the first one hundred acres for Cape Florida State Park on April 5, 1966, with a ceremony and deed transfer held at the Dupont Plaza Hotel on the Miami River. Governor W. Haydon Burns, not a fan of conservation but certainly one vote, called Baggs "foremost" in the campaign to create the park and "the loudest champion of the cause."[15]

When the state finally settled a year later on a financing method for the remainder of the park property, Baggs wrote to Santeiro Garcia once more. "Long after you and I have left this old green planet, children and their parents who cannot afford the private clubs will find a healthy and economical pleasure on the lovely beach front which soon, it appears, is to become the property of the people."[16]

During the early 1960s, the fight to save Biscayne Bay felt like a never-ending boxing match. Just when he thought he had defeated one opponent, another one entered the ring. Eventually, a behemoth in the form of an oil refinery known as Seadade finally awakened South Florida's conservation consciousness. The owner of one of the largest petroleum transport companies in the world, D. K. Ludwig, proposed building an oil refinery on two thousand acres of coastal wetlands in the southern portion of the county, just north of Homestead Bayfront Park in one of the county's most richly diverse and pristine mangroves. The site fell just outside the eastern edge of Everglades National Park and just north of John Pennekamp Coral Reef State Park and the robust fishing grounds off the Florida Keys.[17]

In 1962, the Metro Zoning Appeals Board approved the Seadade rezoning application but asked for a nine-month delay in issuing building permits so that the county could write an antipollution ordinance. Seadade also applied to build a port with a thirty-foot-deep water channel right through the middle of the bay.

If the county had wanted to kill the goose and its golden egg—tourism—it could find no better slayer than Seadade. Lloyd Miller, the chair of the local chapter of the Isaak Walton League, one of the oldest environmental organizations in the United States, went to Baggs to share his concerns about the direction the county was heading.[18]

Baggs gathered studies from University of Miami professors and scientists and other organizations that were looking into Seadade's claims of modern technology that reduced pollution and the impact of oil spills. He sent reporter Verne Williams on a twelve-hundred-mile investigative journey to similar facilities all across America to find out the pros and cons absent the public relations push. Meanwhile, he tried to keep the peace on the cocktail circuit, as his neighbor Mrs. Allen, whose children played with his, sat on the board of Belcher Oil, one of Seadade's biggest partners.

One summary report financed by the National Audubon Society noted that, beyond the destructive environmental impacts, the promise of jobs and tax revenues was suspect. Skilled workers would have to be imported, the report contended, and "heavily industrialized communities in the East have found that polluting industries create slums in their neighborhoods, make great demands on public services and are costly to regulate and police. The tax return is often too low."[19]

After he had digested enough information, he made known his opinion. "Mere agreements are not enough. If we cannot assure ourselves that enforcement will mean the refinery will use, day by day, the most modern technology, and that this modern technology will prevent pollution . . . then the people of this community should not permit a refinery to be established down near Homestead or anywhere near here."[20]

By April 1963, as the nine-month delay drew to an end, Baggs turned up the volume. He had his hands on a confidential memo from a colleague saying that a Phillips Petroleum exec had confided that Florida needed a refinery "like a hole in the head." Because Florida had no oil sources or production, it made no logistical or economic sense to invest in a refinery there.[21]

On April 17, the *News* published an editorial supporting the county commission's delay in making a final decision. One week later, Baggs wrote in his column, "Indeed, the view here is that an oil refinery on that lovely bay of water is a risk this community does not have to take and should not take.... Why not an oil refinery on the Cannes on the Riviera? The tourist industry here is our primary enterprise." The tourists were not his chief concern, however. He pointed out that the federal government, which had been considering a marine biology research center in Miami, would pull the plug because of the refinery's pollutants. He worried about the wading birds and the resplendent roseate spoonbill and "the obligation to pass along a clear bay to our children."[22]

A few days later, Baggs reported that the county commission was considering putting the question to voters, a move he supported because he believed public sentiment would swing against the refinery.[23]

Still, the project limped along until early 1964. The county commissioners reconsidered their original zoning approval, and the state could not reach an agreement with the developers on the channel location. Secretary Udall had also threatened to kill the project by the time the final plans reached the federal-approval stage.[24] Seadade was officially dead.

In December 1965, Miller and the state's chapter of the Isaak Walton League recognized Baggs with a special award for his "outstanding writing in the field of conservation and outdoor recreation."[25]

In the midst of Dade County's environmental wars, Governor W. Haydon Burns asked Baggs to help write Florida's future. Former governor LeRoy Collins's push for a new state constitution finally came to fruition when the Southern District Court found in July 1962 that the state's representational apportionment was, in fact, unconstitutional, effectively forcing the state legislature to create a new plan that would apportion representation according to residency and break the "Old Pork Choppers'" hold on the state.[26]

Baggs was one of thirty-seven men, mostly lawyers and legislators, appointed to the state Constitutional Revision Commission. Baggs had been making the case for reapportionment since he was promoted to columnist in 1949, and every time the subject came before the legislature or during a gubernatorial race, he argued for redistricting and a true two-party system again ... and again.

"To me, this is the single most important issue in this campaign," he'd written in 1954. "Just a single debate on a most important issue. The issue of whether we'll have Democracy, or the same old hypocrisy, in Florida."[27]

When in 1962 the state legislature failed again to do the right thing, his Raccoon told the Wild Turkey, "Old Bird, the humans in Florida can send a man around the world three times and reduce oranges to a magical concentrate. But they cannot divide the state population by so many legislators and come out with the correct answer."[28]

It took until 1965 before the state authorized the commission to begin work. Chairman Chesterfield Smith, founder of the law firm Holland and Knight, appointed Baggs to the judicial branch committee, helmed by a straitlaced state senator from Escambia County named Reubin Askew.[29] The committee's efforts to rework Florida's unwieldy court system ultimately created a streamlined, four-tiered system of checks and balances and clarified roles, including a state supreme court, a court of appeals, circuit courts for juvenile and probate cases, and county courts.[30]

When the entire revision committee met in senate chambers at the end of 1966, Smith purposefully sat Baggs next to Senator Charley Johns, the very man who embodied the old Dixiecrat mentality Baggs had fought for so long.[31] Baggs's questioning of Johns on the issue of reapportionment during the 1955 gubernatorial race had helped sway the contest to LeRoy Collins, something Johns never forgot.

During the contentious committee debates to finalize a new state constitution, Baggs introduced two amendments, both rooted in his sense of equality and fairness. The first was a provision that would have added "or sex" to the equal rights guarantee against discrimination in Section 2 of the revised constitution, so that women would enjoy equal protection under the law. The amendment was indefinitely postponed after a spirited debate and a seventeen-to-fifteen vote.[32]

The second amendment he offered centered on lowering the voting age in the state.[33] If the amendment passed, Florida would become the third state in the country, behind Georgia and Kentucky, to set the voting at age eighteen rather than twenty-one, which had been proposed by President Eisenhower as a national issue a full decade earlier.

Baggs argued that eighteen-year-olds were relegated to being "partial citizens" when they could be legally responsible in business contracts and marriage, had to pay taxes, and assumed roles in society as workers, but nonetheless were denied a vote. "We trust the young men of Florida with artillery in Viet Nam. No one has questioned that a young man of 18 is not old enough to go to war for his country halfway around the world. Doesn't it seem fair that we should trust these young men with a vote?"[34] His argument convinced the full revision commission.

Chairman Smith was so impressed with the editor that he named Baggs one of six members to testify before the full state legislature the following year to urge support for the new constitution's passage. When he did, Baggs drew on Alexander Hamilton's advice to make the U.S. constitution as lean as possible and on John F. Kennedy's appeal to set aside party politics.

"I would beg you ladies and gentlemen," he told the legislature, "to be less Republican and less Democratic as you author the document which is going to determine how the people of Florida are going to govern themselves ... probably for the rest of this century."[35]

CHAPTER 16

1965–1967

Solving problems is the oldest work of man, and it is almost terrifying to reflect after a gaze back through history that 99 percent of these problems have been made by man.—To an angry reader, December 1957

In the late evening hours of September 7, 1965, Ralph McGill made several attempts to reach Baggs by phone. When he finally got through, a frazzled Frec answered.

"I don't know what to do," she said. "William is asleep."

Churning away at 125 miles per hour, Hurricane Betsy was about to make landfall north of Key Largo, just south of Miami, which put the Baggses on the dirty side of the storm. The power in Coral Gables had gone out and the shutters for the house's windows had not gone up.[1]

Baggs eventually awakened and the family weathered Betsy, but not before she took down a forty-year-old mango tree that supplied the fruit for the chutney Baggs sent out as Christmas gifts. He told McGill and Ashmore by letter two days later just how the *News* had bested its rival, whose presses on the bay were flooded by the storm surge. He had convinced the advertising manager, who lived a few blocks away, to drive him into the office.

Gently encouraged into action, the promotion manager was busy telephoning radio and television stations that the *Miami News* would be delivered at the usual time and this announcement during the day most conveniently followed at the heels of the statement by the *Herald* that it simply couldn't get the paper out to its readers. . . . The starter plate went down at 2:09 and the press turned at 2:14. . . . We achieved 90 percent home delivery and not yet has a mother or father of a carrier boy sent me the intention of filing a law suit.[2]

Only ten months later, though, Baggs had to concede a certain measure of defeat.

From a high circulation of 140,000 in the early 1950s, the *News'* readership had dwindled to 112,000 by the mid-1960s—a 20 percent drop. With lengthening commutes caused by increased sprawl and traffic, "people were having to go to work so early in the morning to beat the rush hour that they were leaving before they read their *Herald*. So, when they got home at night is when they first started reading their *Herald*, so who needed the *Miami News*?" recalls Kleinberg, who noticed that the papers remained on the lawns in his neighborhood at nine or ten in the morning when he was headed into the office. By the time he arrived home, Kleinberg could turn on the local and evening news to catch up on the day's events.[3]

On July 29, 1966, the *News* shocked readers when it announced that president and publisher James M. Cox Jr. had signed a joint operating agreement with John S. and James L. Knight, publishers of the *Miami Herald*. Under the arrangement, the *Herald* would assume the advertising, circulation, and printing responsibilities for the *News*.

"We did not seek such an arrangement," wrote John S. Knight on the front page of that day's edition, "We acceded to it to ensure permanent publication of The News, which has suffered large losses in recent years." Knight went on to guarantee readers that the *News*, whose staff would take over the sixth floor of the *Herald*'s Miami Modern fortress on Biscayne Bay, would remain under Baggs "a completely independent editorial entity."[4]

Baggs reassured readers in a companion statement issued alongside those of Knight and Cox. "Miami has avoided the fate which has visited so many American cities. Miami is not going to become a one-newspaper town." To put a finer point on his independence, he added, "Over the years, you have come to expect a vigorous competition between the two newspapers of Miami. Often The News and The Herald have disagreed, and occasionally we have thrown inky stones at each other, and the last time both newspapers shared a common opinion on something important was when Lyndon Johnson was a candidate for President. (Believing in the general worthiness of the Democratic Party to represent the people, we at The News were delighted by that evidence of a new intelligence revealing itself from inside the Herald.)"[5] Yet as he recited these same words when his "What's the Story?" colleague and wtvj anchor Ralph Renick interviewed him for the evening news, Baggs, his booming voice muted, looked down at his notes, never making eye contact with Renick or the camera.[6]

With the joint operating agreement, Baggs had the unhappy task of letting go all of the sales, printing, and circulation staff, including close friend

Huey Stinson, father of young Don. Stinson headed north to work at the *Atlanta Constitution* with McGill.

After the final stick of furniture was moved from the muscular, mid-century building at N.W. 7th Street to the neon-lighted building on his beloved bay, Baggs drove back down Biscayne Boulevard and across the camelback bridge to the empty *News* offices. As he stood on the river's edge looking across the skyline of the city he had come to love and champion, he vomited into the murky waters until there was nothing left.[7]

"The *News* was in trouble for a long time. It was always financially weak," Kleinberg recalls. "You can only tighten your belt so much, you won't be able to breathe anymore."[8]

Nor did it help that Baggs, while deft with people, cared little for the budgeting aspects of administration. He had not balanced the hemorrhaging revenue with the realities of the times, naively figuring it would all work out—*somehow*—because he was doing what he felt was the right thing.

"Bill was a great writer [and] a great individual, [but] he was one of the worst administrators in the history of American journalism," Kleinberg offered in hindsight years later as part of an oral history project. "Bill didn't care about the nickels and dimes of the newspaper. He had things to say, and he said them so well."[9]

Kleinberg still believes that, in addition to television and traffic, Baggs's positions on civil rights, the environment, and his staunch opposition to America's growing involvement in Vietnam cost the *News* hundreds, if not thousands, of readers, which is borne out by the stack of missives from the circulation department among Baggs's papers.

Kleinberg, who ultimately was promoted to editor, said with a wistful sigh that he would not have had it any other way. "Nothing budged Bill Baggs to change the way he was writing. Nothing budged our editorial page people, right down to the last day."[10]

Baggs never shied away from sharing an opinion, even if his views were out of step with his southern heritage or pushed advertisers' buttons. "He [was] the kind of guy [who] would call you a bastard to your face but you wouldn't realize it until twenty minutes later," joked Kleinberg.[11]

Yet as Baggs evolved from reporter to activist in fifteen short years, he was pulled away from the office as well as his family more often and for longer periods of time. His profile got a big boost when, in late 1961, Baggs accepted an invitation from Robert Maynard Hutchins to join the board of the Center for the Study of Democratic Institutions, the liberal think tank Hutchins founded in Santa Barbara, California, and where Ashmore served as executive vice president. All at once, Baggs was in conversation on a regular basis with other fellows and board members, including the likes of Supreme Court justice William O. Douglas, Arkansas senator J. William Fulbright, biochemist Linus Pauling, and political scientist and novelist Harvey Wheeler.

"He was enamored of ideas," Frec sighed one afternoon in 2007 as she looked out her living room window. Her wan smile conveyed a still-palpable frustration.

During the darkest days of the Cuban Missile Crisis in October 1962, Pope John XXIII, who was battling inoperable cancer, found the energy and the courage to write what many considered his "last will and testament," *Pacem in Terris*, or *Peace on Earth*. During Holy Week the following April, the pope unveiled this final encyclical, a groundbreaking delineation of the moral imperative for human rights—including the end of racial discrimination, a call to equal rights for women, and the admonishment that political authority must serve the greater good. It was the first time in history, according to religious scholar and journalist Dr. Peter Steinfels, that "a papal encyclical was addressed not only to the bishops, clergy, and faithful, but 'to all men of good will.'"[12]

For the first time since meeting Reverend Gibson, in whom he recognized such grace, Baggs found a spiritual message he could rally around. He committed his 1963 Maundy Thursday editorial to sharing the pope's earnest plea, which was "no generalized peace appeal from an ivory tower." To his readers "down on Flagler Street," he wrote, "The Pontiff seems to be saying that the world is smaller, weapons are deadlier, nations are being pulled closer together and that mankind had better rediscover its God-given brotherhood if it is to survive."[13]

Inspired, Baggs asked Bishop Coleman Carroll of the Diocese of Miami to find him a bust of Pope John XXIII. After the contentious discussions he and Baggs had held over the years, the shocked bishop obliged, and Baggs placed the pope's likeness next to Abraham Lincoln's on his bookshelves.[14] For Baggs, *Pacem in Terris* flipped a switch inside of him, confirming that the role of a newspaperman was more than just to inform and engage a public readership; it was to challenge and to lead readers to new ways of thinking, sorely needed as the volatile 1960s devolved into domestic and international turmoil.

For his part, Hutchins, according to Ashmore's memoir *Hearts and Minds*, saw in the pope's encyclical "a possible breakthrough in the Cold War." He envisioned the pope's moral and spiritual requirements for peace as a foundation for an unofficial discussion, through the Center for the Study of Democratic Institutions, among diplomats, representatives, and scholars on both sides of the Iron Curtain to find and implement secular avenues to achieve peace. Hutchins put Ashmore in charge of organizing a convocation.[15] Ashmore, in turn, enlisted Baggs's help.

For three days in February 1965, an international conference on *Pacem in Terris* was convened at the United Nations building overlooking the East River in New York City. "The guest list would have done credit to a U.N. charter meeting or a state funeral: the Secretary-General of the U.N., the president of the Assembly and two former presidents; the Vice President and Chief Justice of the U.S., an associate justice and four U.S. senators . . . all told, 2,000 delegates from 20 nations of the communist, neutralist and free worlds," wrote *Life* magazine correspondent John K. Jessup, who covered the entire conclave. The sessions were recorded and broadcast on more than ninety educational television and radio stations across the United States and other countries. Those gathered debated such eternal questions as "When man is both killer and saint, how do we proceed from there?" and "How do you distinguish wars of national liberation from wars in defense of democracy, as the dual concerns of Israel and Vietnam illuminated?"[16]

Speaking to the delegates, Hutchins reported that a 1962 U.N. study revealed that the nations of the world were spending more than $120 billion annually on military operations. Thus, war had become a powerful economic engine and a real threat to the complicated business of making of peace. "To redeploy this force for non-military purposes," Hutchins warned, "is an operation large enough to give rise to important problems of economic and social adjustment."[17]

The overall theme of the conference appeared to be that, while it may be difficult for human nature to evolve—"Was mankind even capable of peace?" one theologian asked—the institutions that governed men could.

Standing in the great hall, Chief Justice Earl Warren implored the United Nations to live up to its potential of perfecting international law. "Perhaps that was excusable during the centuries of isolation because of slowness of transportation and communication, but there can be no excuse in this latter part of the twentieth century," he said.[18]

Luis Quintanilla, the flamboyant and gregarious former Mexican ambassador to the United States, agreed with Warren's suppositions. Quintanilla, who had nominated the atom bomb for the Nobel Peace Prize in years past, had often pushed the U.N. to position itself as a world government. He suggested making all countries of the world members, with voting power weighted by population, to which Adam Schaff of Communist Poland offered the idea that rational ideological warfare still could be pursued without resorting to shooting.[19]

Throughout the three days of meetings, Baggs took notes, shook hands, connected with world leaders and intellectuals, and penned columns to reach the readers of his paper—all while growing more involved in actual day-to-day efforts toward peace.

Three U.N. undersecretaries and veteran diplomats followed up the Pacem in Terris conference with a meeting in Santa Barbara at the headquarters of the Center for the Study of Democratic Institutions. After the Gulf of Tonkin Resolution in 1964, the war in Vietnam had escalated, with U.S. pilots saturating the North with bombs and U.S. and civilian casualties rising in the South. The Center initiated back-channel discussions with private emissaries to bring China, at least, to the table.[20] Baggs served as the Center's contact with the U.S. State Department, which proved as thorny and as distrustful of the press and private citizens as some of the communist countries the Center was dealing with. Baggs constantly had to tell Ashmore to remind the Center's members to be discreet.[21]

Amid what was becoming an all-consuming focus on Vietnam, Baggs had put off looking after his own well-being. By December 1965, however, he was in the hospital, where doctors injected radioactive tracers to get a better view of what was happening with his kidneys.

McGill's wife had died from chronic kidney disease, so he was particularly concerned about Baggs's health. He implored his friend to give up the wet straw-smelling Erik cigars he smoked constantly, to drink less, and to exercise. McGill finally wrote to Ashmore, hoping to get some reinforcement: "Our friend Dr. Baggs came back from the New York meeting ... and has really been having a pretty bad time with kidney bleeding."[22]

Still, Baggs pushed on. He met with President Johnson and others again in February 1966, at which time the president shared his "inner thoughts relating to Viet Nam, the Soviet Union, and China." In providing his notes to Hutchins and Ashmore, Baggs stressed to the latter that "the White House is very sensitive about giving any indication that it has conferred with private groups. So, for God's sake, make sure that this report stays in only two pair of hands—the one belonging to you and the one belonging to the Abbot [Hutchins]."[23]

Baggs and Ashmore met again in Geneva in June 1966 as part of the planning effort for Pacem in Terris II. While there, Baggs reported from France and Switzerland, gaining a deeper understanding of how much the Vietnam War was impacting the world. "Europeans of various political persuasions, conservative and liberal and Socialist, seek out Americans to talk about the war in Viet Nam. And the concern really doesn't appear as much that Europe is going to become involved in the war, but that just about every trouble in the world goes unattended because of Viet Nam."[24] Out of the planning effort came a concerted all-hands-on-deck approach to getting representatives from Hanoi, Saigon, Peking, and other Southeast Asian nations to the Pacem in Terris II meeting, set for May 28–31, 1967.

From Geneva, Baggs traveled to Israel, where he walked the "plain of Armageddon" to see how Israeli ingenuity had turned the barren lands into verdant fields of produce.[25] He visited Arab families along the Jordanian border, who applauded Egypt's Gamal Nasser as he called for the destruction of Israel even as their lives had been improved with electricity, running water, and television since the founding of the state.[26] He stood on the border of Syria in full view of a machine gun nest, where an Israeli asked him, "Do you know how we define someone who is anti-Semitic?"

"No," Baggs answered.

"We define an anti-Semitic fellow as someone who hates the Jews more than necessary."[27]

Meanwhile, Quintanilla, the retired Mexican diplomat, journeyed in October to Peking (now Beijing), where his personal invitation to China's foreign minister to attend Pacem in Terris II was politely declined. Quintanilla took advantage of the proximity to North Vietnam and finagled a private meeting with President Ho Chi Minh. Although Ho had already rejected an invitation to attend the upcoming Geneva conference, he did indicate that he would welcome discussions with Center representatives.[28]

Three days after Christmas 1966, Baggs and Ashmore were on a plane headed to North Vietnam.

CHAPTER 17

January–March 1967

Some things a President thinks is [*sic*] in the national interest shouldn't be published . . . no sympathy whining to a newspaperman. Every President I have known since FDR manages news. Job of newspaperman is to discover what news Pres. is managing and then manage it themselves.—Handwritten notes for speech, undated

Baggs and Ashmore were not the first private citizens who had tried to open channels of communication between Washington and Hanoi. Just one month before Baggs headed east, a complex network of communications orchestrated through Poland and Italy, called "Marigold," had ended abruptly when President Johnson ordered more air strikes in and around North Vietnam's capital city.[1] And while Baggs, Ashmore, and Quintanilla, who joined them for the mission, assessed the damage from Operation Rolling Thunder, Great Britain and Moscow were trying to produce the first direct talks between American and North Vietnamese envoys in an initiative dubbed "Sunflower."[2] The U.S. State Department thought so little of Baggs and Ashmore as the Center's gardeners that the department never even gave their attempt at diplomacy a sweetly scented code name.

The department did, however, see the opportunity to "exchange exploratory views without compromising the official position of either side."[3] It hesitantly gave its blessing and prepped these unofficial and nonprofessional diplomats for the journey. Assistant Secretary of State William Bundy, Undersecretary of State Nicholas Katzenbach, and Deputy Assistant Secretary of State for Far Eastern Affairs Len Unger briefed Baggs and Ashmore for two days straight on U.S. policy in Vietnam. Repeatedly, they emphasized that the Center was not acting on behalf of the U.S. government and that Baggs and Ashmore were representing only themselves as private individuals. They did, however, ask the two to convey a request to the Democratic Republic of Vietnam (DRV) that it invite the International Red Cross to establish contact with American prisoners of war.

Baggs agreed to keep the meeting secret, as requested by the department, but he was quite candid that on his return he intended to write articles about what he had seen and learned in Hanoi. He promised to leave out the diplomatic parts.[4]

Bundy and Katzenbach had met Baggs on occasion through the years, beginning with the Kennedy administration, and had no reason to distrust him, other than the fact that their current boss had been unhappy with the critical press he had received from someone he once considered a friend. Katzenbach, however, believed Ashmore was a loose talker.[5] Bundy thought Ashmore had leaked to a reporter the story of another private peace mission, this one by Italian politician Giorgio LaPira, during the Christmas season of 1965.[6]

One week and ten thousand miles later, Baggs, Ashmore, and Quintanilla were stalled in Phnom Penh, Cambodia. They had the necessary DRV-approved visas and an established communication channel to Hanoi. What they didn't have was the International Control Commission (ICC) plane, the only way in and out of Hanoi, which would not arrive until January 6—three days away. It was going to be hard for the three men to remain inconspicuous, so they joined groups of tourists at museums and traveled to the ancient city of Siem Reap to explore Angkor Wat, a place Baggs considered "floating poetry."[7]

The ICC's arthritic Boeing 317, built in 1946, arrived as scheduled on January 6, and finally they were headed to Vietnam. For safety reasons—sharing air space with U.S. bombers—the plane could fly only after dark. It stopped in Vientiane, Laos—a poor city in a poor nation that Ashmore called the "Mississippi of Southeast Asia"—where they connected with U.S. Ambassador William Sullivan, who would serve as a point of contact and conveyer of any information they needed to get back to the U.S. government.[8] By the time they reached Hanoi in the late evening, their clandestine mission had already been uncovered by *New York Times* correspondent and managing editor Harrison Salisbury.[9]

Salisbury was the first American journalist (Baggs was the second) granted a visa by the DRV since the U.S. aerial assault had commenced in February 1965, and he was the first to report that what scant information the generals provided to the American press differed from what was actually occurring on the ground. Salisbury had seen Baggs, Ashmore, and Quintanilla's names on the ICC flight manifest before departing Hanoi and outed them in the press when he filed his first stories days later.[10] Baggs and Ashmore would not learn of this breach until they returned to U.S. soil.[11]

A delegation offering bouquets of gladiolas met them at the airport. The small group, including an interpreter and Luu Quy Ky, vice chairman of the Committee for Cultural Relations with Foreign Countries, was led by Hoàng Tùng, editor of the DRV's official newspaper *Nhân Dân* and president of the Vietnam Journalistic Association. He was a minister of and spokesman for the government as well, and clearly had President Ho Chi Minh's ear.

As they rode in the back of a Soviet-made GAZ Volga sedan, Baggs, Ashmore, and Quintanilla were subjected to the prevailing message that, while the North Vietnamese despised "American aggression," they harbored deep respect for the American people. They wanted independence and peace, but not peace on its own, and they were prepared to survive war as they had for twenty-five years, fighting first the Japanese and then the French.

All Baggs wanted at that moment was sleep. He noted, however, that the Long Bien Bridge, reported by UPI to have been destroyed, remained intact as they drove across it into a pockmarked Hanoi.[12]

Like all diplomats, intellectuals, and activists from Western nations, the three men were delivered by their greeters to the Thong Nhat Hotel, a once-opulent turn-of-the-century French colonial gem where writer Graham Greene set his novel *The Quiet American* and celebrities Charlie Chaplin and Paulette Goddard honeymooned after their secret wedding in 1936. Formerly named the Hotel Metropole, it had been rebranded the "Reunification Hotel" in 1954 after the fall of the French at Dien Bien Phu. The soft textures and muted elegance of the art nouveau decor had been extinguished, replaced by the drab utilitarian furnishings common to the Soviet Union. Even the toilet paper was rationed.

During that first full day in Hanoi, January 7, Baggs was getting his bearings in a city that reminded him much of Paris with its broad sidewalks, townhomes, and foliage-covered courtyards. He noted that the breweries had moved outside of the city, dispersed along with school children and soldiers. Every few feet, thirty-six-inch-wide concrete pipes had been planted into the ground with perforated manhole covers to be used as easy-access bomb shelters when the air sirens blared. One of the guides informed him that the pipes would be used for a sewer system after the war.

The better part of their first day was spent visiting sites the North Vietnamese claimed had been destroyed by U.S. bombs. As a former bombardier, Baggs had a particular interest in assessing damage made by planes that could fly much closer and hit with more firepower and greater accuracy than the B-24s he had flown in over Eastern Europe. At a rise alongside the Red River, Baggs documented three hundred homes that had been burned, but noticed no blast damage among the ruins. The destruction could have been caused by incendiary bombs or Vietnamese antiaircraft missiles that had fallen back, he surmised. "People here say that Hanoi was bombed on June 29, Dec. 2, 3, 13 and 14," he scribbled in his navy blue leather-bound notebook.

At the School for Trade Unions, southwest of Hanoi, roofs were torn off buildings and a student dormitory was cut in half. The resulting bomb craters measured twenty feet across and thirty feet deep. About a third of a mile northeast of downtown Hanoi, in the city's most densely populated residential area, fifty-two homes were destroyed, and the entire roof of a Buddhist pagoda was missing. The only possible legitimate "steel and concrete" target in the area was a rail line that led to Haiphong.[13] It remained untouched. The Viet Ba grammar school on Highway One, in the countryside five kilometers south of Hanoi, was bombed, but the truck base a mile away remained unscathed.[14]

These images stood in stark contrast to the precise hits in the industrial suburbs they had seen on the drive into the city the night before. "Our subsequent examination of the results would reveal that our countrymen either were guilty of inordinately sloppy bombing or were carrying on a macabre heckling campaign," Baggs and Ashmore later wrote in their chronicle of events.[15]

After Baggs published his articles about his trip to Vietnam, Paul Warnke, general counsel to the secretary of defense, was called in to investigate the veracity of Baggs's reports. Warnke confirmed that civilian targets had been hit. "Now, you never know whether that's inadvertence, or whether it's recklessness on the part of a particular pilot. People don't always behave terribly well under the pressure of war," he later concluded.[16]

Everywhere they went, Baggs spoke with children, the elderly, and laborers, a sort-of Man in the Middle for Southeast Asia. And everywhere

Baggs and company toured, they had to run for cover when the air alerts sounded.

Later that evening, Baggs, Ashmore, and Quintanilla shared an intense conversation with Vice Chairman Ky, who at one point asked, "Why does America continue bombing if it wants peace?"

As instructed by the State Department, Baggs was careful with his answer, telling Ky that "every country wished to conclude [the] war, including the U.S., and that the work ahead of us was not to change attitudes but to agree on a technical approach to begin conversation." He offered the carrot that economic and cultural development throughout Southeast Asia could begin after the war's end.

He also cautioned that anyone telling the North Vietnamese that the protests against the war were about to change American foreign policy was fooling them. "We don't carry placards," Baggs said of his own unofficial delegation, "just news back to the people who make decisions in the U.S. these days."[17]

Most Americans, said Baggs, respected their flag and country and would follow both. Not only did his prediction prove wrong, it also reflected a degree of naivety regarding the swell of public opinion that would grow over the next few years. But Baggs was hardly naïve, given his involvement with the civil disobedience of the civil rights movement. Unsure of his footing in his dual role of both accidental diplomat and journalist, Baggs may have spoken in the language of the State Department, which conflicted with his role as objective observer.

The following day, Baggs and Ashmore drove to Hà Nam Province in the Red River delta. Highway One was barely two lanes wide. Because it was not safe to travel after 3:30 p.m. Hanoi time, when the bombing was most likely to begin, they stayed in a farmhouse surrounded by rice paddies in My Trung village. The next day, Baggs and Ashmore made their way before the bombing began along a one-lane causeway to reach Nam Dinh, a city of ninety thousand people. Their guide told them the city, a textile center, had been bombed fifty-three times. The U.S. State Department had told them Nam Dinh was a rendezvous point for supplies headed to the Viet Minh and the Viet Cong fighting in the south.

Air alerts sounded just as they arrived and they had to wait for an all clear before they could take stock of the results of previous saturation bombing. They found thirty-two gouges from a rocket blast in the exterior walls of a school and three to four acres of homes obliterated. In the city center, six square blocks of homes, churches, and pagodas had been destroyed. The power plant and textile mill were still in operation.

On their return to Hanoi they stopped in Phu Ly, a virtual ghost town thirty-six miles outside of the capital city. In an article he published on his return, Baggs wrote, "the town is a vista of rubble."[18]

On the evening of their return to Hanoi, Hoàng Tùng arranged a meeting with DRV leaders and intellectuals. The resulting conversation proved robust, centering on President Johnson's April 1965 speech at Johns Hopkins University in which he stated that the reason for American intervention in Vietnam was to defend an independent South from a communist takeover by the North Vietnamese and China.[19] The DRV representatives believed there was no need for talks if the U.S. president's position remained so intractable. When the DRV attorney general asserted that the United States was ambitious for a Pax Americana, Ashmore flatly denied it, saying "both sides have an obligation to end the war."

Hours later, however, by the end of the night, the group had settled on some noncommittal conditions that they hoped would lead to future conversations between their nations. According to Baggs's transcribed notes, the DRV wished to end the war honorably and viewed a cease-fire as an agreement between two equals. They all concurred that the first meeting required no agenda, but the DRV did not believe that the other political faction, the National Liberation Front (NLF) and its military arm, the Viet Cong, needed to be present at the initial meeting. Rather, the DRV would consult with the NLF should any agreement be reached with the United States.

On January 11, they met with Col. Hà Văn Lâu of the DRV military high command, who "recited figures like an accountant," including the number of South Vietnamese troops who had deserted, been captured, killed, or wounded, and planes downed. He cited specific war crimes and America's use of chemical weapons. Baggs recorded nearly every number, but made it clear that he could not use the colonel's figures in print because they could not be verified. Still, he promised to share them with the U.S. government.[20]

That evening, the Committee for Cultural Relations staged a concert. "Every song but one was a stirring patriotic rendition," wrote Baggs. "The one exception, played in honor of two visiting Americans, was 'Get Along Little Doggie,' and you have never heard 'Get Along Little Doggie' until you've heard it played on a monochord."[21]

The following morning, Hoàng Tùng requested that Baggs and Ashmore meet him at his newspaper office. When Baggs inquired why he had not replaced the broken windows, which let in so much cold air, Tùng smiled and said, "I do not fix the broken windows, because your Mr. McNamara may send the planes again." As if on cue, the windows rattled from a bomb strike in the distance.[22]

Then, for the next few hours, Ashmore and Baggs peppered Tùng with questions: Would the DRV be willing to meet privately in exploratory talks with the United States? Were indirect communications possible between the two governments until the time was right for direct communication? Could the International Red Cross be allowed into North Vietnam?

Tùng's answers always circled back to his assertion that, "if the United States government is willing to end the war, and shows some concrete example of good intention, then something can be done. The DRV is not unreasonable."

When the meeting finally ended, the Americans returned to the Thong Nhat Hotel. By the time they got to their rooms, Tùng had sent word that President Ho Chi Minh wanted to meet with them.[23]

In clear English, the spry, alert Ho greeted the men and welcomed them to the sparely furnished former French governor's estate, a colonial manor surrounded by gardens that now served as the presidential palace. Quintanilla had rejoined the group, along with Tùng and an interpreter.

"Please, forget protocol," said Ho. "Please feel at home."

Baggs and Ashmore reiterated that they were visiting as private citizens. While they would use the utmost respect and discretion, they would report on their conversation to the U.S. government and to Robert Hutchins at the Center for the Study of Democratic Institutions.

Ho reaffirmed his position that there was "no possibility of conversation with the United States until the bombing stopped. No new troops should be introduced in the south by the United States during any truce while conversations were going on."

As Baggs would later note, "He was, Ho said, a businessman, and he wanted to see the goods before the price was established. We took this to mean an act of good faith by the United States. . . . He is not going to negotiate under duress."

Ho spoke often of peace during their two hours together. Just as often, he referred to the lengthy campaign for Vietnam's independence from the French and the Japanese.

"This may be difficult for you to believe," he told Baggs. "I am grieved not only when the Vietnamese people are killed. I am also grieved when American soldiers are killed. I sympathize with their parents."

At no time did Ho mention China or the Soviet Union. He referred to them always as "our socialist brothers." Nor did he insist that the NLF, the communist faction, had to be represented in any possible talks.

When Baggs, Ashmore, and Quintanilla rose to leave, they suggested to Ho that an acceptance by the DRV of an exploratory conference would not be regarded in any way as a sign of weakness by the United States. Ho assured them in reply that "neither would the willingness of the U.S. to meet be in any way considered a sign of weakness or irresolution by the DRV."

Tùng offered to accept and share any future correspondence and suggested that it could come through the DRV representation in Phnom Penh. Ho nodded and said, "Of course, that is all right, but why not send it direct to me?"[24]

At a stop in Hong Kong on their way home, Baggs sent film canisters and raw stories ahead to Kleinberg, who had been promoted to news editor. In the packet, he sent instructions to managing editor Ed Pierce to ensure that the series was presented in an unbiased fashion so that neither Baggs nor the paper would be accused of aiding and abetting the enemy—charges that had been leveled at the *Times'* Salisbury after his articles had run just weeks earlier. Baggs wanted the reader to assess the facts and "make up his own mind," but many a reader could draw similar conclusions from Baggs's accounts as they did from Salisbury's, which called into question the veracity of the Johnson administration's claims that the United States was winning the war.[25]

On Monday, January 16, 1967, Baggs's nine-part series of dispatches from Vietnam debuted. Baggs led off with his interview with Ho, whom he quoted: "We will never surrender our independence for peace. We have battled too long for our independence and freedom."

The series was picked up nationwide by the Associated Press and carried across all Cox publications, including the *Atlanta Constitution*, which under McGill held firm to the Johnson administration's line on Vietnam—so much so, that the president wrote thank-you letters to McGill for his stead-fastness. The *News* took out daily ads in the *Miami Herald* to announce the next day's articles.

On January 17, Ashmore and Baggs flew to Washington and met with William Bundy and Heywood Isham, a career diplomat, at the Jefferson Hotel around ten that night. Bundy directed the men to dictate their notes to the State Department the following day. Afterward they reviewed their report with Ambassador-at-Large Averell Harriman and Undersecretary Katzenbach.

Both U.S. Representative Dante Fascell of Florida and Senator J. William Fulbright of Arkansas asked Baggs and Ashmore to speak before their legislative committees. However, the two men respectfully declined because of their promise to keep in confidence their private diplomacy.[26]

While in Washington, they called McGill, who later reported to publisher Jack Tarver that he "had the great pleasure last night of talking for a while with Ho Chi Minh's two envoys."[27] Although the message seemed to be in keeping with the ruthless teasing these men traded in, it was the first real sign of a fracture in their relationship. As elsewhere in the nation, the Vietnam War came between fathers and sons.

Reader responses to Baggs's articles ran the gamut from encouraging to inflamed.

"What amazes me is the conviction of Mr. Baggs in traveling to the country of the enemy in order to find the truth and bring it to the American people," wrote Nathan S. Davis of North Miami Beach. "In my opinion, Mr. Baggs's visit will make a great contribution to the long-desired peace talks."

R. J. Farrell of Hialeah could not have felt less inclined to agree. "As a Marine Corps veteran of World War II and the Korean police action, let me say, if I were a combat GI in the mud and filth of Vietnam, who had the misfortune to receive a copy of Mr. Baggs' [sic] epic, seemingly edited by Mr. Salisbury of the *New York Times*, I honestly feel my hate for the Communist would be focused right here near Biscayne Bay."[28]

Both Salisbury and Baggs were nominated for the Pulitzer Prize. Neither won. In fact, no reporting about the war received recognition that year. Even in 1967, the majority of newspapers in the U.S. still offered tacit approval of the war.

CHAPTER 18

May–September 1967

Events here could easily persuade a visitor that he should have dressed in a suit of armor.—"Reds Pull Out of Geneva Conference," *Miami News*, May 29, 1967

Senator Fulbright, chair of the Senate Foreign Relations Committee and a vocal critic of U.S. policy in Vietnam, visited Baggs in Miami in late January 1967 after Baggs had returned from Hanoi. When Fulbright learned that neither Baggs nor Ashmore had shared their report with President Johnson, he approached the president days later at a White House event.

"I'd like to see them, Bill," the president was reported saying, "but you know I can't talk with everybody who's been over there talking with Ho Chi Minh."[1]

As far as anyone knew (and still knows), the only people who had spoken directly with Ho in all the secret peace missions that had taken place (and failed) were Quintanilla, Baggs, and Ashmore.

Fulbright subsequently summoned Baggs and Ashmore to a meeting in Katzenbach's Washington office. They traveled to D.C., and after a series of back and forth conversations and drafts with Katzenbach, Bundy, Harriman, and the senator in attendance, a letter for Ashmore's signature was produced. The letter, which sought to keep the lines of communication open with Ho, requested some reciprocal restraint by the DRV in the form of a pledge that it would not use the talks for military advantage. Bundy presumably received approval from the White House and Secretary of State Dean Rusk to send the letter to Tùng, which Ashmore did on the afternoon of February 5, 1967.[2]

Baggs stayed in touch with Harriman and Katzenbach all through March and April, letting them know if Ashmore had heard from Tùng. On behalf of the board of the Center for the Study of Democratic Institutions, Baggs had invited North and South Vietnam to send representatives to the upcoming Pacem in Terris II conference in Geneva, and he had asked for Harriman's help in getting the president to encourage Vice President Hubert Humphrey to attend and participate.[3] Baggs and Ashmore did not find out until months later, however, that President Johnson had sent a letter of his own to Hanoi, hardening the United States' stance in favor of a military rather than a negotiated resolution. It was sent through a less-direct channel in Moscow a few days before Ashmore had sent his.

According to Ashmore and Baggs, Fulbright warned them in private, after their February meeting in D.C., that "these State Department people figure they're entitled to use you, in any way they see fit, to further what they call the national interest, but the national interest is whatever they decide it is and can sell to the president. Their big weapon is secrecy; they let you have just as much of the pertinent information as serves their purpose and hold back the rest. . . . When you cross them, they begin leaking out whatever they've got that can serve to discredit you."[4]

At the end of May in Geneva, Switzerland, the Center convened Pacem in Terris II: A Second International Convocation to Examine the Requirements for Peace. Frec accompanied Baggs on this trip, and she noticed a man staying on their hallway who always left his hotel room at the same time they did and who appeared in many of the same places around town. When she asked her husband if he was part of the conclave, Baggs told her not to worry, he was probably one of Johnson's guys and that their rooms were most likely bugged.[5]

Four times as many nations joined the conference in Switzerland as had attended two years before in New York.[6] The *Miami News* reported that the first order of business was to examine the sources of the contemporary conflicts in the Middle East, Africa, and Southeast Asia and determine how they could best be defused.[7]

However, just before the convocation officially began, the DRV representatives who had considered attending after Baggs and Ashmore's visit rescinded their acceptance of the Center's invitation. South Vietnam sent its representative, foreign minister Tran Do, anyway. Not able to do much more than observe because of the DRV's absence, he left. Then, Moscow pulled out of the gathering to protest the United States' escalation of the war, which now included a commitment of nearly half a million combat troops. The four diplomats from East Germany followed the lead of Moscow, but they eventually returned. Representatives from Thailand,

Indonesia, Cambodia, Laos, and the Philippines broke away to hold their own Southeast Asian conference to discuss the formation of a regional organization to promote social, economic, and cultural cooperation and to spur development and investment.[8]

In spite of the fits and starts, the convocation began on a high note. Baggs was in the audience when Dr. Martin Luther King Jr. took the stage on May 29 to set the tone for the day's discussions.

> If in my remarks, statements are made that are critical of my nation's foreign policy, this must not be construed as a rejection of my country. I criticize America because I love her and because I want to see her stand as the moral example of the world. The war in Vietnam is more than a local conflict taking place on Asian soil. It is a nightmarish struggle that involves and threatens the whole world. I cannot help but feel that the present crisis in the Middle East is indirectly related to the U.S. involvement in Vietnam. War anywhere intensifies the possibility of war everywhere.

King let no one and no nation off the hook for the struggles plaguing the world, which surely caused discomfort among many of the delegates, not least of all those from the United States. "The maintenance of peace," he continued in his rolling cadence, "requires the promotion of justice, and for almost 75 percent of the world's population, justice requires development. When progress and development are neglected, conflict is inevitable. We of the West must come to see that the so-called wars of liberation which loom on the world horizon are attempts of the people of underdeveloped nations to find freedom from hunger, disease, and exploitation."[9]

The convocation continued for a few more days, but participants grew anxious as tensions rose in the Middle East. Just as the meetings broke up in Geneva, the Six-Day War broke out.

Baggs had already flown home with Frec when he received a call on June 9 from Ashmore, who had stayed on in Switzerland to wrap things up and take a few days' rest. Mai Van Bo, the DRV's ambassador to France, had been instructed by his government to request a meeting with Baggs and Ashmore, to take place in Paris on June 12. It seemed to both Baggs and Ashmore that Ho had trusted them enough to keep the lines open, even though he had not responded to the February letter.

Baggs contacted Katzenbach, who thought the meeting would be useful and asked Baggs to provide a full report on his return. Then, Baggs caught a plane back to Europe.[10]

Mai Van Bo showed interest in the concept of the regional Southeast Asian organization that had come out of Pacem in Terris II, even if political cooperation could not be achieved right away, but he expressed his government's inability to trust the United States. Every time Hanoi had said it would be open to talks, the United States escalated the bombing.

"What kind of war is this?" Mai Van Bo asked. "We see that this is an American war of aggression against a people struggling for independence and freedom."

Baggs reiterated that he was speaking only as a private citizen and not as a representative of the U.S. government. He also assured Mai Van Bo that there would be no public report of this meeting, which contradicted his role as journalist, observer, and chronicler. The man who bristled at news being managed was himself managing the news. Perhaps Baggs believed, as he had during Miami's desegregation efforts, that the less publicity there was, the easier it would be to achieve the desired results.

Baggs spoke of the mutual distrust between their nations being based on inaction on the part of the DRV in response to previous attempts to open a discussion of the path to peace. "There is in the American government a considerable skepticism that Hanoi is genuinely interested in negotiation at this time and doubts that North Vietnam wishes to conclude the war."

Baggs further acknowledged that there had been untimely military actions, and that two factions in the U.S. government were fighting for prominence on the issue of the war. One wanted a military solution and the other wanted a negotiated solution.[11]

Ashmore proposed that the Center help coordinate private, informal talks, if necessary. He then asked whether it would be possible to set up a limited and private meeting, simply to establish an agenda for a discussion that would take place only when the bombing stopped. Mai Van Bo thought the proposal might be a way forward.[12]

While Baggs and Ashmore were meeting with Mai Van Bo in Paris, the State Department had authorized Operation Pennsylvania, in which a friend of a friend of Harvard professor Henry Kissinger was to meet with a DRV representative somewhere else in France. This effort, too, fell apart when President Johnson okayed additional bombings. Instead of diminishing the North Vietnamese, it only strengthened their resolve, which would be demonstrated in the Tet Offensive the following January.

Former Undersecretary of State George Ball admitted three years later how ridiculously complicated even the attempt at negotiations had become, because of the egos involved. "We really weren't prepared to concede anything significant, because we weren't asking for a negotiated solution," Ball said. "We were asking the other side to capitulate, in effect, to give up everything they had been striving to do for twenty-five years. And this I was convinced they were not going to do."[13]

At home, Baggs tried to share some of his experiences with his sons. He brought back artwork that he had framed for the walls of their home and passed out the colorful paper money of Laos and Cambodia. He taught the boys in the neighborhood how to say "Go to hell" in Vietnamese. He thought the rather sing-songy lilt of *cùt đi* sounded like a fast and imprecise "good day," and he suggested they say it when they got mad at one another to avoid a fight. He would laugh when he heard them curse this way around the pool or in the courtyard.[14]

If only those words could have diffused some of the frustrations he was feeling. At one of the community cocktail parties in French Village, Baggs listened as his neighbors carried on conversations about things he no longer could identify with—the music and the fun were not enough to brighten his mood. During the party, a call came that he took in the study. Afterward, Bill left Frec a note, then disappeared upstairs: "Pressure is mounting, but pressure doesn't bother me that much. However, the pap I have heard this evening is more than I wish to hear. So, I sleep. Wish I had a tape of what was said to me on the telephone. Sorry I left the party—really am—but this business I find I am involved in probably is worthwhile, even, raising the wrath of a lovely woman who happens to be your wife."[15]

That pressure came from the discovery of Johnson's hardline letter, which prompted Ashmore to pen a scathing piece for *The Center* magazine entitled "The Public Relations of Peace," which was published on September 18, 1967. In it, Ashmore charged the Johnson administration with deception and concerted efforts to undercut any negotiated peace settlement to end the war. Thus, the cover of their secret diplomacy was blown, which prompted—as Fulbright had warned them—the wrath of the State Department and every measure to discredit them by suggesting the president had only been doing a favor for Fulbright in approving their visas in the first place. Bundy placed any future failure of peace talks at their feet because, obviously, "the present disclosure will not reassure Hanoi that such private contacts will be kept secret."[16]

On September 19, 1967, the day after Ashmore's story hit, Senator Robert Kennedy sent a Western Union telegram to Baggs's office: "I think he [Johnson] dislikes you more than he dislikes me. Bob."[17]

Soon thereafter, President Johnson sent his own message. It was a framed eleven-by-seventeen-inch print of "A Roman General's Opinion of 'Military Critics,'" from the 1797 translation by George Baker of Titus Livius's *History of Rome*.

> In every circle, and, truly, at every table, there are people who lead armies into Macedonia; who know where the camp ought to be placed; what posts ought to be occupied by troops; when and through what pass that territory should be entered; where magazines should be formed; how provisions should be conveyed by land and sea; and when it is proper to engage the enemy, when to lie quiet.
>
> And they not only determine what is best to be done, but, if anything is done in any other manner than what they have pointed out, they arraign the consul, as if he were on trial before them. . . .
>
> What then is my opinion?
>
> That commanders should be counselled, chiefly, by persons of known talent; by those who have made the art of war their particular study, and whose knowledge is derived from experience; from those who are present at the scene of action, who see the country, who see the enemy; who see the advantages that occasions offer, and who, like people embarked in the same ship, are sharers of the danger.

He signed it, "To Bill Baggs—Warm regards, Lyndon Johnson."[18]

Baggs, the new editor, presides over the dedication of the *Miami Daily News* building on the Miami River in October 1957. He is flanked by general manager James Brumby (left) and James M. Cox Jr. (right). *HistoryMiami Museum/Miami News Collection*

Baggs stamped white postcards with "This is not a simple life, my friend, and there are no simple answers," and mailed them to readers who sent him hate mail. *Photo by Amy Paige Condon*

"Bobby," who changed his name to "Mahoney," joined the family in 1961.
Courtesy Craig and Mary Baggs

As editor, Baggs developed lasting friendships with world leaders, including former president Harry S. Truman. *HistoryMiami Museum/Miami News Collection*

In December 1967, Baggs received the Eleanor Roosevelt-Israel Humanities Award from Ambassador Avraham Harman. *HistoryMiami Museum/Miami News Collection*

The Jordan Marsh department store in downtown Miami hosted a book signing event in its tea room in October 1968 when *Mission to Hanoi* was published. Baggs, smoking one of his ubiquitous Erik cigars, had let his hair grow out of his typical crew cut, for which Ralph McGill teased him. *HistoryMiami Museum/Miami News Collection*

The last headshots taken of Baggs for the *Miami News*. *HistoryMiami Museum/Miami News Collection*

Baggs rarely looked directly at the camera when having his headshots taken. The *News'* humor writer called Baggs "the most gregarious loner in the world." *Courtesy of Mahoney and Valerie Baggs*

Cape Florida

Baggs began writing about the preservation of the Cape Florida Lighthouse in 1958. He finally succeeded in convincing the landowner to sell it and the surrounding five hundred acres for a state park in 1965. *HistoryMiami Museum/Miami News Collection*

In 1974, Frec Baggs and Florida Governor Reubin Askew spoke at the ceremony to rename Bill Baggs Cape Florida State Park. *HistoryMiami Museum/Miami News Collection*

Pacem in Terris

At a reception for the Pacem in Terris convocation in 1965, Baggs chats with Senator Robert F. Kennedy and biochemist/peace activist Linus Pauling. *Courtesy of Craig and Mary Baggs*

When Harry Ashmore became executive vice president of the Center for the Study of Democratic Institutions, he asked Baggs to serve on the board, which launched Baggs's efforts to seek peace in Vietnam. *William C. Baggs Papers, Courtesy of Special Collections, University of Miami Libraries, Coral Gables, Florida*

Vietnam

Baggs climbs over what is left of a housing complex destroyed by American bombers in Hanoi, March 1968. *William C. Baggs Papers, Courtesy of Special Collections, University of Miami Libraries, Coral Gables, Florida*

Residents clear the rubble left after American bombers destroyed
a housing complex in the North Vietnamese village of Nam Dinh,
January 1967. *William C. Baggs Papers, Courtesy of Special Collections,*
University of Miami Libraries, Coral Gables, Florida

Baggs often spoke with people on the street and around the margins
to get an on-the-ground account of life in North Vietnam, March 1968.
*William C. Baggs Papers, Courtesy of Special Collections, University of
Miami Libraries, Coral Gables, Florida*

A number of churches and Buddhist pagodas were destroyed by U.S. bombs, even though the official U.S. line was that American pilots were targeting only "concrete and steel" that supported the North Vietnamese war effort. *William C. Baggs Papers, Courtesy of Special Collections, University of Miami Libraries, Coral Gables, Florida*

Memorials

Baggs kept a penny bubble gum machine in his office for staff and their children. At the end of the year, he would donate the money raised by the machine to UNICEF or another child-welfare organization. *HistoryMiami Museum/Miami News Collection*

Baggs's office as he left it on December 26, 1968—the imprint of his body still on the leather chair. *HistoryMiami Museum/Miami News Collection*

Among the pallbearers who accompanied Baggs's casket: (on the left) Former Florida Governor LeRoy Collins, managing editor Howard Kleinberg, Harry Ashmore, NBC news correspondent Sander Vanocur; (on the right) Senator Edward M. Kennedy, Cox Media's James M. Cox Jr., and *Miami Herald* publisher John S. Knight. *HistoryMiami Museum/ Miami News Collection*

Seven months after Baggs's death, his close friend, Rev. Canon Theodore Gibson, dedicated an African mahogany altar marked with the symbol for peace at Christ Episcopal Church in Coconut Grove. *HistoryMiami Museum/Miami News Collection*

PART IV

From There to Here

CHAPTER 19

October 1967–April 1968

A statesman once said making peace is harder work than making war.
—Baggs on Adlai Stevenson

And then, the war came between the brethren.

To challenge the national press's prevailing acceptance of the Johnson administration's dismissal of him and Baggs as no more than amateurs jockeying for the Nobel Peace Prize, Ashmore submitted a letter to the editors of multiple newspapers throughout the country, including the *New York Times* and the *Atlanta Constitution*.[1] McGill, however, gave no ink to Ashmore's missive, nor did he run Baggs's editorial imploring readers to accept the facts surrounding their efforts in North Vietnam, if not the conclusions drawn by Ashmore.[2]

McGill defended his decision in an internal memo to president James M. Cox Jr. "Patterson returned the letter to me with his own notation, saying that he thought Harry later on would thank us if we didn't run it. He concurred that we had no obligation to run so long and argumentative a letter on a subject which the people wouldn't know about nor in which they had shown any interest. . . . He seems largely to be arguing with himself."[3]

McGill was covering his behind because Baggs had already sent a letter to Cox, indicating his great dissatisfaction.

Later that December, when McGill sent a letter seemingly to congratulate Baggs on being awarded the Eleanor Roosevelt-Israel Humanities Award, the chasm between the two men grew wider, and it seemed all of the brethren might fall into the abyss.

> However, there is one puzzling little matter—and you will forgive me if I
> bring it up. I, too, was one of the ardent supporters in the war of Israel against
> the Arab states. I was not in favor of peace at that moment, but of victory in

war by the valiant forces of the armies of Israel and the air force . . . but again, I ask if you will pardon me. I am a little puzzled by those who are for war in one part of the world and insistent on peace in another. Mr. [Harry] Golden is also puzzled by this. This is a small matter and of no great importance, but nonetheless, all of us are happy to see you in the position of an Israeli hawk.

In the postscript, McGill further chided Baggs. "I am sure that since you have for so long been an ornament of the Judaic-Christian civilization, you will, in your new position as recipient of one of Israel's major awards, not have failed to see the recent message from Vatican City in which the Pope condemns the protest movements and other interferences with those engaged in the defense of liberty and justice."[4]

Baggs responded and copied Ashmore, Golden, Popham, and Tarver, just as McGill had done.

As I understand it, you are puzzled by those who are for war in one part of the world and insistent for peace in another. Oh, Doctor, you are today, in all of western civilization, the gilded monument to the theory that man should not be a slave to consistency.

It is true that I was dismayed that the democratic loving peoples in Washington, headed by Lyndon Baines Johnson, stood mute, or hid in the closet, when the Arab hordes sought to smother the little State of Israel. I, too, was puzzled on that occasion. I couldn't understand why we would keep watering the Jeffersonian garden being tended by General Cao Ky and other assortments in Saigon, but that we are not of mind to help what is at least a promising democratic experiment on the shores of the Mediterranean Sea.

Like you, I am a soldier, not so old, but aging, and am not horrified by war when it is necessary. My only argument about the war in Vietnam is that we are fighting on the wrong side. Any old Confederate, below or above the battalion level, can sniff and know if he is fighting on the wrong side. Have you tried sniffing lately, Doctor?

I was intrigued by your postscript. I noticed where the Pope condemned the protest movements, and I hope the mayors of Detroit and Washington Federal City thanked him by prompt cable. But knowing how they grease the works in Baghdad-on-the-Potomac these days, I am afraid that this wedge entered slightly more is going to reveal the first U.S. foreign aid bill for the Pope. Such blessings abroad . . . come with high price tags these days.[5]

And thus, the Christmas Eve party in 1967 was quieter than usual, but it was a bumper crop for avocadoes that year and everyone received a flat of them from Baggs, including McGill and "non-candidate" Robert Kennedy.

Just after the new year, Aunt Grace died. Baggs had not been to Colquitt in years, but her loss only deepened his melancholy over a war he believed was destroying the soul of the nation. More than five hundred thousand U.S. troops were already deployed in Southeast Asia, and Senator Fulbright indicated to Baggs that the generals were going to request another two hundred thousand American soldiers. Despite Defense Secretary Robert McNamara's assertion that the North Vietnamese were losing ground and spirit, the North's Viet Minh fighters joined with the Viet Cong and launched the Tet Offensive on January 30, and the body count on all sides skyrocketed.

On February 3, Baggs did the only thing he knew to do. He sat down and wrote an uncharacteristically serious letter to Robert Kennedy, who had been waffling on whether or not to challenge President Johnson and Senator Eugene McCarthy of Minnesota for the Democratic Party nomination. Baggs laid out a long-term strategy for Kennedy, whom he envisioned as the future of the party and someone who could bring the country back together.

> It is my opinion, for whatever it is worth, that you have only two choices. Either you contest the President as a candidate for the nomination, or you represent more strongly your differences with him. I believe the first is the best choice, because I think you and your views lose out anyway if you don't become a candidate. It also seems to me that in losing a contest for the nomination, which the political arithmetic would indicate as the likeliest prospect, you could actually emerge as a more influential member of the Democratic Party.
>
> I say this because I believe our views of the domestic rebellion in our cities and of the questionable war in Asia are hard right, and the correctness of these views is going to become more and more visible to the American people in the next few years. If you are identified with these opinions, then surely the voters in the next few years are going to appreciate you more. And, what better way to identify yourself with these opinions than as a candidate for the nomination.[6]

Later that month, having heard nothing from Kennedy as the senator weighed his options, an impatient Baggs wrote the "Reluctant Dragon" (Kennedy) and asked, "Robert Francis, why don't you answer your mail?"[7]

A hopeful letter of a different sort arrived on leap year day from Hoàng Tùng, after many months of silence. "I think that so far your government has not been serious about negotiations to end its war of aggression in

Vietnam. President Johnson's San Antonio formula reflects a stand for continued intensification of the war through the setting forth of conditions that we cannot but reject. In practical deeds, the U.S. Government is taking every step to escalate the war. I hope that more and more Americans will take strong action to bar this dangerous path."[8]

Could it be an opening for another conversation?

On March 11, Ashmore cabled Tùng to see if he would entertain another visit. On March 19, Tùng answered yes and said that visas for Ashmore and Baggs were already available in Phnom Penh. Baggs left immediately for Washington, D.C., for a meeting with Bundy to learn "the level of the bidding" and to get an updated briefing on current policy in light of Tet. There, State Department officials gave Baggs instructions on how to discuss a potential prisoner exchange. Bundy considered that an exchange might lead to other avenues of cooperation, although he did not think Hanoi would negotiate too seriously until after November's presidential election. From Katzenbach, Baggs secured tentative agreement that he and Ashmore could testify to the executive committee of the Senate Foreign Relations Committee on their return.[9]

As Baggs left the State Department, Bundy said there would not be any bombing of Hanoi for several days. "You shouldn't have any personal considerations."

The presidential race heated up as Baggs and Ashmore were making plans to depart. Both men watched closely, for personal and diplomatic reasons. Senator McCarthy scored a close second to President Johnson in the New Hampshire primary, making the election a referendum on Johnson's leadership. Then, on March 16, Robert Kennedy announced his candidacy. Baggs's mood soared.

When the ICC flight touched down in Vientiane on March 29, Robert Hurwitch, the consul for the U.S. embassy in Laos, whom Baggs remembered from his role in negotiating the release of Miami-based Cuban exiles taken prisoner during the Bay of Pigs Invasion, informed them that three North Vietnamese sailors would be boarding the flight as part of a prisoner exchange. "The arrival of the [sailors] on the same plane might indicate to the DRV your association with the business of exchanging prisoners," Hurwitch told them.[10]

Tùng met Baggs and Ashmore at the Hanoi airport with his cohort and more bouquets of flowers. The bright and fragrant blossoms could do nothing to mask the change in Hanoi's landscape. The Long Bien Bridge had been "surgically bombed," and the Volga had to make its way across the Red River on a pontoon bridge. The number of trucks and cars had increased. Young women armed with rifles served as military police to control traffic.[11]

Within ten minutes of settling in at the Thong Nhat Hotel, an air-raid siren wailed. Baggs and Ashmore, who had hurt his leg and hip on the flight by falling into an open hatch, had to dash downstairs and across the patio to the shelter. There, they hunkered down with author and intellectual Mary McCarthy, who was on her own fact-finding mission for the *New York Review of Books*. She and Ashmore, whose daughter Anne was a student at Vassar, McCarthy's alma mater, passed the time creating a new group. "The company consisted of eight Chinese, one Pole, Charles Collingwood, three Czechs, and your Uncle William Calhoun Baggs. It's hell all over," Ashmore wrote to his daughter.[12]

Twenty minutes later they got the all clear. Another air raid came at 2:20 a.m., but this time their alert came in the form of a young boy knocking on their door and leading them with a candle downstairs to the shelter. Another air raid followed fewer than five hours later. Baggs was struck by the "delicate" barmaids and waitresses who grabbed their rifles and buttressed the antiaircraft system from rooftops and patios.

They were exhausted when they met Tùng later that morning at his newspaper offices, where all the window panes were now gone. "Westmoreland's calling card," Tùng said and smiled. "I understand Mr. McNamara gave up making war for banking."

The three men spoke easily and wondered whether, if they were not at war, they could be friends. They might even guest edit one another's papers.

When they finally got down to business, Tùng began by saying, "The Vietnamese people, north and south, should determine their own future." He did not mention anything about China or the Soviet Union. Nor was he in a hurry to set a date to reunify the country.

For the next three hours, Baggs and Ashmore shared their thoughts, couching each one in specific language. If it was something Baggs had discussed with Bundy, he would preface, "We know our government would be interested in. . . ." If the ideas were his own, he would say, "Speaking as a private citizen. . . ."

Tùng asked that they write down in detail each of their key suggestions, as a way of moving toward a proposal for a future meeting where representatives of all parties would collaborate on an agenda to end the conflict. Nothing could progress, he reaffirmed, until the U.S. bombing of North Vietnam had ceased, without conditions. He had no qualms about bombing in the south, because that was where the fighting was.

"Peace can only be made step by step," Tùng offered. He added that the North Vietnamese would not instigate any combat while their two countries talked, but that they would resume should no agreements be reached.

When it came to prisoner exchanges and the welcome of the International Red Cross, Tùng said he would take it under advisement with the Central Committee. He flatly refused to allow Baggs and Ashmore to visit with any of the prisoners.

On an entirely different matter, Kleinberg had asked Baggs to take pictures with an "idiot-proof" camera. Baggs had already broken it after only twelve pictures, so Tùng offered Baggs one of his photographers to borrow while he was in the country.

Baggs and Ashmore had no idea how long it would take for Tùng to confer with the DRV government and they took the time to wander, examine new bomb damage, and meet the people on the street. During the early morning hours of March 31, Hanoi time, Baggs, awakened by his kidneys and the relentless, heckling bombing in the suburbs, rousted Ashmore out of bed. Alone, without interpreters or escorts, the two men walked to a Buddhist temple that Baggs had seen the day before.

"The temple was deserted, except for a very old woman who scuttled away from the altar," recalled Ashmore. Baggs "took her place, knelt, and recited a version of the Episcopal liturgy, while a benign Buddha looked down across the flickering candles. Early the next morning came word that Lyndon Johnson had cleared the skies of bombers north of the nineteenth parallel."[13]

On April 1, Hanoi time, President Johnson's address to the nation came over the radio airwaves in Hanoi. He had decided to halt the bombing in the north, except for a specified area north of the Demilitarized Zone. When he said he would neither seek nor accept his party's nomination for the presidency, Mary McCarthy gathered Baggs and Ashmore into a boisterous bear hug in the lobby of the Thong Nhat Hotel.

The men made a beeline for Tùng's office and asked him to confirm in writing what he thought the president's message would mean for future talks. As for his own government, Tùng suggested that the DRV ambassador in Moscow would call the U.S. ambassador within seven days after the bombing's cessation to arrange a first meeting involving direct contact between government representatives. All questions would be open: representation of the NLF, the future of Saigon, a cease-fire, exchange of prisoners, phased withdrawal of troops, and political questions on the future of Vietnam. They cabled this information to Bundy through the Indonesian embassy and waited for a formal proposal from the DRV government. Tùng cautioned that the proposal could take some time because they had to be certain the bombing had ceased. Already, American pilots had been unleashed in an area to their north.

During the downtime, Baggs and Ashmore received permission to travel back into the countryside, again to Hà Nam province. Fourteen months after their last visit, more destruction from bombing was evident. Some villages lay wasted, while in others industrious Vietnamese were stacking bricks in craters to keep the roads passable.

On their way, an air raid forced them off the road and they ended up taking shelter in the same farmhouse in My Trung where they had stayed before. The runner would find them there after searching for more than half a day.

When they returned to the Thong Nhat Hotel, Baggs found a telegram waiting: "Greatly appreciate you or Harry Ashmore file to New York Times current appraisal negotiations situation include if possible what role you've therein, best regards to all, Harrison Salisbury."[14]

Tùng met Baggs and Ashmore and suggested they move to a private villa for the remainder of their stay so that they could talk more securely. Over the next day and half, the three men went back and forth on the details of the DRV's official response to President Johnson's speech, constantly making sure that nothing was lost in translation. In the dimming light of April 5, Hanoi time, Tùng delivered the DRV's final official response, what he called the *aide-mémoire*, with six key points that ranged from provisions for prisoner exchange to a request for clarification of President Johnson's term, "limited bombing." The aide-mémoire stipulated that the DRV ambassador was ready to meet with a representative of equal rank in the U.S. government, the place of contact could be Phnom Penh or somewhere else mutually agreed, and the United States could specify the date when the unconditional cessation of U.S. bombing would occur. Tùng repeatedly stressed that the aide-mémoire was to remain secret and delivered only to the U.S. government.

Just after they had received the news of Martin Luther King Jr.'s assassination, before they left for the airport on their way to Vientiane to deliver the document to U.S. Ambassador Sullivan, Tùng turned to Baggs and Ashmore and said, "Ho sends his good wishes. He hopes some peace would come of these efforts this week and that you can return soon to Hanoi as ordinary tourists."[15]

CHAPTER 20

May–September 1968

The ideals introduced by the president in 1961 do not languish. . . . I would serve those ideals with any man, but with no man would I serve to stall their growth.—To Robert Kennedy, August 1964

After his return from the grilling at the State Department and another roasting before Fulbright's Foreign Relations Committee, Baggs was forced to take vacation because of his kidneys and what he brushed off as a chest cold. Of course, there was no rest. As Hurricane Abby scraped up the west coast of Florida with seventy-five-mile-per-hour winds, threatening to strengthen and move across the state into Miami, he worked on his part of the *Mission to Hanoi* manuscript that would be published by Putnam in the fall. Three years ago, he had promised Frec a book, although this one probably was not what she had in mind. But reading it, she would come to know better what her husband had been up to all these years: trying to make the world safer for their sons.

He kept watch on the conditions in Vietnam, where the death toll for American and South Vietnamese soldiers steadily climbed, even as Harriman, carrying the aide-mémoire they had brought out of Vietnam, was embroiled in the early days of the Paris Peace Talks, arguing over an exact date for the bombing to end and where each party would sit around the table, shape and size still to be determined. As those discussions dragged on, Baggs followed the scuttlebutt out of Washington that both the Democrats and the Republicans were considering Miami Beach to host their conventions in August.[1]

Between two and three o'clock on the morning of June 5, the phone rang. The results of California's Democratic Primary would be in, so Baggs took the call downstairs in his study. It was someone—Frec thought later that it may have been Sander Vanocur—letting Baggs know not of Robert Kennedy's victory, but that the senator had been shot.

Frec met her husband in the hallway when he finally came upstairs.

"I have to go," he told her. Devastated, he never got back to sleep that night.

In the afternoon edition of the *News*, Don Wright's illustration of a single bullet with the words "As American as Apple Pie" ran beside Baggs's editorial asking, "What the Devil Is Wrong?"

"We are reminded once again of a lesson in history," he wrote, "that the United States, like the Roman Empire or any nation of great influence, is rarely destroyed by its enemies from abroad. It is corrupted and ruined by enemies from within—in our case the enemies of the civilized, democratic process."

A second call came later that day, confirming that Robert Kennedy had died. Baggs sat down at his typewriter and wrote the next day's editorial, a rambling one trying to discern, but not really finding, some meaning out of tragedy. He touched on gun control, the need for Secret Service coverage of presidential candidates (not the practice at that time), the need to give the youth of this country some semblance of leadership.[2] By the time the paper went to print later that morning, Baggs was on his way to New York to stand vigil at St. Patrick's Cathedral and to bid farewell to his friend.

He was there when Kennedy's plain mahogany casket arrived, and he watched as Ted Kennedy, the only surviving son among Joe and Rose's nine children, mourned in a nearby pew. He was struck by how the crowd gathered around Rose to protect her from photographers trying to capture this most private grief.[3] Then, after the service on Saturday, June 8, he boarded the train and rode it all the way to Washington, D.C., balancing his role as witness and mourner.[4] As Robert Kennedy was laid to rest in Arlington National Cemetery that afternoon, the *Miami News* reported that King's assassin, James Earl Ray, had been apprehended in London.[5]

A week after Kennedy's death, Baggs penned a personal tribute to him, a man he considered "the most misunderstood politician of rank in this country." Because Baggs had been present for meetings that he had never written about, he had had a glimpse behind the public persona crafted in much of the media, which profiled Kennedy as a "grown-up brat" who could be "cruel" and "feisty."

"He was none of these," Baggs affirmed, telling of the parties Kennedy would throw for children of Justice Department employees and of how he had been working on long overdue legislation to aid Native Americans. "In all, those who knew RFK well knew he was a gentle, sensitive and committed human being who cared about his country as much as he cared about his own family. He was a large American, and there is a hole left in our society since he left it."[6]

Baggs may well have been talking about the hole left in his own heart. The friendship between the two men had first blossomed not during the tense days of the Cuban Missile Crisis or the fight for civil rights, but in those first awful days after President Kennedy's assassination. Baggs had written to the attorney general just after they hung up the phone, when Robert Kennedy had asked Baggs to help with gathering oral histories for the future JFK Library.

> Last evening, I was thinking of a conversation I had with the President and I feel I should pass on to you a comment that he made. We were discussing, I believe, racial injustice and he, in his fine and polite style, doubted some comment of mine. I suggested to him that if he were the host of a doubt he should perhaps ask you to examine the matter. No, he said, because you were involved in . . . and he tapped off five or six enterprises which were demanding long days of you already. Your brother then paused and the only time I have ever heard him sigh was then. He looked into my eyes and said: "I wish so very much I had two Bobbies."[7]

For nearly a month, Baggs struggled with what to say to Ethel. Finally, on July 1, 1968, he tapped out a message of hope on his typewriter. "I do believe what we all kicked off some years ago, with Jack and then Bob carrying the standard, had the intelligence and integrity to change this country for the better, and you know there are enough of us left around to make sure that that standard is carried on."[8]

On the same day, he sent a letter to Ted: "Word comes from our mutual confederates that you are angry and not disposed at all to politics, and Lord knows this is understandable. But, what your brothers stood for and what friends of your brothers stood for, and tried to promote in our young and needing society, really demands that all of us promote these ideals. It would seem to me that to do otherwise would be obscene."[9]

On the eve of the 1968 Republican Convention in Miami Beach, Baggs and Frec hosted a welcome party at their Coral Gables home for visiting media. It was a thrilling evening for many reasons. For one, the guests included Sander Vanocur, Walter Cronkite, Chet Huntley, David Brinkley, John Chancellor, Eric Severeid, and Kay Graham. Second, Frec had prepared pan after pan of cornbread and gallons of Brunswick stew to give the catered event a down-home feel. The only problem was that she was afraid a mishap in storing the stew would give everyone food poisoning and cause a media blackout.[10] Third, the journalists in the old Gutenberg trade decided it was time to teach the glamorous broadcast reporters a lesson for accelerating the news cycles, changing standards, diverting advertising dollars, and, ultimately, making their business harder, so they threw a fully clothed Cronkite into the pool. Cronkite emerged looking steaming mad, but then he let out a mad howl and offered to buy everyone a gin and tonic at the open bar.[11]

The Baggs's party seemed as if it was going to provide the only excitement during the monumentally boring convention of "elephant-riders," but as Richard Nixon made his acceptance speech—as expected, despite a crowded field of nominees that included Dixiecrat Strom Thurmond, Nelson Rockefeller, Winthrop Rockefeller, George Romney, and Ronald Reagan—a riot erupted in Liberty City. It was Miami's first. The violence sparked on August 7 after a white *Miami Herald* reporter and television crew showed up to cover a Black empowerment rally where both basketball star Wilt Chamberlain and civil rights icon Ralph Abernathy were expected to speak. The ensuing violence, exacerbated by aggressive police presence, resulted in gun battles in the streets and looting of storefronts along the commercial corridors. The anger and unrest caught fire and spread into Overtown. More than two hundred people were treated at Jackson Memorial Hospital. Three people were killed by gunshot wounds, including two men who were caught in the crossfire. The city instituted an 8:00 p.m. curfew.

"The strange piece in all this business, which is the business really of finally making it [this country] a democracy, and actually emancipating 105 years later, is that it gets more difficult the more you do," Baggs wrote the day after the riots.[12]

Together, Baggs and Reverend Gibson walked the streets of Liberty City, just listening to stories of the young and the old and the frustrated. They both recognized that the strides they had made together in the earlier part of the decade had achieved access for Miami's Black citizens but had not resulted in demonstrable economic and social shifts in Dade's society. The young Black citizens had grown weary of waiting and their patience with their esteemed elders had run out. By now, Medgar, Malcolm, and Martin were all dead.

In their words, Baggs heard the echoes of King's Poor People's Campaign. "The demands are for a fair employment opportunity," he wrote a week after the riots. "The Negro wants to escape that little house squeezed in by a little house on either side. He wants something other than the sidewalk as a playground for his children. And so many times in recent years has the writer heard the Negro father and mother admit it may be too late for them, but they are bound and determined their child is going to have a good educational opportunity."[13]

No sooner had Baggs left Miami's unrest than he stepped into the chaos of violent demonstrations and police beatings in Chicago's Lincoln Park. Ashmore, still limping on a cane, met Baggs at the Democratic Convention, but the political gathering held none of the intrigue and strategy of years past. McGill and Baggs's friendship remained strained, and Baggs had not recovered from the disappointment that Robert Kennedy would never have the chance to lead the country. He had been looking forward to re-connecting with Senator Fulbright, but even the man from Arkansas decided to stay home. The convention was a circus and Baggs hated every minute of it.[14] He could barely muster enough enthusiasm for the nominee, Vice President Hubert Humphrey, a man he liked but for whom he had lost respect for toeing the Johnson line on Vietnam.[15]

When he returned home, he focused on the upcoming release of his and Ashmore's book, *Mission to Hanoi: A Chronicle of Double-Dealing in High Places*, their personal account of the efforts at private diplomacy in North Vietnam. He went back out on the speaking circuit, telling the Miami Kiwanis, "In my opinion, gentlemen, this is a war no one really wants, with the exception of China, who apparently believes it's in the national interest of China to sustain this conflict."

When he and Kleinberg went to the Miami Club for lunch, he wore a Mao pin on the lapel of his unpressed seersucker suit, just to needle the readers who called this World War II veteran a "pinko," a "Red," a "Commie sympathizer." One fellow diner got so angry with Baggs that he threw up on the editor's shoes.[16]

Kleinberg and others, though, noticed that Baggs had lost weight and his energy had waned. On September 23, when Baggs was admitted to the Miami Heart Institute, he told Ashmore that it was ostensibly "so that the physicians can find out why I have been hurting lately. The actual reason I have been hurting lately is because I have eyes and can see what is going on in this country."[17]

CHAPTER 21

October 1968–February 1969

In the process of history, there have been some remarkable men, who gave themselves in admirable efforts of individuality to make this a better world. Socrates and Mencius, Aristotle and Buddha, Confucius and Mohammed. However, the day of celebration today belongs to the Rabbi of Nazareth who spent his life trying to distribute the doctrine of telling man [*sic*] to learn to love one another.—"The Adoration of the Magi," *Miami News*, December 25, 1968

Baggs remained in the hospital into October with a stubborn infection and another bout of kidney stones, none of which stopped his neighbor, Dr. Beverly Jones, from sneaking pitchers of martinis in on visits. Among his other well-wishers was Ethel Kennedy, who sent him a bright bouquet of flowers. Despite his discomfort, Baggs's thank-you note winked with his inimitable playful banter. After thanking her for setting up an adoption of a Newfoundland puppy from the same breeder that begat the Kennedys' famous Brumis, Baggs wrote, "The flowers cheer the room, but what I can't understand is that the bouquets I got from Lyndon Johnson and Dean Rusk were twice as large."[1]

Ashmore visited Baggs in Miami to plan for the upcoming rollout of *Mission to Hanoi*, which Putnam had set to release on October 19. Baggs had every intention of accompanying Ashmore to New York and Washington, D.C., where they had scheduled back-to-back radio and television interviews, plus a lunch with Ethel Kennedy.

In a thawing of the frost that had formed on the edges of their friendship, McGill, the wannabe doctor, sent a letter that good-naturedly ribbed his protégé. "These learned medical men observe that if a person begins to pour Bloody Mary mixtures down his throat, beginning at breakfast time and continuing into the evening, the combination of acids . . . sets up an irritation in the parathyroid and thyroid glands. Dr. Ashmore and I have consulted about this, and we both agree that it is time you emulated him and me, along with some of your other friends, and begin to show a certain maturity which enables a man to look after himself physically. Please do not let this happen again."[2]

A month later, however, Baggs scuttled plans to meet Ashmore for their book's publicity tour. Instead, he followed doctor's orders and stayed close to home because of a persistent case of pneumonia. A friend who saw him at a lunch and book signing at the Miami Rotary Club took note of Baggs's increasingly gaunt appearance.

"You have run your physical condition to the brink," his friend chastised. "I dislike organizing memorial foundations, particularly for people the community needs so badly."[3]

Even son Craig was worried. When he asked his dad to take a break, all Baggs could offer was, "What do you want me to do, just quit?"

"I'm not sure he knew how to relax," reflects Craig. "People pulled him from all directions."

The pressure on Baggs was as relentless as his drive. He continued to rattle cages with his mighty pen on issues from poverty and hopelessness to the increasing death toll in Vietnam. He kept contact with Ambassador-at-Large Harriman on the progress, albeit slow, of the Paris Peace Talks.

On October 31, just ahead of the presidential election, President Johnson announced a cessation to the bombing in North Vietnam. The following day, the *Miami News* carried several articles about Johnson's surprise announcement, including a damning piece by Fred Hoffman, the Associated Press's military reporter, on the human, financial, and emotional costs of the failed Operation Rolling Thunder. Above the fold, Baggs's article, "Bombing Halt Is Just Part of LBJ-Hanoi Negotiation," cited unnamed American diplomats and sources inside Hanoi that tied the announcement to the first requirement of the aide-mémoire for beginning earnest discussions for de-escalation and peace. What others were claiming as a cheap election-year stunt by Johnson, Baggs was connecting to the long line of public and private diplomatic efforts. Still, the State Department flatly denied Baggs's article, stating that the president's announcement had nothing to do with any private diplomacy and no deal had been reached.[4] What Johnson and his team knew that Baggs did not was that Nixon had been working with GOP fundraiser Anna Chennault, who had convinced South Vietnamese President Nguyen Van Thieu to sabotage the peace talks in the hopes that it would hurt Democratic candidate Vice President Hubert Humphrey and give Nixon an edge in the election.[5]

Nixon won the White House four days later by a razor-thin 0.7 percent margin over Humphrey. Baggs's close friend and former governor LeRoy Collins got trounced in his bid for the U.S. Senate seat from Florida, but the revised Florida Constitution they both had fought so hard for was approved.

Baggs summoned the goodwill to purchase a reprint of King's *The Measure of a Man* for Humphrey and inscribed it with encouraging words.

Dear Hubert,

With your commitment over the years, I think you will find this "little book" most pertinent to what the Republic should be.

Fondly,

Wm Baggs

He set the book in his study with every intention of sending it.[6]

Good news arrived in early December. First, Rory Kennedy, the eleventh child of Robert and Ethel Kennedy, was born. Baggs asked Ashmore to deliver a red rose to Ethel on his behalf while Ashmore was in Washington. Then, Reverend Gibson was named canon of the South Florida Diocese of the Episcopalian Church. Baggs's buttons nearly burst for his dear friend, and he worked with the *News* staff to publish a series on Gibson's long history of civic and spiritual contributions to Miami. Gibson, who never forgot how Baggs rescued his faith at the moment when he considered leaving the church, asked the bishop for special dispensation to allow Baggs to deliver the sermon at the service rather than a member of the clergy. In the invitation to the tea he and Frec were hosting at their home following the ceremony, Baggs wrote, "In short, in my opinion [Father Gibson] has been one of the most valuable persons in our community."

Baggs then spent three days with Ashmore in D.C. While there he met with his congressmen on Capitol Hill to lobby for funding to build a downtown campus for Dade County Junior College. Ever the mischief, he pinned a Mao button to the wreath on Nicholas Katzenbach's door as he departed a meeting about progress in the ongoing peace talks.[7] He made it home in time for the annual Baggs Christmas Eve party. In the midst of the festivities and Santa's arrival, Craig noticed his father was experiencing shortness of breath, but Baggs just smiled from across the room and trained his attention on his guests and the stars in the sky. That night, in a live broadcast, the Apollo 8 crew orbited the moon, giving humans their first glimpses of its far side and "dirty sand" surface as well as a new perspective on the Earth.

Baggs's personal physician, among the well-wishers, told him to come to the hospital for a checkup. The editor looked even more frail than he had before Thanksgiving.[8]

Baggs never stopped fighting, though. The day after Christmas, his column bitterly calculated that twelve thousand more U.S. troops had died in Vietnam since April, when he and Ashmore had returned from Hanoi with an outline for peace. He left work early that day with a fever.

On December 27, as the paper was covered in news about the returning astronauts, Baggs pushed for an equally bold initiative, a complete redesign of downtown Miami from the ghetto to the bay. "So, say the large city, such as Miami, can actually rebuild its downtown, creating a kind of urban tranquility in the tastes and designs of the buildings, establishing areas for play for children, not skimping on trees and grass, making boulevards. This could become the example."[9]

On Sunday, he was in the study talking with younger son Mahoney when he fainted. As he came to, he pleaded with his son, "Please, don't tell your mother."[10]

A scared and defiant Mahoney ran for Frec, who called for an ambulance. For the next several days, the doctors at the Miami Heart Institute attempted an all-out assault on the tryptic of pneumonia, influenza, and kidney infection attacking every major organ, including Baggs's brain. He had an adverse reaction to the massive doses of steroids, while antibiotics produced only modest success. Even though the *News* reported in Tuesday's paper that his condition had "improved," the doctors warned Frec that it would be days before they were out of the danger zone.

Meanwhile, the Newfoundland pup arrived the day after Baggs was admitted. Ethel Kennedy had taken care of the $300 adoption fee as well as the dog's delivery. The boys called the black-and-white male Tarver, keeping alive the tradition of naming their pets for honored friends. Frec's mother, who had come for the holidays, stayed with the boys while Frec spent her days at Bill's side. Frec kept the faith, never truly considering that her still-young husband, who had always bounced back from adversity, would not survive.

On Tuesday, January 7, 1969—the same day the new Florida State Constitution went into effect and President Johnson bid farewell to the nation—Baggs was still breathing. He showed continued improvement throughout the day, enough so that Frec felt she could take a coffee break late that afternoon. When she returned to his room, the doctors were in tears as Baggs's monitors beeped in distress. Frec rushed to his side, and, as she wrote in her memoir, "I took his hand, still unaware that he was not going to make it, leaned over to kiss him, and said, 'Bill, won't you get well and come home? We need you.'"

Baggs, only forty-five years old, whispered that he was sorry, then took his last, labored breath.[11]

By the time a shocked and shaken Frec made the half-hour drive from Miami Beach to Coral Gables, her home was filled with *Miami News* staff, neighbors, and other members of the large network of friends who had come to think of Baggs as their own. Word of his death had already been delivered on the evening's local newscast.

Editorial writer Jack Kassewitz found Rev. Canon Gibson weeping in the corner of Baggs's study. "I guess you don't know that as recent as eight years ago, Bill Baggs saved my life," he told the newsman, then finally revealed the secret pact the two had made back in Baggs's office when they first met nearly ten years prior.

Craig and Mahoney, who were allowed to visit their father only once in the hospital, were inconsolable. Mahoney believed then as he does now that the war took his father's life. "His name is not on that wall," he says, "but Vietnam killed him just the same."

In Atlanta, McGill received a phone call telling him that Baggs had died at 6:05 p.m.

"That was how hope ended," he wrote for the next day's column. In print, McGill recalled a conversation he and Baggs had had about the poet Keats, who died so young at age twenty-six and on whose gravestone was inscribed, "Here lies one whose name was writ in water."

"We wondered about the why of that. . . . I found myself thinking of our talk after the call came that Bill Baggs was dead. His name was etched deeply in the hearts of all who knew him and in the records of journalism that he had served so well and with so much honor."

Back in Miami, Kleinberg and his news staff set about planning the next day's newspaper.

"Frec would call me and say, 'Howie, I hope he doesn't die on *Herald* time.' She didn't want [them] to have the first story of Bill's death," Kleinberg says. But the *Herald* got it, and for the first time as managing editor, Kleinberg did not care that he got scooped. He welcomed the extra time to plan a proper tribute to his boss while helping his writers grieve.

"It was crushing to the staff," Kleinberg says, wincing at the memory. "It was crushing to the city. He [was] a cultural liberal, but he also meant something to the guy who liked the wild turkey in the Everglades. He wrote seriously . . . but he was clever."

Kleinberg assigned a staff photographer to capture Baggs's office just as he had left it the week before. A piece of legal-sized yellow wire-service paper still rolled into the typewriter showed that he had been about to pen one of his CIA cable parodies. His chair remained debossed with the curve of his body, as if his restless spirit had settled, book in hand, foot perched on the edge of the desk. An Adlai Stevenson poster and pictures of Jack and Bobby hung with no sense of decor, only a thought to where they could be seen in order to inspire. A marmalade jar brimming with pencils. The penny bubblegum machine.

Reporter Milt Sosin took on the unenviable task of calling friends in Florida, Georgia, Washington, D.C., New York, and throughout the world to deliver the sad news and gather statements. Once these people, who came from all walks of religious, academic, journalistic, and governmental life, overcame the shock of his passing, they talked about his friendship and the void left in his wake.

Walter Cronkite summed up the general feelings of all. "It's a tragedy for his family and friends, but it's a greater tragedy at a time when the world can ill afford to lose journalists with old-fashioned zeal for the truth. The zeal for the truth motivated Bill's whole life."[12]

Sports columnist Morris McLemore lamented how the pleas for Baggs to slow down and take care of himself went unheeded. The usually jocular John Keasler wrote the most personal of benedictions.

And all we know for sure, or begin to grasp in this bad time, is that it's not just every lifetime you get to meet and learn from a gentle maverick who somehow led the herd. . . . Empty is a word with more dimension now to those who knew Bill Baggs, newspaperman, always the stylist, the most gregarious loner in the world; Georgia boy who became an intimate of the great and the lowly, throwback editor of eerie agelessness, who had unbelievable hordes of friends and who drove his enemies further frantic because they sensed he rather loved them.[13]

On the day of the funeral, January 10, 1969, the entire staff of the *Miami News* gathered in the lobby where they were joined by a contingent from the *Herald*, including publisher John S. Knight and general manager Alvah Chapman. They walked en masse in the rain the one block to the soaring Trinity Cathedral for the fallen editor's service. Kleinberg and James Cox Jr. led the way.[14] Alumni of the *News*, like James Bellows, joined in the procession.

When they arrived, the church's pews were filled with hundreds of mourners from all across the city, from the janitor at the *News*' old Freedom Tower office to the head of Wometco Enterprises. Tarver, Ashmore, and Vanocur came to lay their brother to rest. Before the funeral began, Vanocur passed among them a note in imitation Baggs penmanship that read, "Sorry I won't make it today, so don't save me a seat."

"More than a few people inappropriately burst out laughing," says Don Stinson. "Bill would have loved the humor."[15]

Former governor LeRoy Collins and Senator Edward M. Kennedy appeared and requested to walk beside the brethren as pallbearers. McGill was there, too, but blended deep into the background, mourning in private.

Later, Kleinberg admitted that he was surprised to learn how far and how high Baggs's friendships ran. "Baggs told stories I didn't know whether to believe or not. I didn't believe his Kennedy connection until he died, and there's Teddy."[16]

Kleinberg had to look no further than the black Smythson Featherweight diary that Baggs always carried in the breast pocket of his seersucker suit—the final one from 1968, embossed with his name and the year in gold. In neat print made with his steadfast fountain pen, Baggs's list of names and numbers ran from Aunt Grace to the Oval Office. In between were the office and home numbers for Kay Graham, Ben Bradlee, and the late Robert Kennedy, columnist Art Buchwald, high-ranking members at the State Department, his nephews, admirals and governors, North Vietnamese envoy Mai Van Bo, and every member of his news and editorial staff. Tucked within the pages were his driver's license and AAA card, vibrant paper currency from Laos, and a reminder to order the next year's diary.

As one last laugh, there was the note passed between him and author Philip Wylie when they found themselves on the same flight. In Wylie's tight script it reads, "Please pass P. Wylie through the lines. A. Lincoln." Baggs's sardonic response, "Oh yeah? J. W. Boothe [sic]."[17]

Over the next several days and weeks, letters, cards, and telegrams expressing surprise and solace poured into the office from all over the country and world, even from President Nixon. Florida senator Claude Pepper read Keasler's poetic tribute to Baggs into the Federal Register. The City of Miami, Dade County, and the State of Florida passed resolutions in Baggs's honor.

That rainy Friday after the service, Frec took her husband back to Georgia for burial. Baggs was laid to eternal rest in the Carr family plot located at the top of a grassy terrace overlooking a valley by the Oconee River, across from "Big Craig" and near the stillborn child Baggs never had the opportunity to hold.

Two days later, Craig returned to Proctor Academy on a brutally cold evening. He walked from the bus stop to his dorm in the snow. "I felt like my guts had been kicked out of me and I was really alone in the world."

A warm wind arrived a couple of weeks later in the form of a letter from his godfather. McGill had just returned from Nixon's inauguration.

"I was very proud of you when I was down in Miami," he wrote in encouragement. "A very harsh destiny has made it necessary for you to play the role of a man at a very early age, but you certainly played it, and I know you will keep on doing it."

McGill finally shared with Craig what he and only a few of the brethren had known: that Baggs had been in failing health for at least two years. "Remember him not as the man troubled by sickness, but as a real fine, great fellow who made many, many valuable contributions to journalism and to his region."

Before signing off, McGill seemed to sense his own dwindling hours. "I am getting to be an old-timer, Craig, and along the way I lost two children, one three days old and one five. There have been other losses, but these I remember the most. I can tell you that the passing of time will help a lot. You will never forget, and you would not want to forget, but time will dull some of the feeling of loss and resentment at the great inexplicable mystery of life and death."

On February 3, McGill called Ashmore to talk. Baggs's death had been troubling his mind. Ashmore followed up with a letter the next morning. In it, he encouraged McGill not to put too much stock in Baggs's fevered ramblings at the end or their unresolved tensions over Vietnam.

"Anyway, I think we have to close that last painful chapter," he comforted. "Bill, of course, had his share of all the confederate weaknesses—including a broad sentimental and romantic streak—but this is what made him the lovely man that he was. Our favorite joke had to do with our natural-born capacity to wind up with the losers. When I see who's winning these days, I would not have had it different."[18]

Ashmore never sent the letter. Later that morning, he received the news that McGill was gone.

His heart had given out at the dinner table, two days shy of his seventy-first birthday. McGill, the father figure chosen by Baggs, was buried in Westview Cemetery, across the rolling hills from where C. C., the father Baggs never knew, was laid to rest.

CHAPTER 22

August 1969–

When Bill Baggs took up a cause you knew it, and it did not matter whether it was your cause or even precisely the right cause. What mattered was that it was the better for his having taken it up. Restless, driven, he knew just about everybody in his profession, and an awful lot of people all over the world for it was his intention to see it all, and he pretty nearly did.—William C. Baggs Obituary, *Washington Post*, January 10, 1969

Seven months after Baggs's death, the Rev. Canon Theodore Gibson welcomed a standing-room-only crowd into the sanctuary of his historic Coconut Grove church. The occasion was the dedication of an altar built from a single piece of African mahogany, the same type of wood used to make Robert Kennedy's casket. The front of the altar was adorned with the "px" symbol used by early Christians to signify "pax" or "peace," and a small plaque that read, "This family altar is dedicated to the glory of God in loving memory of William Calhoun Baggs."

Rabbi Joseph R. Narot of Temple Israel read from Ecclesiasticus 44: "There were those who ruled in their kingdoms, and made a name for themselves by their valor; those who gave counsel because they were intelligent; those who spoke in prophetic oracles; those who led the people by their counsels and by their knowledge of the people's lore; they were wise in their words of instruction."[1]

Ashmore followed the rabbi with a eulogy he could only give after the gift of time and distance.

"Cleaning out a man's desk, he told me, is an office that ought to be carried out posthumously by an understanding friend," recalled Ashmore. "In a way this is the office many of us here have been performing in the months since we lost Bill."

He recalled Baggs's quiet generosity and how it reshaped the community, how his lack of awe allowed for comfort in the presence of kings as well as cabbies, how his relentless humor was matched only by his earnestness for a good cause.

"I doubt the case for ending the war in Vietnam was ever made more eloquently than he made it in our long private audience with Ho Chi Minh, and, in turn, in the inner reaches of the State Department."

Then, he came full circle back to the friendship between Baggs and Gibson as the greatest evidence of the man.

> I think in many ways the proudest day of his life came when Theodore Gibson was ordained a canon of that one-time white citadel, the Episcopal Diocese of South Florida. And certainly, the most moving moment of mine came when I stood outside the cathedral while thousands of Bill's mourners filed away and heard Canon Gibson say: "I owe Bill Baggs my life—more than that, much more, for he saved my faith. . . . I began to hate, to lump white people together and hate them all, and it ate away at me like acid until I thought I had no right to wear the cloth. I was at the point of leaving the church when I met Bill Baggs. It wasn't so much what he did, but the way he was, that showed me that there is still love and grace in the world, and that a man who is not blind or afraid can find it if he looks. He restored my faith, and as long as I live Bill Baggs lives in me."[2]

In May 1969, the State of Florida finalized the purchase of the full nine hundred acres for Cape Florida State Park.

Five years later, Governor Reubin Askew and his cabinet voted unanimously to rename the park in honor of Baggs. In introducing legislation in the Florida House of Representatives to do the same, Miami Beach state representative Paul Steinberg said, "We wish to honor a man who was a conservationist before it became fashionable and used the power of the pen for this good purpose." The bill passed without dissent.[3]

And so, on March 12, 1974, between seventy and eighty of Baggs's compatriots gathered at the entrance of the newly christened Bill Baggs Cape Florida State Park for the unveiling of a new sign and a plaque bearing his words. Governor Askew, who credited Baggs with encouraging him to run for office in the first place, spoke of the park's wildness being a fitting tribute to the legendary journalist. Frec followed, recalling how her husband had loved the song "The Impossible Dream" from Broadway's *Man of La Mancha*, and, addressing Bill, called the park "your impossible dream come true."

The Rev. Canon Gibson was there, too. He offered a blessing and represented the City of Miami as a city commissioner.[4]

Eighteen years later, in late August 1992, Hurricane Andrew's Category 5 (165 mph) winds nearly destroyed the historic lighthouse and denuded the hammocks and dunes of the park. Now fully restored and flourishing, its more than one million annual visitors stretch out on the beach's velvet sands and catch a shimmering vision of the remaining Stiltsville houses on its southernmost horizon. There, beachcombers find waters as gin-clear as the dry martinis Baggs used to drink—two olives in, with extra olive juice on the side. There is no question why he worked so hard to save this place. For the peace found here, at the very least, is everlasting.

EPILOGUE   *Miami, December 1988*

I almost feel like there's been a death in my family.—Eloise Harris, Letter to the Editor, *Miami News*, October 15, 1988

In the wake of Baggs's death, a distressed reader asked, "Who is going to speak for us . . . for the people?"[1]

The editorial staff of the *News* answered that they would, and they did for almost twenty years. From redesigns and staff changes through Watergate and the cocaine cowboys, the *News* upheld Baggs's principles. But a quarter-century after Cox Media made the deal with the *Herald*, Miami became the one-paper town that Knight and Baggs had fought so hard to prevent. The *Miami News* published its final afternoon edition on December 31, 1988.

Avid reader F. M. Roth offered a solution that seems frightening today. "You mean there's something around Donald Trump is not buying? I thought he bought everything for sale."[2]

Kleinberg, who served as the paper's final editor, joked that if every person who wrote in lamenting the paper's demise had actually subscribed, they wouldn't have needed to stop the presses for good. In all his years with the paper, Kleinberg never wavered in maintaining an editorial voice independent from that of the *Herald*, and his newsroom was just as feisty and committed to telling a good story as ever. His last column challenged the *Herald* to keep reporting as if it still had able competition.

For 92 years, the *Miami News* has tried, with imperfect efforts and results, to lead public opinion along the sinuous, uphill and endless path toward social justice, equality, and opportunity based on individual achievement.

The *News* has retained its integrity by adhering to its beliefs that the use of stereotypes undermines attempts to promote equal opportunity, that a community and a nation are only as strong as their weakest members, that natural resources must be protected rather than exploited, that public corruption breeds public and private cynicism, that unpopular defenses of constitutional rights protect the rights of all, that improved public education is essential to overwhelm the ignorance which subjugates the poor, that the people of the world share common desires and goals which must, if the world is to survive, transcend the often self-serving political differences that separate governments.

Although this is its final edition, the *Miami News* will always remain on the high moral plateau where it has stood upright for so long, and so often alone, to be discovered again and again by historians, archivists and average citizens interested in learning how Miamians lived and what some of them stood for from May 15, 1896, until the last day of 1988. . . . Who can look at the prevailing conditions and not see a country and a world in transition? Who can look at the transition and not see opportunity? In more favorable circumstances, this *Miami News* would continue to prod Americans to spread the benefits their society must offer everyone. Now the *News* leaves to others the burden, the challenge and the earnest desire to carry ever higher the banner of concern for all people, and to do so with unrelenting passion, conviction and logic.[3]

ACKNOWLEDGMENTS

No book of this scope rests in a single author's hands, and there are many people to thank.

First and foremost, the Baggs family. Frec invited me in and allowed me to listen as she reminisced about the great love of her life. Mahoney and Valerie gave me an envelope that held the missing pieces of Bill's childhood. Craig and Mary opened their home and their hearts and allowed me to unearth long-buried memories and family lore—sometimes confronting emotions they had not tended in years. We shared tears and deep belly laughs along with wistful wonderings of what might have been. They are family now.

My former boss and mentor, Howard Gregg, taught me how to dig deep for the stories of place. State park ranger Art Levy shared the initial Baggs research that captured my imagination.

That foundation led me to the University of Miami's Special Collections department, where Nicola Sabine Hellman-McFarland patiently aided me year after year as I worked through the boxes of Bill's professional life. Sasha Coles, Ph.D., served as my eyes at the University of California, Santa Barbara, where Harry Ashmore's papers and those of the Center for the Study of Democratic Institutions are preserved. Graduate writing intern Kelsey Sanchez spent two quarters enthusiastically helping to build a profile of Bill's career as a reporter—an invaluable and sometimes tedious task. Britt Scott formatted photographs for publication. Betty Darby caught my mistakes.

Howard Kleinberg showed me the famous rubber stamp—a memento, a talisman—which he has held onto all these years. His stories, as did those of Mel Frishman, brought the *Miami News* newsroom back to life. Rev. Terrence Taylor introduced me to Thelma Gibson, Rev. Canon Theodore Gibson's widow, who recalled her husband's friendship with Bill. The ever-generous Jerry Whiting, historian for the 485th Bomb Group, talked me through the missions flown by the Fifteenth Air Force out of Venosa, Italy. He served as verifier and networker, leading me to Michael Kempffer, whose father flew during the same time and with the same bomb group as Bill.

Journalist and crusader Hank Klibanoff gave me the great gift of his wisdom and enthusiastic counsel. His book, *The Race Beat*, written with Gene Roberts, should be required reading for all American history and journalism classes.

Patrick Allen gave the best piece of advice, "You can't know everything," which freed me from the tyranny of the rabbit hole of too much research. He and the team at UGA Press have my eternal gratitude for their patience and support.

I am indebted to the organizers behind TEDxSavannah, who provided me a platform to bring the idea of this book to a broader audience.

Many thanks to Melany Martin Ash and Carol Garvin, who were up for research and writing adventures. The members of the True Lit Writing Group—Katherine Oxnard Ellis, Judy Fogarty, Tina Kelly, and Nancy Remler—kept me sane with wisdom, thorough reads, good eats, and steadfast encouragement. Nancy Fullbright and Heidi Fedak asked tough questions and lifted me with encouraging quotes from RuPaul. My mother-in-law, Rosalyn Condon, fed and sheltered me on the many trips back to Miami. Annabelle Carr, Cheryl Day, Maggie Harney, Brianne Halverson, James Lough, Jonathan Rabb, Beth Concepcion, and Lee Griffith—thank you all for your friendship, guidance, and support. Gratitude to Terry Toole, Harold Moore, and Lorraine Shaw for your insights on Colquitt.

To my mother, Barbara Lee Polly—oh, how I wish you could hold a copy of this book in your hands. You understood my need to write it.

And to my love, my dearest, my Brian, who did not hesitate when I asked back in 2008 if it would be okay to completely upend our lives and veer off the well-worn path for the grassier one. The past few years have been fraught with big moves, financial insecurity, writer's angst, fast-food takeout, and lots of distraction from my living in my head. Yet somehow, some way, we've never been happier or felt more alive.

The narrative thread of Bill's life is woven in and among all of our stories now. Let us, then, make a pact, you and me, that we will not leave this place until we have helped it live up to our highest ideals.

NOTES

PROLOGUE. Hanoi, April 1968

1. Baggs, "Notes on Missions to North Vietnam," written 1967–68, transcribed April 1968, unpublished, 23–25.

2. Ashmore and Baggs, *Mission to Hanoi*, 157–58.

3. Howard Kleinberg, "Other Great Lives Tied to King's Memory," *Miami News*, January 17, 1987.

4. Kleinberg interview, November 28, 2016.

5. Ashmore and Baggs, *Mission to Hanoi*, 159–64.

CHAPTER 1. 1923–1936

1. Birth certificate for William Calhoun Baggs, September 30, 1923, File No. 17111, Georgia State Board of Health, Bureau of Vital Statistics. A copy of Baggs's certified birth certificate was among military records provided to the author by the National Personnel Records Center, National Archives, St. Louis, Missouri. The date of Baggs's birth has caused some confusion, but the birth certificate confirms that he was born in 1923. He filled out paperwork throughout his life that noted September 30, 1922, as his birth date, and that is the date etched on his headstone at Oconee Hills Cemetery in Athens, Georgia. A clerical error on military paperwork, when he was required to register for the reserves in 1951, listed his birth year as 1920. Baggs, who maintained a boyish appearance throughout his life, often told people he was older than he actually was.

Death certificate for Crawford C. Baggs Sr., October 18, 1923, File No. 28588, Georgia State Board of Health, Bureau of Vital Statistics, obtained by author through the Georgia Archives, Atlanta, Georgia. The death certificate lists "intestinal obstruction" as the cause of death. In one of his war letters from 1944, however, Baggs mentions that his father "was a drinking man" and died of "poisoned whiskey," something the powers that be may have wanted to keep quiet during the early days of Prohibition, when obtaining the support of the evangelical temperance movement was critical to getting elected to office.

2. "Crawford Baggs Dies at Wesley Memorial," *Atlanta Constitution*, October 19, 1923.

3. 1930 United States Census (Population Schedule), Atlanta, Fulton County, Georgia, Sheet No. 20A, family 211, lines 30–34, April 9, 1930.

4. Death certificate for Katherine Bush Baggs, January 11, 1936, File No. 1118, Georgia State Board of Health, Bureau of Vital Statistics, in author's possession.

5. Letter from Judge Alex W. Stephens, Court of Appeals of the State of Georgia, to Calhoun Baggs, January 11, 1938, private collection.

6. William Beers, "My Song of the South," and Robert Beers, chapter 3 of draft biography of William C. Baggs, unpublished manuscripts, private collection.

7. Raymond L. Chambers, "Miller County," *New Georgia Encyclopedia*, December 10, 2005, https://www.georgiaencyclopedia.org/articles/counties-cities-neighborhoods/miller-county.

8. "Swamp Gravy: Georgia's Official Folk-Life Play," https://swampgravy.com.

9. Email to author from Terry Toole (publisher, *Miller County Liberal*), July 2, 2018.

10. William Beers, "My Song of the South," and Robert Beers, draft biography of William C. Baggs.

11. Robert Beers, draft biography of William C. Baggs.

12. Letter from Laverne Kimbrell Shaw to author, July 9, 2018.

13. Harold Moore phone interview, July 27, 2018.

14. "Calhoun Baggs is Honor Student and Class Speaker," *Miller County Liberal*, May 16, 1941.

15. In his book *David and Goliath: Underdogs, Misfits, and the Art of Battling Giants* (New York: Little, Brown, 2013), author Malcolm Gladwell explores the phenomenon of "eminent orphans," high-achieving children who lost their parents early in life.

CHAPTER 2. 1936–1939

1. Robert Beers, chap. 3 of draft biography of William C. Baggs, 4, unpublished manuscript, private collection.

2. Dan Mahoney, The Publisher's Corner, *Miami Daily News*, December 30, 1950.

3. Baggs, "Opening Minds," View of the News, *Miami News*, March 10, 1961.

4. Robert Beers, draft biography of William C. Baggs, 5.

5. Telegram from Baggs to Robert Maynard Hutchins (founder, Center for the Study of Democratic Institutions), November 30, 1967, MSS 18, box 61, folder 5, Center for the Study of Democratic Institutions Collection, Davidson Library, University of California, Santa Barbara.

6. Robert Beers, chap. 3 of draft biography of William C. Baggs, 5.

7. William Beers, "My Song of the South," unpublished manuscript, private collection.

8. Robert Beers, draft biography of William C. Baggs.

9. According to the Equal Justice Initiative in Montgomery, Alabama, and its catalog of more than 3,800 racial-terror lynchings in America between the years 1880 and 1940, the state of Georgia was second only to Mississippi in the number of murders. The most active part of the state was the rural southwest. The EJI's supplemental report to its landmark study *Lynching in America: Confronting the Legacy of Racial Terror* recorded nearly thirty-five murders in Miller County and neighboring Early County. As EJI's senior attorney, Jennifer Taylor, acknowledged in an email to the author on July 19, 2018, "the list will never be exhaustive. The very nature of lynching and racial terrorism in this country meant that many victims' fates were unknown or undocumented, obscured through lies, cover-ups, corruption and indifference. Memories were silenced through fear and intimidation."

10. E. E. Cox, "Congressman Cox Resents Passage of the Unjust Bill," *Miller County Liberal*, January 31, 1940.

11. Louis P. Masur, "Why It Took a Century to Pass an Anti-lynching Law," *Washington Post*, December 28, 2018.

12. Robert Beers, chap. 3 of draft biography of William C. Baggs, 6–7.

CHAPTER 3. 1939–1943

1. Charles Crawford Baggs Jr. phone interview, August 31, 2018. His father, Baggs's older brother, was a member of the Civilian Pilot Training Program and became a noncommissioned officer on loan to Canada. As a partner in the British Commonwealth Air Training Plan, Canada then sent Charles to Poland to train Polish Air Forces. After the invasion of Poland, Charles and the Polish flyers fell back to England and fought the Germans in the air.

2. "Miss Baggs, Mr. Beers Take Vows Wednesday," *Miller County Liberal*, June 7, 1939.

3. Alan Taylor, "The 1939 New York World's Fair," *Atlantic*, November 1, 2013.

4. Calhoun [Bill] Baggs, "A Challenge," valedictorian speech, private collection.

5. "Announcement," *Miller County Liberal*, May 23, 1941.

6. Greg Robinson and Maxime Minne, "The Unknown History of Japanese Internment in Panama," discovernikkei.org.

7. A recording of the Pearl Harbor announcement can be heard at "Pearl Harbor Attack Emergency Radio Broadcast Announcement," VeteransToday, n.d., YouTube video, 2:21, https://www.youtube.com/watch?v=s_f9A3fwn6w.

8. The United States did not have an air force at the start of the war, nor did it have much in the way of war-ready planes. The Mighty Eighth was the first air

force established by the U.S. and it flew B-17s out of England. Civilian pilots became noncommissioned officers and went into training.

9. Mercedes K. Morris, "The *Star & Herald*—An Epitaph," *Canal Record*, December 1988, 81.

10. Letter from Frec Baggs to Bill Baggs, November 20, 1945, private collection.

CHAPTER 4. 1943–1944

1. Frec Baggs interviews, June–July 2007. At the encouragement of her mother, Anne Nichols Wood held onto Baggs's letters for years, even after she married. According to his widow Frec Baggs, Anne was startled to see the sign for Bill Baggs Cape Florida State Park during a visit to Miami for a Realtors convention, and she wondered if the park was named for the same man she had known so many years before. During a luncheon, a fellow Realtor introduced Wood and Frec, who was also working as a real estate agent at the time. They became fast friends and Wood gave Frec the letters to add to her collection.

2. Army Air Forces Pre-Flight School Final Grade Sheet, Ellington Field, Texas, Class 43-19 B, June 21, 1943, National Personnel Records, National Archives and Records Administration.

3. St. John, *Bombardiers of WWII: A History*, 11–12.

4. Dorr, B-24 *Liberator Units*, 11.

5. Malcolm Gladwell, "The Strange Tale of the Norden Bombsight," filmed July 15, 2011, in Edinburgh, Scotland, TED video, 14:54, https://www.ted.com/talks /malcolm_gladwell_the_strange_tale_of_the_norden_bombsight.

6. Ibid.

7. William C. Baggs, ed., *Bombs Away*, 44-1 (Midland, Tex.: Army Air Forces Bombardier School, 1944); available at http://aafcollection.info/items/list .php?item=000842.

8. Letters, short stories, and other ephemera, private collection.

9. Frec Baggs, *I Thought He Hung the Moon*, 26–27.

10. Dorr, *B-24 Liberator Units*, 11.

CHAPTER 5. 1944

1. National Personnel Records and email to author from Jerry Whiting (historian for 485th Bomb Group), October 31, 2018.

2. Whiting, *Don't Let the Blue Star Turn Gold*, 14–15.

3. The account here is based on an oral history by ball-turret gunner Harold "Red" Kempffer, "Life at Venosa Airfield during World War II," http://www.storiedelsud .altervista.org/Venosa PSP/PSP RED ENGLL.htm. Kempffer's service in the 485th HBG/830th squadron in Italy overlapped with Baggs's, and is supplemented by Whiting's *Don't Let the Blue Star Turn Gold*, 8, 87–98, and Michael Kempffer interview, November 12, 2018.

4. Whiting, *Don't Let the Blue Star Turn Gold*, 87–98; Kempffer, "Life at Venosa Airfield."

5. Dorr, *B-24 Liberator Units*, 8–16.

6. Using Baggs's service scrapbook, letters, and the 485th Bomb Group's *Missions by the Numbers*, Jerry Whiting and the author were able to verify which missions Baggs flew.

7. Dorr, *B-24 Liberator Units*, 37.

8. Schneider, *Missions by the Numbers*, 38.

9. *Miller County Liberal*, date unknown, most likely published when Baggs was on leave in October 1944.

10. Schneider, *Missions by the Numbers*, 37–53, and Whiting email to author, October 31, 2018.

11. Ralph McGill's column, *Atlanta Constitution*, January 8, 1969, as well as obituaries and family members in interviews mention that Baggs was forced to bail out twice. A search through official escape statements, however, did not reveal the exact conditions, dates, and experiences surrounding his bailouts. According to Whiting, if crews bailed out over the island of Vis, "a safe-haven for allied airmen in the Adriatic, there would have been no Escape Statement. Vis was occupied by Partisans." Whiting also suggested that long gaps in letters home could signal periods when airmen were making their way back to base after having bailed. There are no letters from Baggs during June and August of 1944.

12. Schneider, *Missions by the Numbers*, 54.

13. Servicemen were provided with pocket-sized Armed Services Editions of classic novels and nonfiction books on history and current events. According to Brett McKay and Kate McKay, "soldiers had a surprisingly keen interest in understanding more about the context of the war," which Lippman's book explored. McKay and McKay, "Literature on the Frontlines: The History of Armed Services Edition Books," The Art of Manliness, last updated April 16, 2019, https://www.artofmanliness.com/articles/literature-on-the-frontlines-the-history-of-armed-services-edition-books.

14. Letters from Baggs to Anne Nichols, July 4, 16, and 28, 1944, private collection.

15. Email from Whiting to author, May 11, 2018.

16. National Personnel Records, National Archives and Records Administration.

CHAPTER 6. 1944–1945

1. Letter from Baggs to Anne Nichols, October 16, 1944, private collection.

2. Gary R. Mormino, "Midas Returns: Miami Goes to War, 1941–1945," Tequesta, no. 57 (1997): 7.

3. Ibid., 5–52.

4. Frec Baggs, *I Thought He Hung the Moon*, 3.

5. "R. C. Orr Dies at 71; Landscaper," *Atlanta Constitution*, December 10, 1962.

6. Frec Baggs, *I Thought He Hung the Moon*, 4.

7. Ibid., 35.

8. Letter from Baggs to Joan Orr, December 8, 1944, private collection.

9. Letter from Baggs to Joan Orr, December 1944.

10. Letter from Baggs to Joan Orr, February 28, 1944

11. Letter from Baggs to Joan Orr, March 27, 1944.

12. At the time, John Wayne and Ward Bond were filming John Ford's *They Were Expendable* with Robert Montgomery and Donna Reed on Key Biscayne and other small barrier islands in Biscayne Bay.

13. Letter from Frec Baggs to Shareef Malnick (owner, The Forge), March 2009, private collection.

CHAPTER 7. 1945–1946

1. Letter from Baggs to Joan Orr, May 15, 1945, private collection.

2. Frec Baggs, *I Thought He Hung the Moon*, 26, and Frec Baggs and Craig Baggs interviews, 2007 and 2018, respectively.

3. Frec Baggs, *I Thought He Hung the Moon*, 36–37, and letter from Joan Orr Baggs to Sally Orr (mother), July 9, 1945, private collection.

4. Letters between Bill and Frec Baggs, October–November 1945, private collection.

5. Frec Baggs, *I Thought He Hung the Moon*, 36–37.

6. A 1946 Academy Award–winning drama, directed by William Wyler, about war veterans readjusting to civilian life, *The Best Years of Our Lives* is one of the first films to address topics such as post-traumatic stress disorder and the emotional, financial, physical, and personal struggles veterans faced when they returned home.

7. Letter from Frec to Bill Baggs, October 15, 1945, private collection.

8. Letter from Bill to Frec Baggs, October 13, 1945, private collection.

9. Letter from Frec to Bill Baggs, November 20, 1945, private collection.

10. Craig Baggs interview, August 11, 2018.

11. Letter from Frec to Bill Baggs, November 21, 1945, private collection.

12. Frec Baggs, *I Thought He Hung the Moon*, 49.

13. Ibid., 60.

14. Ibid., 61.

15. Robert Beers, draft biography of William C. Baggs, unpublished manuscript, private collection.

16. Letter from Baggs to Hoke Welch (managing editor, *Miami Daily News*), February 20, 1946, private collection.

17. Letter from Hoke Welch to Baggs, February 25, 1945, private collection.

18. Frec Baggs, *I Thought He Hung the Moon*, 63.

1. Theresa Van Dyke, "Miami's Second Ghetto" (master's thesis, Florida Atlantic University, 1994), 14.

2. The phrase is often attributed to Phil Graham, the late publisher of the *Washington Post*. For an exploration of its origins, see Jack Shafer, "Who Said It First? Journalism Is the First Rough Draft of History," *Slate*, August 30, 2010, https://slate.com/news-and-politics/2010/08/on-the-trail-of-the-question-who -first-said-or-wrote-that-journalism-is-the-first-rough-draft-of-history.html.

3. Howard Kleinberg, "History of the *Miami News* 1896–1987," *Tequesta*, no. 47 (1987): 5–30.

4. Governor Cox ran on the Democratic ticket in 1920 with a young running mate by the name of Franklin Delano Roosevelt. Because of their fierce support for the United States joining the League of Nations, they suffered the worst defeat in U.S. presidential history to Warren G. Harding and Calvin Coolidge.

5. "Cox Buys the *Metropolis*," 75th Anniversary Special Section, *Miami News*, May 14, 1971.

6. Kleinberg, "History of the *Miami News*," 6.

7. "Hoke Welch, Former Editor of *Miami News*," UPI Archives, July 11, 1981.

8. "A Man of Considerable Dimensions," *Miami Daily News*, January 24, 1953.

9. Golden Anniversary Special Section, *Miami Daily News*, May 12, 1946.

10. Arthur Robinson, "Miami's Fast Air Growth Started from Daring Pioneer Flight in 1911," Golden Anniversary Special Section, *Miami Daily News*, May 12, 1946.

11. Baggs, "3 Miamians Build Airline," *Miami Daily News*, July 18, 1946.

12. Frec Baggs, *I Thought He Hung the Moon*, 64.

13. Bill to Frec Baggs, October 31, 1946, and Frec's handwritten notes, private collection.

14. On the Wing by Grace Wing, *Miami Daily News*, January 7, 1947.

15. Baggs, "Airlines Wage Fight on Ticket Scalpers," *Miami Daily News*, December 29, 1946.

16. Baggs, "Miami's Growing Air Horizons," *Miami Daily News*, June 22, 1947.

17. Carlton Montayne, "A Day Spent in Lauderdale," Monty Says, *Miami Daily News*, January 23, 1953.

18. Kleinberg, "History of the *Miami News*," 18–20.

19. Baggs, "You Just Grab the Rattlesnake," *Miami Daily News*, July 27, 1947.

20. Baggs, "Florida, Cuban Officials Lead PAA Celebration," *Miami Daily News*, October 28, 1947.

21. Letter from Bill to Frec Baggs, July 7, 1948, private collection.

22. Mahoney, The Publisher's Corner, *Miami Daily News*, December 30, 1950.

23. Letter from Bill to Frec Baggs, July 6, 1948, private collection.

24. Letter from Bill to Frec Baggs, July 15, 1948, private collection.

25. Letter from Bill to Frec Baggs, August 16, 1948, private collection.

26. Baggs, "Reds Face Ouster as Union Leaders Plan Housecleaning," *Miami Daily News*, June 14, 1948.

27. John Keasler, "The Man—Littered, Literate, Unique; Waystop between a Wild Irreverence and a Deep Belief," *Miami News*, January 8, 1969.

28. Baggs, Paul Crouch series, *Miami Daily News*, May 9–16, 1949.

CHAPTER 9. 1949–1957

1. Philip Wylie, "Vipers Created a Furor," *Miami News*, October 25, 1971.

2. Wylie, "Wylie Bats for Baggs," *Miami Daily News*, February 8, 1951.

3. Baggs, In the Bag, *Miami Daily News*, May 17, 1950.

4. Baggs, In the Bag, *Miami Daily News*, February 19, 1950.

5. Baggs, "Photograph Raises Intriguing Questions on 'Flying Saucers,'" *Miami Daily News*, March 29, 1950.

6. John Keasler, "The Man—Littered, Literate, Unique; Waystop between a Wild Irreverence and a Deep Belief," *Miami News*, January 8, 1969.

7. Fred Clampitt, "Odds, Ends about that Guy Baggs," *Miami Daily News*, February 12, 1951.

8. Baggs, "The Worst Dressed," *Miami Daily News*, February 9, 1955.

9. Fuller Warren, Letters to the Editor, *Miami Daily News*, February 15, 1955.

10. Dan Mahoney, The Publisher's Corner, *Miami Daily News*, April 21, 1951.

11. Letter from Bill to Frec Baggs, July–August [?] 1950, private collection.

12. Martin, *Ralph McGill, Reporter*, 121–23.

13. Baggs, "Italy Needs Leader to Curb Commies, Worker Declares," Man in the Middle, *Miami Daily News*, April 11, 1951.

14. Baggs, "Yugoslavs Struggle against High Prices, Food Shortages," Man in the Middle, *Miami Daily News*, April 15, 1951.

15. Baggs, "Yugoslavian Editor Points with Pride to Paper's 'Freedom,'" Man in the Middle, *Miami Daily News*, April 19, 1951.

16. Baggs, "Yugoslavs Struggle against High Prices,"

17. Ralph McGill, "A Hi, a Smile, and a Joke," *Miami News* and *Atlanta Constitution*, January 8, 1969.

18. Baggs, "Video Begins Here Tomorrow Night on Station WTVJ," Television Edition, *Miami Daily News*, March 20, 1949.

19. "Miamian Wins Merit Award, Fellowship," *Tampa Bay (St. Petersburg) Times*, June 25, 1952.

20. "News Will Sponsor TV's 'Meet the Press,'" *Miami Daily News*, August 31, 1956.

21. Art Grace, "Bill Baggs and the News," Gracefully Yours, *Miami News*, June 24, 1959.

22. John Egerton, "Possum on Terrace: The Southern Life and Times of Johnny Popham and Some of His Friends" (unpublished manuscript, 1987).

23. Frec Baggs, *I Thought He Hung the Moon*, 86.

24. Baggs, "And Spring Came," *Miami Daily News*, February 18, 1953.

25. Ralph McGill, "A Thin Wail in the Night," *Atlanta Constitution*, February 19, 1953; ellipsis in original.

26. Letter from Governor James M. Cox to Baggs, March 31, 1953, box 8, file 8, MS-2, James M. Cox Papers, Special Collections and Archives, University Libraries, Wright State University, Dayton, Ohio.

27. Baggs, "The Dove Is Out," *Miami Daily News*, April 1, 1953.

28. Letter from Ralph McGill to Baggs, October 7, 1953, box 5, file 9, Ralph E. McGill Papers, Special Collections, Stuart A. Rose Manuscript, Archives and Rare Book Library, Emory University, Atlanta, Georgia.

29. "Palm Tree Politics," *Tampa Bay Times*, July 23, 1955.

30. Letter from James M. Cox to Baggs, February 15, 1955, Cox Papers.

CHAPTER 10. 1957–1969

1. "James M. Cox Dies at 87," *Dayton Daily News*, July 15, 1957.

2. "The Dayton Daily News turns 120," Staff Report.

3. "Announcement," *Miami Daily News*, July 28, 1957.

4. Ibid.

5. "The Press: Meet the Press," *Time*, September 15, 1958. See also "Bill Baggs, 48, Dies of Pneumonia," *Miami News*, January 8, 1969.

6. Earl Wilson, "One Society," *Springfield Leader and Press*, March 6, 1958.

7. Bellows, *The Last Editor*, 72.

8. "Second in Miami; First on Cuba," *Time*, November 16, 1962.

9. Kleinberg interview, November 28, 2016.

10. Julian Pleasants, "Don Wright," unpublished transcript, Florida Newspapers Oral History Collection, Samuel Proctor Oral History Program, Department of History, University of Florida.

11. John Keasler, "The Man—Littered, Literate, Unique; Waystop between a Wild Irreverence and a Deep Belief," *Miami News*, January 8, 1969.

12. William Tucker, "Hoke Welch Ends 15 Years as County Aide," *Miami News*, October 7, 1975.

13. Frishman and Kleinberg interviews.

14. Kleinberg interview, November 28, 2016.

15. Frishman phone interview, September 17, 2018.

16. Bellows, *The Last Editor*, 72. Bellows became known as a mercy editor, rescuing newspapers that had fallen on hard times. On the recommendation of Baggs, Bellows left the *News* in December 1961 to take the job as executive editor of the storied *New*

York Herald Tribune. It, too, was an underdog newspaper, so he took a cue from Baggs to focus on strong, human storytelling with a hyperlocal focus. Bellows hired journalist Jimmy Breslin as the local columnist and brought on Clay Felker to head up the paper's Sunday supplement, *New York*, which ultimately became *New York* magazine—the bastion of Tom Wolfe, Gloria Steinem, and New Journalism.

17. Hurricane Donna Special Section, *Miami News*, September 16, 1960.

18. Bellows, *The Last Editor*, 75.

19. Ibid., 76.

20. "Second in Miami: First on Cuba," *Time*, November 16, 1962.

21. Kleinberg interview, November 28, 2016. Kleinberg still has the stamp.

22. Baggs, "Harry's Stature Grows," *Miami News*, February 17, 1960.

23. From Craig Baggs to editor, *Miami News*, October 18, 1988, private collection.

24. Don Stinson interview, August 17, 2018.

25. Baggs, "There Is Indeed This Santa Claus," *Miami Daily News*, December 24, 1951.

26. Mahoney Baggs interview, December 12, 2017, and Frec Baggs, *I Thought He Hung the Moon*, 98–99.

27. Charles Allen interview, January 19, 2019.

28. Dr. Alec Jones and Lacy Jones Ashton interview, January 25, 2019.

29. Bellows, *The Last Editor*, 85.

30. Jones and Ashton interview.

31. Ibid.

32. Baggs Papers, Special Collections, University of Miami, Florida.

33. Letters from Bill Baggs to Richard M. Nixon, October 24, 1960, and from Nixon to Craig Baggs, October 26, 1960, series 320, box 59, Richard Nixon Presidential Library and Museum.

34. Letter from Baggs to Richard M. Nixon, November 1, 1960, Nixon Presidential Library.

CHAPTER 11. 1958–1962

1. Baggs, "Operation Bootstrap," *Miami Daily News*, November 13, 1952, and "Operation Bootstrap in Puerto Rico," View of the News, *Miami Daily News*, September 10, 1957.

2. Baggs became an expert on Puerto Rico and wrote a case study on the Caribbean island's history and progress for the 1962 Britannica Book of the Year, *World without Want*. His hope was that it would inspire other Latin American and U.S. leaders to take a development approach to U.S. foreign policy.

3. Baggs, "The New World," *Miami Daily News*, August 10, 1954.

4. Hal Hendrix, "Firm U.S. Policy Is Urged to Discourage Dictators," *Miami News*, August 16, 1958.

5. Letter from Baggs to Richard M. Nixon, April 21, 1959, Nixon Presidential Library.

6. Ibid.

7. For more on Fidel Castro's efforts to court American media, see Leonard Ray Teele's *Reporting the Cuban Revolution: How Castro Manipulated American Journalists* (Baton Rouge, La.: LSU Press, 2015), which offers, among other highlights, a detailed account of the reporters to whom Castro awarded gold medals during his first trip to the United States after the Cuban Revolution.

8. Letter from Jay Mallin to Baggs, undated, private collection.

9. "News' Jay Mallin Scores Cuban Beat," *Miami News*, January 2, 1959.

10. Letter from Baggs to Fidel Castro, April 21, 1959, private collection.

11. On January 18, 1959, the *News* published an exclusive letter from Castro on its front page. In the letter, Castro speaks of restoring "rights for all" and denounces dictators such as Khrushchev in the Soviet Union, Trujillo in the Dominican Republic, and Franco in Spain.

12. Baggs, "A Midnight Visit with Fidel Castro," *Miami News*, April 26, 1959.

13. Letter from Baggs to Fidel Castro, April 21, 1959, private collection.

14. Letter from Baggs to Richard M. Nixon, April 21, 1959, Nixon Presidential Library.

15. Letter from Richard M. Nixon to Baggs, May 18, 1959, Nixon Presidential Library.

16. Baggs, "The Sad Story of Castro," View of the News, *Miami News*, November 3, 1959, and "Red Schoolhouses," *Miami News*, May 25, 1961.

17. Letter from Baggs to Mrs. Bernard S. Klayf, October 29, 1965, Baggs Papers.

18. Maria Anderson, "Pedro Pan: A Children's Exodus from Cuba," *Smithsonian Insider* (blog), July 11, 2017.

19. "That Long, Long Line," *Globe-Gazette* (Mason City, Iowa), September 21, 1962.

20. Letter from Baggs to Mrs. Bernard S. Klayf.

21. Kleinberg interview, November 28, 2016.

22. Tye, *Bobby Kennedy*, 241.

23. Thomas Maier, "Inside the CIA's Plot to Kill Fidel Castro—with Mafia Help," *Politico*, February 24, 2018.

24. Kleinberg interview, November 28, 2016. See also Glenn Garvin, "The Miami Herald, the CIA, and the Bay of Pigs Scoop That Didn't Run," *Miami Herald*, April 17, 2015. The reporter, David Kraslow, began his career in sports at the *News*, and returned as the publisher of the *News* in the 1980s until it folded in 1988.

25. David P. Hadley's *The Rising Clamor* (Lexington: University Press of Kentucky, 2019) explores the relationship between U.S. intelligence agencies and the press.

26. Letters from Baggs to Governor Luis Muñoz Marín, February 8, March 10, and May 16, 1960, Baggs Papers.

27. Tye, *Bobby Kennedy*, 242.

28. Letter from Baggs to Harry Ashmore, November 29, 1960, Harry Ashmore Papers, MSS 18, box 61, folder 5, Davidson Library, University of California, Santa Barbara.

29. Baggs, "War and Discipline," View of the News, *Miami News*, April 21, 1961.

30. Baggs, "A Chance to Show What Democracy Can Do," View of the News, *Miami News*, June 4, 1961.

31. Letter from Baggs to John F. Kennedy, September 16, 1961, Baggs Papers.

32. "Bill Baggs to Attend Caribbean Conference," *Miami News*, September 3, 1961.

33. "JFK Greets Emerging Caribbean," *Miami News*, September 7, 1961; ellipsis in original.

34. Letter from Baggs to Harry S. Ashmore, undated, Baggs Papers.

35. Letter from Baggs to Dean Rusk, January 26, 1962, Baggs Papers.

36. Tye, *Bobby Kennedy*, 249.

37. Internal cover memo from Federal Bureau of Investigation to Attorney General re: Baggs's report of misconduct by CIA employees in Florida, October 4, 1962, U.S. Department of Justice, Federal Bureau of Investigation, FOIPA Request no. 1366398.

38. Clarke Ash, "Miami Crawled with CIA Men," *Palm Beach Post*, October 18, 1987.

39. Ibid. Many years after they worked together at the *News*, Ash and Hendrix reconnected in Palm Beach, where they were both living. According to an account Ash published on the twenty-fifth anniversary of the Cuban Missile Crisis, Hendrix never relied solely on his CIA contacts. He had an unnamed source deep in Cuba who would get information to him through family members living in Miami, and he had another unnamed source right inside the White House, whose identity he took with him to the grave.

40. Kleinberg interview, November 28, 2016.

41. In a 1977 *Rolling Stone* article, journalist Carl Bernstein explored the findings of the Church Commission, which revealed that some well-known and respected journalists, such as Joseph and Stewart Alsop (who were syndicated columnists published by the *News*, among many other top newspapers), were paid informants and often mouthpieces for the CIA. He asserts in his article that as many as four hundred journalists and editors, including Hal Hendrix, were Agency assets. According to an email dated January 9, 2019, from David Hadley, author of *The Rising Clamor*, the CIA believed certain reporters were assets, even though the Agency did not direct their reporting activities or pay them for their services. These same reporters simply viewed the CIA as one of many legitimate sources for information and would share details they had learned in the process of reporting with CIA contacts in order to obtain confirmation or denial.

1. The existence of this phone has been confirmed separately with Frec, Craig, and Mahoney Baggs, as well as Howard Kleinberg and Mel Frishman. Kleinberg and another *News* colleague learned about it by pure accident. During one of the storied Baggs Christmas Eve parties, he and another writer needed to follow up on a scoop, so they headed into Baggs's study, picked up the first receiver they saw and heard an official voice on the other end of the line before they had even dialed a number.

2. Notes for a speech, undated, Baggs Papers.

3. "Editor Raps News Control," *Miami News*, February 20, 1963.

4. My account here is based on interviews with Frec Baggs and Howard Kleinberg, review of *Miami News* coverage and retrospectives, and chapters 2 and 3 of Robert Beers, draft biography of William C. Baggs, unpublished manuscript, private collection.

5. Kleinberg interview, November 28, 2016.

6. "Cuban Missile Crisis," Special Section, *Miami News*, October 15, 1982.

7. "Cuba Raps U.S. in Wild U.N. Session" and "Prisoner Airlift Awaited," *Miami News*, October 8, 1962. The prisoners were freed on Christmas Eve 1962, for a ransom of $53 million in tractors, food, and medical supplies.

8. William Tucker, "We'll Hit All Ships to Cuba, Alpha 66 Threatens," *Miami News*, October 11, 1962.

9. Baggs, "Testing Ground," View of the News, *Miami News*, October 13, 1962.

10. Baggs, "U.N. Reports 1–4," View of the News, *Miami News*, October 15–18, 1962.

11. Baggs, "Here Are the Real Issues in '62 Campaign," View of the News, *Miami News*, October 21, 1962.

12. Frec Baggs, *I Thought He Hung the Moon*, 106.

13. Kleinberg interview, November 28, 2016, and "Castro Affects Our Town," *Miami News*, Special Seventy-Fifth Anniversary Edition, May 14, 1971.

14. "Second in Miami; First on Cuba," *Time*, November 16, 1962.

15. Frec Baggs, *I Thought He Hung the Moon*, 106.

16. Charles Kessler, "JFK Roasts GOP, Reds," *Miami News*, November 19, 1963.

17. Frec Baggs, *I Thought He Hung the Moon*, 107.

18. Milt Sosin, "Just a Few Feet Away," *Miami News*, November 19, 1983.

19. Baggs, "The Man," *Miami News*, November 23, 1963.

20. John Keasler, "The Man—Littered, Literate, Unique; Waystop between a Wild Irreverence and a Deep Belief," *Miami News*, January 8, 1969.

21. Todd Bookman, "John F. Kennedy Diary Reveals Shift from Journalist to Budding Politician," NPR, April 25, 2017.

22. Email from Don Stinson to author, December 5, 2018.

23. "Benjamin Franklin: In His Own Words: Transcript of Benjamin Franklin, Epitaph," Library of Congress website, https://www.loc.gov/exhibits/franklin/bf-trans61.html.

24. Craig Baggs interview, August 11, 2018.

25. Letter from Baggs to Jacqueline Kennedy, January 1964, Baggs Papers.

26. According to Craig Baggs, the accompanying note from the former First Lady did not survive. Frec, angry that her husband had not introduced her to the president when he had visited Miami the week before the assassination, ripped it up.

CHAPTER 13. 1949–1960

1. Raymond A. Mohl, "'South of the South?' Jews, Blacks, and the Civil Rights Movement in Miami, 1945–1960," *Journal of American Ethnic History* 18, no. 2 (Winter 1999): 7.

2. Theresa Van Dyke, "Miami's Second Ghetto" (master's thesis, Florida Atlantic University, 1994), 66.

3. Jack Mann, "The Defender . . . In Priestly Garb," *Miami News*, December 4, 1968.

4. Van Dyke, "Miami's Second Ghetto," 35–42.

5. Baggs, In the Bag, *Miami Daily News*, May 16, 1950.

6. Baggs, In the Bag, *Miami Daily News*, May 23, 1950.

7. Baggs, In the Bag, *Miami Daily News*, May 3, 1950.

8. Baggs, "Death Trap," View of the News, *Miami News*, October 19, 1961.

9. Baggs, "A Negro Man Was Worried," *Miami Daily News*, July 23, 1952.

10. Baggs, "You Could Call it 'Bedsheet Fiction,'" *Miami Daily News*, April 21, 1957.

11. Mohl, "'South of the South?,'" 5.

12. Desegregation letters to the editor, Baggs Papers, box 19, folder 519.

13. Baggs, "Anonymous Fiction," View of the News, *Miami News*, November 7, 1961.

14. Baggs, "Opening Minds," View of the News, *Miami News*, March 10, 1961.

15. Van Dyke, "Miami's Second Ghetto," 68.

16. Baggs, "Don't Kid Yourself on Desegregation," *Miami Daily News*, December 5, 1954.

17. Baggs, "Abolish Our Schools?" *Miami Daily News*, December 6, 1954.

18. Baggs, "The First Negro Judge in Dixie," *Miami Daily News*, December 7, 1955.

19. Baggs, "Orr's Plan Might Be Answer," *Miami News*, September 25, 1958.

20. Haines Colbert, "Eldridge Tops Orr, But Debate Still On," *Miami News*, October 1, 1958.

21. Baggs, "Press Has a Great Duty to Tell Both Sides," *Miami Daily News*, October 8, 1957; Baggs, "Segregation, Dollars & Sense," *Miami Daily News*, February 8, 1959.

22. Desegregation letters to the editor, Baggs Papers.

23. Baggs, "Segregation, Dollars & Sense."

CHAPTER 14. 1960–1968

1. Jack Kassewitz, "Covenant of Brotherhood," *Miami News*, January 10, 1969, and "New City Commissioner Offers Political Paradox," *Miami News*, April 20, 1972.

2. Gibson biographical sketch, Reverend Canon Theodore Gibson Collection, Black Archives, History and Research Foundation of South Florida, Inc., 1.

3. Jack Mann, "The Defender . . . In Priestly Garb," *Miami News*, December 4, 1968.

4. Gibson biographical sketch, 1.

5. Mann, "The Defender."

6. Gibson biographical sketch, 1.

7. Jack Mann, "Gibson Breaks Witch Hunt in State Led by Johns," *Miami News*, December 5, 1968.

8. Ibid.

9. Gibson biographical sketch, 2.

10. Jack Mann, "Gibson Firm on Ideals—but He Was 'Hurt Inside,'" *Miami News*, December 6, 1968.

11. Gibson biographical sketch, 3.

12. Harry S. Ashmore remarks, memorial service for Baggs, Christ Episcopal Church, Miami, August 10, 1969, private collection.

13. Jack Kassewitz, "Covenant of Brotherhood," *Miami News*, January 10, 1969.

14. Tye, *Bobby Kennedy*, 124–31.

15. Ashmore remarks, memorial service.

16. Multiple obituaries and writings about Baggs mention that he helped secure the release of Dr. King from a Georgia state penitentiary in October 1960. There are no specific details provided. Considering his deep connections in Georgia, his friendship with the Kennedys, and his pragmatic approach to race relations, it seems plausible that Baggs provided advice to either Senator John Kennedy or his brother or one of the campaign aides.

17. "Another Editor in the Baggs-McGill Tradition," *Miami News*, May 4, 1971.

18. Baggs, "Violent Hucksters," *Miami News*, August 9, 1968.

19. Raymond A. Mohl, "'South of the South?' Jews, Blacks, and the Civil Rights Movement in Miami, 1945–1960," *Journal of American Ethnic History* 18, no. 2 (Winter 1999): 3.

20. Howard Kleinberg, "Littered and Literate—and a Force for Positive Change," *Miami Herald*, October 25, 1994.

21. Letter from C. B. Potter to Baggs, November 14, 1961, Baggs Papers.

22. Letter from Baggs to Louis F. Oberdorfer, June 12, 1963, Baggs Papers.

23. "Civil Rights: Meeting with Religious Leaders," digital archives, JFKPOF-097-011-p0003, June 17, 1963, Papers of John F. Kennedy, Presidential Papers, Presidential Office Files, John F. Kennedy Presidential Library and Museum, Boston, Massachusetts, National Archives and Records Administration.

24. Baggs, "Accusing Spirits," *Miami News*, July 23, 1963.

25. Baggs, "For a Key Man," *Miami News*, July 24, 1963.

26. Letter from Vice President Lyndon B. Johnson to Baggs, July 25, 1963, Baggs Papers.

27. McGill's secretary Grace Lundy sent the photo of McGill cheering at his desk to Baggs after McGill learned he had been awarded the Pulitzer Prize. "I wish I had been there," Baggs wrote McGill on May 5, 1959. "I would have supplied you some of my white kidney medicine for spiking the coffee."

28. Letter from Ralph McGill to Harry S. Ashmore, April 10, 1961, McGill Papers.

29. Gene Roberts and Hank Klibanoff, "The Embrace of Principled Stands," *Neiman Reports* 60, no. 2 (Summer 2006): 88.

30. Jeanne Theoharis, "Don't Forget That Martin Luther King Jr. Was Once Denounced as an Extremist," *Time*, January 12, 2018.

31. Roberts and Klibanoff, "Embrace of Principled Stands," 88.

32. Martin S. Ochs, "The Sage of Atlanta," *Virginia Quarterly* 75, no. 3 (Summer 1999): 589; emphasis in original.

33. Letter from Baggs to Montgomery Curtis, American Press Institute, October 21, 1959, papers of the Center for the Study of Democratic Institutions.

34. Ibid.

35. Letter from Grace Lundy to Harry Ashmore, June 3, 1971, Harry Ashmore Papers.

36. Letter from Baggs to John Popham, managing editor, *Chattanooga Times*, April 28, 1960, Baggs Papers.

37. Letter from Baggs to Harry S. Ashmore, August 19, 1960, Papers of the Center for the Study of Democratic Institutions.

38. Letter from Ralph McGill to Philip Coombs, assistant secretary of state for education and culture in the Kennedy administration, February 29, 1960, Harry Ashmore Papers.

39. Letter from Baggs to Harry S. Ashmore, May 22, 1962, Papers of the Center for the Study of Democratic Institutions.

40. Baggs, "Hatred," *Miami News*, January 13, 1963.

41. Frec Baggs, *I Thought He Hung the Moon*, 97; Craig Baggs interview, August 11, 2018.

42. Jones interview, January 26, 2019.

43. Letter from Baggs to Col. Michael Twitty, retired commander of SouthCom at Homestead Air Force Base, February 24, 1964, Baggs Papers.

44. Craig and Mahoney Baggs, Howard Kleinberg, and Alexander Jones all mentioned the revolving book case to the author, most often preceded by the question, "Has anyone told you about the secret passage yet?"

CHAPTER 15. 1955–1968

1. "Misery's Calendar," *Miami News*, December 25, 1958, and "We're Grateful, Proud," *Miami News*, May 5, 1959; https://www.pulitzer.org/prize-winners-by-category/209.

2. Howard Van Smith obituary, *Tampa Bay Times*, August 17, 1986.

3. "It's Our Third Pulitzer," *Miami News*, May 7, 1963.

4. Carl Bernstein, "The CIA and the Media," *Rolling Stone*, October 20, 1977.

5. Haines Colbert, "Don Wright Took Just Four Years to Win Pulitzer," *Miami News*, May 3, 1966. Wright had been the paper's photo editor and had threatened to quit after an argument with another editor. Baggs, who had long sought a skilled cartoonist for the newspaper, liked the drawings Wright had shown him and encouraged him to stay on staff and move into a newly created editorial cartoonist position.

6. Ben Schneider, "Developers Buy on Key Biscayne," *Miami News*, February 3, 1958.

7. "Preserve Cape Florida Light," *Miami News*, July 26, 1958.

8. "We Can Save the Lighthouse," signed editorial, *Miami News*, August 24, 1958.

9. Craig Baggs interview, August 11, 2018.

10. Dade County Commission, "Proposed Cape Florida State Park," July 21, 1964, Baggs Papers.

11. Baggs, "An Offer," *Miami News*, May 16, 1965.

12. Elena Santeiro Garcia, "'I'd Like Cape to Be Park,'" *Miami News*, May 23, 1965.

13. Baggs, "Cape Florida . . . Gift to Our Heirs," *Miami News*, June 27, 1965.

14. Baggs, "Our Bay a Great Asset," View of the News, *Miami News*, June 23, 1960.

15. Bob Corchoran, "Cape Florida Deed Presented to Burns," *Miami News*, April 5, 1965.

16. Letter from Baggs to Elena Santeiro Garcia, May 16, 1967, private collection.

17. Dudley R. Parsons & Co., "Summary Report on the Proposed Seadade Port and Refinery on Biscayne Bay, Florida," March 11, 1963, Baggs Papers.

18. Baggs, "The New Conservationists, Color Them Green," *Miami News*, May 20, 1972.

19. Press release by public relations firm Dudley L. Parsons & Co., March 18, 1963, Baggs Papers.

20. Baggs, "Oil Refineries," View of the News, *Miami News*, August 27, 1962; ellipsis in original.

21. Confidential Memo, August 24, 1963, Baggs Papers.

22. Baggs, "Unnecessary Risks," View of the News, *Miami News*, April 25, 1963.

23. Baggs, "Courthouse Birds," View of the News, *Miami News*, April 30, 1963.

24. Paul Einstein, "Seadade Suffers 2 Jolts," *Miami News*, January 23, 1964.

25. "An Award for Baggs," *Miami News*, December 14, 1965.

26. Adkins, *Making Modern Florida*, xxiv–xxv.

27. Baggs, "Want to Debate This?," *Miami Daily News*, May 17, 1954.

28. Baggs, "Reapportionment," View of the News, *Miami News*, September 7, 1962.

29. Adkins, *Making Modern Florida*, 69.

30. Ibid., 87–92.

31. Ibid., 77.

32. Ibid., 125–30.

33. Rich Oppel, "Voting at 18 Up for Debate," *Tallahassee Democrat*, December 1, 1966.

34. "Lower Vote Age, Says Bill Baggs," *Miami News*, November 30, 1966.

35. Charles F. Hesser, "Baggs Urges Nonpartisan Constitution," *Miami News*, July 13, 1967; ellipsis in original.

CHAPTER 16. 1965–1967

1. Letter from Ralph McGill to Harry S. Ashmore, September 8, 1965, Baggs Papers.

2. Letter from Baggs to Ralph McGill and Harry S. Ashmore, September 10, 1965, Papers of the Center for the Study of Democratic Institutions.

3. Julian Pleasants, "Howard Kleinberg FNP 71," unpublished transcript, Florida Newspapers Oral History Collection, Samuel Proctor Oral History Program, Department of History, University of Florida, 16.

4. "Statement by John S. Knight," *Miami News*, July 29, 1966.

5. "Statement by Bill Baggs," *Miami News*, July 29, 1966.

6. Interview with Ralph Renick, *WTVJ Evening News*, video, private collection.

7. Craig Baggs interview, August 11, 2018.

8. Kleinberg interview, November 28, 2016.

9. Pleasants, "Howard Kleinberg FNP 71," 12.

10. Kleinberg interview, November 28, 2016.

11. Pleasants, "Howard Kleinberg FNP 71," 13.

12. Remarks by Dr. Peter Steinfels, Inaugural Lecture, Pacem in Terris Lecture Series, Georgetown University, October 10, 2003.

13. Baggs, "A Spiritual Leader's Down-to-Earth Plea," *Miami News*, April 11, 1963.

14. "Bill Baggs Had 2 Idols: Lincoln and John XXIII," The Voice of Ralph Renick, *The Voice* (Archdiocese of Miami), January 17, 1969, private collection.

15. Ashmore, *Hearts and Minds*, 415.

16. John K. Jessup, "Peace on Earth?," *Life*, March 5, 1968, 33A.

17. Baggs, "Peace," *Miami News*, February 21, 1965.

18. "The Ways to Peace Searched," AP Wire, *Miami News*, February 19, 1965.

19. Jessup, "Peace on Earth?," 34A–35A.

20. Ashmore and Baggs, *Mission to Hanoi*, 5.

21. Letter from Baggs to Harry S. Ashmore, December 27, 1965, Baggs Papers.

22. Letter from Ralph McGill to Harry S. Ashmore, December 13, 1965, McGill Papers.

23. Letter from Baggs to Harry S. Ashmore, February 3, 1966, Baggs Papers.

24. Baggs, "Bill Baggs in Switzerland," *Miami News*, June 13, 1966.

25. Baggs, "Determination at Armageddon," *Miami News*, June 15, 1966.

26. Baggs, "For Arabs, a Free Country," *Miami News*, June 16, 1966.

27. Baggs, "Stubborn Enough to Exist," *Miami News*, June 14, 1966.

28. Ashmore and Baggs, *Mission to Hanoi*, 5.

CHAPTER 17. January–March 1967

1. Gordon M. Goldstein, "'Marigold: The Lost Chance for Peace in Vietnam,' by James G. Hershberg," book review, *Washington Post*, January 27, 2012.

2. Robert K. Brigham, "A Lost Chance for Peace in Vietnam," *New York Times*, June 16, 2017.

3. Ashmore and Baggs, *Mission to Hanoi*, 7.

4. Baggs, "Notes on Missions to North Vietnam," written 1967–68, transcribed April 1968, unpublished, 1.

5. Nicholas Katzenbach, LBJ Oral History Collection, LBJ Presidential Library.

6. William Bundy, LBJ Oral History Collection, LBJ Presidential Library.

7. Baggs, "Notes," 4.

8. Ibid., 6.

9. Ashmore and Baggs, *Mission to Hanoi*, 6.

10. While Baggs was in Hanoi, Salisbury fought on the home front for his own journalistic credibility—a situation Baggs would face once his first reports from Hanoi were published. Both men were called propagandists and traitors, among other names. Because in his articles Salisbury quoted the DRV's casualty figures, which differed significantly from the U.S. military's tallies, had spoken with members of the Viet Cong, and had written of the devastation caused by American bombs to villages, schools, and hospitals, he was roundly condemned not just by the Johnson administration, but by readers and television pundits. One of Salisbury's conclusions would prove prescient: the Viet Cong were growing increasingly independent of Ho's influence and less submissive to the aims of Hanoi, although the VC still strove for reunification of the country. Baggs agreed and would come to believe that peace talks would amount to nothing if the VC were not invited to the negotiating table.

11. Ashmore and Baggs, *Mission to Hanoi*, 6.

12. Baggs, "Notes", 7–8.

13. The Johnson administration repeatedly claimed that American pilots were bombing only steel and concrete—e.g., rail yards and munitions factories—that supported the war effort.

14. Baggs, "Notes," 10–11.

15. Ibid., 11–12.

16. Paul Warnke, LBJ Oral History Collection, LBJ Presidential Library.

17. Baggs, "Notes," 13–15.

18. Ibid., 20.

19. Speech by President Lyndon B. Johnson, "Peace without Conquest," April 7, 1965, LBJ Presidential Library.

20. Baggs, "Notes," 25.

21. Baggs, "Baggs Tells How Hanoi Takes Life as City at War," *Miami News*, January 17, 1967.

22. Baggs, "Notes," 27.

23. Ibid., 29.

24. Ibid., "Notes," 30–34.

25. Baggs's handwritten notes to editors for Vietnam series, January 1967, Baggs Papers.

26. Baggs, "Notes," 37.

27. Internal memo from Ralph McGill to Jack Tarver, publisher, Atlanta Newspapers, Inc., January 19, 1967, McGill Papers.

28. Letters to the Editor, *Miami News*, January 24, 1967.

CHAPTER 18. May–September 1967

1. Ashmore and Baggs, *Mission to Hanoi*, 65. In an oral history compiled by the LBJ Presidential Library, Harrison Salisbury confirmed this account, having had the same conversation with Senator Fulbright about his own trip to Hanoi.

2. Ibid., 69–71.

3. Baggs, "Notes on Missions to North Vietnam," written 1967–68, transcribed April 1968, unpublished, 38.

4. Ashmore and Baggs, *Mission to Hanoi*, 69.

5. Frec Baggs, *I Thought He Hung the Moon*, 116.

6. Baggs, "Reds Pull Out of Geneva Peace Conference," *Miami News*, March 29, 1967.

7. "World Peace Session Will Open Sunday," *Miami News*, May 26, 1967.

8. Baggs, "Notes," 40.

9. Dr. Martin Luther King Jr.'s speech to the Pacem in Terris II convocation, Part A, Program 435, University of California Library Digital Collections, Santa Barbara, http://digital.library.ucsb.edu/items/show/4971.

10. Baggs, "Notes," 39.

11. Ibid., 42.

12. Ibid., 42–44.

13. George Ball, LBJ Oral History Collection, LBJ Presidential Library.

14. Craig Baggs interview, August 11, 2018.

15. Handwritten note from Baggs to Frec, undated, private collection.

16. Robert W. Lucas, "Maybe Ashmore 'Goof' was Planned," *Press and Sun-Bulletin* (Binghamton, N.Y.), September 19, 1967.

17. Telegram from Robert Kennedy to Baggs, September 19, 1967, Baggs Papers.

18. As seen by author, private collection.

CHAPTER 19. October 1967–April 1968

1. Harry S. Ashmore, "The Ashmore Controversy," Letters to the Editor, *Baltimore Sun*, October 11, 1967.

2. "Ashmore's Charges: Take a Good Look at the Facts," *Miami News*, September 19, 1967.

3. Internal memo from Ralph McGill to James M. Cox Jr., November 6, 1967, McGill Papers.

4. Letter from Ralph McGill to Baggs, December 15, 1967, McGill Papers; ellipsis in original.

5. Letter from Baggs to Ralph McGill, December 20, 1967, Baggs Papers.

6. Letter from Baggs to Robert Kennedy, February 3, 1968, Baggs Papers.

7. Letter from Baggs to Robert Kennedy, February 23, 1968, Baggs Papers.

8. Letter from Hoàng Tùng (editor, *Nhân Dân*) to Baggs, February 29, 1968, Baggs Papers.

9. Baggs, "Notes on Missions to North Vietnam," written 1967–68, transcribed April 1968, unpublished, 2.

10. Ibid., 5.

11. Ibid., 6.

12. Letter from Harry S. Ashmore and Baggs to Anne Ashmore, April 6, 1968, private collection.

13. Harry S. Ashmore remarks, Baggs Memorial Service, August 10, 1969.

14. Cable from Harrison Salisbury to Baggs, April 4, 1968, Baggs Papers.

15. Baggs, "Notes," 34.

CHAPTER 20. May–September 1968

1. Baggs, "Demo, GOP Chiefs Like Miami Beach," *Miami News*, May 17, 1967.

2. Baggs, "Robert Francis Kennedy, Man of Courage," *Miami News*, June 6, 1968.

3. Baggs, "I Saw a New York Cop Crying," *Miami News*, June 7, 1968.

4. Telegram invitation from Kennedy family to Baggs, June 7, 1968, Baggs Papers.

5. Associated Press, "King Suspect Is Arrested," *Miami News*, June 8, 1968.

6. Baggs, "RFK Myth," *Miami News*, June 12, 1968.

7. Letter from Baggs to Robert Kennedy, December 11, 1963, Baggs Papers; ellipsis in original.

8. Letter from Baggs to Ethel Kennedy, July 1, 1968, Baggs Papers.

9. Letter from Baggs to Edward Kennedy, July 1, 1968, Baggs Papers.

10. Frec Baggs, *I Thought He Hung the Moon*, 122–23.

11. Craig Baggs interview, August 11, 2018.

12. Baggs, "The Violent Hucksters," *Miami News*, August 9, 1968.

13. Baggs, "Frustration," *Miami News*, August 16, 1968.

14. Letter from Bill to Frec Baggs, August 28, 1968, private collection.

15. Baggs, "Absentees," *Miami News*, August 26, 1968.

16. Kleinberg interview, November 28, 2016.

17. Letter from Baggs to Harry S. Ashmore, September 23, 1968, Baggs Papers.

CHAPTER 21. October 1968–February 1969

1. Letter from Baggs to Ethel Kennedy, October 7, 1968, Baggs Papers.

2. Letter from Ralph McGill to Baggs, October 29, 1968, McGill Papers.

3. Frec Baggs, *I Thought He Hung the Moon*, 126.

4. "Editor Charges LBJ-Hanoi Deal," *Pensacola Times*, November 1, 1968.

5. John A. Farrell, "When a Candidate Conspired with a Foreign Power to Win an Election," *Politico*, August 6, 2017.

6. Baggs never sent the book, and it remains in Craig Baggs's library.

7. "Another Editor in the Baggs-McGill Tradition," Special Anniversary Section, *Miami News*, May 14, 1971.

8. Kleinberg interview, November 28, 2016.

9. Baggs, "Why Not Re-do City from Ghetto to Bay," *Miami News*, December 27, 1968.

10. Mahoney Baggs interview, December 12, 2017.

11. Frec Baggs, *I Thought He Hung the Moon*, 125.

12. "World Leaders Honor Him as Peace Crusader," compiled by Milt Sosin, *Miami News*, January 8, 1969.

13. John Keasler, "The Man—Littered, Literate, Unique; Waystop between a Wild Irreverence and a Deep Belief," *Miami News*, January 8, 1969.

14. Kleinberg interview, November 28, 2016.

15. Don Stinson email to author, December 5, 2018.

16. Kleinberg interview, November 28, 2016.

17. Baggs's 1968 pocket address book, private collection.

18. Letter from Harry S. Ashmore to Ralph McGill, February 4, 1969, Harry Ashmore Papers.

CHAPTER 22. August 1969–

1. Program for William C. Baggs Memorial Service, August 10, 1969, private collection. The verse is Ecclesiasticus (Sirach) 44:2–3 (New Revised Standard Version).

2. Harry S. Ashmore remarks, Baggs Memorial Service, August 10, 1969.

3. Rick Eyerdam, "Baggs Park OK'd by House," *Miami News*, April 13, 1973.

4. Ian Glass, "Your Impossible Dream Has Come True, Bill Baggs," *Miami News*, March 13, 1974.

Epilogue. Miami, December 1988

1. "A Policy Based on People," editorial, *Miami News*, January 9, 1969; ellipsis in original.

2. Donna Gehrke and Dan Christensen, "Like a Death in the Family, Reader Says," *Miami News*, October 15, 1988.

3. Howard Kleinberg, "The *Miami News* Ends; The Causes Continue," *Miami News*, December 31, 1988.

BIBLIOGRAPHY

Books

Adkins, Mary E. *Making Modern Florida: How the Spirit of Reform Shaped a New State Constitution.* Gainesville: University Press of Florida, 2016.

Ashmore, Harry S. *Hearts and Minds: A Personal Chronicle of Race in America.* Cabin John, Md.: Seven Locks, 1988.

Ashmore, Harry S., and William C. Baggs. *Mission to Hanoi: A Chronicle of Double-Dealing in High Places.* New York: G. P. Putnam's Sons, 1968.

Baggs, Frec. *I Thought He Hung the Moon: A True Love Story.* Miami, Fla.: printed by author, 2008.

Baggs, William C., ed. *Bombs Away, 44-1.* Midland, Tex.: Army Air Forces Bombardier School, 1944. Available at http://aafcollection.info/items/list.php?item=000842

Bellows, Jim. *The Last Editor: How I Saved the* New York Times, *the* Washington Post, *and the* Los Angeles Times *from Dullness and Complacency.* Kansas City, Mo.: Andrews McMeel, 2002.

Dorr, Robert F. *B-24 Liberator Units of the Fifteenth Air Force.* Oxford: Osprey, 2000.

Martin, Harold H. *Ralph McGill, Reporter.* Boston: Little, Brown, 1973.

McCarthy, Mary. *Hanoi.* New York: Harcourt, Brace & World, 1968.

Schneider, Sammy, ed. *Missions by the Numbers: Combat Missions Flown by the 485th Bomb Group (H).* 2nd ed. Walnut Creek, Calif.: Tarnaby Books, 2008.

St. John, Philip A. *Bombardiers of WWII: A History.* Nashville, Tenn.: Turner, 1993.

Tye, Larry. *Bobby Kennedy: The Making of a Liberal Icon.* New York: Random House, 2016.

Whiting, Jerry W. *Don't Let the Blue Star Turn Gold: Downed Airmen in Europe in WWII.* 2nd ed. Walnut Creek, Calif.: Tarnaby Books, 2016.

Interviews

Allen, Charles. Interview by author, Miami, Florida, January 19, 2019.

Ashmore, Anne. Telephone interview by author, Savannah, Georgia, August 31, 2018.

Baggs, Charles Crawford. Telephone interview by author, Savannah, Georgia, August 31, 2018.

Baggs, Craig. Interviews by author, Savannah, Georgia, July 13, 2018; Ocala, Florida, August 10–12, 2018.

Baggs, Frec. Interviews by author, Miami, Florida, June 2007–July 2008.

Baggs, Mahoney. Interview by author, Miami, Florida, December 12, 2017.

Frishman, Mel. Telephone interview by author, Savannah, Georgia, September 17, 2018.

Gibson, Thelma. Interview by author, Miami, Florida, December 16, 2017.

Jones, Dr. Alexander. Interview by author, Savannah, Georgia, January 26, 2019.

Kempffer, Michael. Telephone interview by author, Savannah, Georgia, November 12, 2018.

Kleinberg, Howard. Interview by author, Miami, Florida, November 28, 2016.

Moore, Harold. Telephone interview by author, Savannah, Georgia, July 27, 2018.

Stinson, Don. Telephone interview by author, Savannah, Georgia, August 17, 2018.

Letters, Notes, and Unpublished Manuscripts

Ashmore, Harry S. "Remarks by Harry S. Ashmore: Memorial Service for William C. Baggs, Christ Episcopal, Miami, 10 August 1969." Privately held.

Baggs, William C. (Bill). Letters and other ephemera. Privately held.

———. "Notes on Missions to North Vietnam." Written January 1967–April 1968, transcribed April 1968, unpublished. Privately held.

Beers, Robert. Chapters 1–3 of draft biography of William C. Baggs. Last modified 2012. Privately held.

Beers, William. "My Song of the South." Unpublished manuscript. Privately held.

Libraries and Archives

Ashmore, Harry S. Papers. Special Collections, Davidson Library, University of California, Santa Barbara.

Baggs, William C. (Bill). Papers. Special Collections, University of Miami Libraries, Coral Gables, Florida.

Center for the Study of Democratic Institutions. Special Collections, Davidson Library, University of California, Santa Barbara.

Cox, James. M. Papers. Special Collections and Archives, University Libraries, Wright State University, Dayton, Ohio.

Gibson, Father Theodore R. Papers. The Black Archives History and Research Foundation of South Florida, Miami.

McGill, Ralph Emerson. Papers. Special Collections, Stuart A. Rose Manuscript, Archives and Rare Book Library, Emory University, Atlanta, Georgia.

Dissertations, Theses, Oral Histories, and Manuscripts

Egerton, John. "Possum on Terrace: The Southern Life and Times of Johnny Popham and Some of His Friends." Unpublished manuscript, 1987. Emory University. https://southernspaces.org/sites/default/files/Possum-on-Terrace-Egerton.pdf.

Pleasants, Julian. "Don Wright." Unpublished transcript. Florida Newspapers Oral History Collection, Samuel Proctor Oral History Program. Department of History, University of Florida. http://ufdc.ufl.edu/UF00005544/00001.

———. "Howard Kleinberg FNP 71." Unpublished transcript. Florida Newspapers Oral History Collection, Samuel Proctor Oral History Program. Department of History, University of Florida. http://ufdc.ufl.edu/UF00091471/00001.

Van Dyke, Theresa. "Miami's Second Ghetto." Master's thesis, Florida Atlantic University, 1994. https://fau.digital.flvc.org/islandora/object/fau%3A11825.

Newspaper Columns and Articles by Bill Baggs

"3 Miamians Build Airline." *Miami Daily News*, July 18, 1946.

"Abolish Our Schools?," *Miami Daily News*, December 6, 1954.

"Absentees." *Miami News*, August 26, 1968.

"Accusing Spirits." *Miami News*, July 23, 1963.

"Airlines Wage Fight on Ticket Scalpers." *Miami Daily News*, December 29, 1946.

"And Spring Came." *Miami Daily News*, February 18, 1953.

"Anonymous Fiction." View of the News, *Miami News*, November 7, 1961,

"Baggs Tells How Hanoi Takes Life as City at War." *Miami News*, January 17, 1967.

"Bill Baggs in Switzerland." *Miami News*, June 13, 1966.

"Britons Favor M'Arthur Ouster." Man in the Middle, *Miami Daily News*, April 18, 1951.

"Cape Florida . . . Gift to Our Heirs." *Miami News*, June 27, 1965.

"A Chance to Show What Democracy Can Do." View of the News, *Miami News*, June 4, 1961.

"Courthouse Birds." View of the News, *Miami News*, April 30, 1963.

"Death Trap." View of the News, *Miami News*, October 19, 1961.

"Demo, GOP Chiefs Like Miami Beach." *Miami News*, May 17, 1967.

"Determination at Armageddon." *Miami News*, June 15, 1966.

"Don't Kid Yourself on Desegregation." *Miami Daily News*, December 5, 1954.

"The Dove Is Out." *Miami Daily News*, April 1, 1953.

"The First Negro Judge in Dixie." *Miami Daily News*, Dec. 7, 1955.

"The First Step." View of the News, *Miami News*, Sept. 14, 1961.

"Florida, Cuban Officials Lead PAA Celebration." *Miami Daily News*, October 28, 1947.

"For a Key Man." *Miami News*, July 24, 1963.

"For Arabs, a Free Country." *Miami News*, June 16, 1966.

"Frustration." *Miami News*, August 16, 1968.

"Harry's Stature Grows." *Miami News*, February 17, 1960.

"Hatred." *Miami News*, January 13, 1963.

"Here Are the Real Issues in '62 Campaign." View of the News, *Miami News*, October 21, 1962.

"I Saw a New York Cop Crying." *Miami News*, June 7, 1968.

In the Bag, daily column, *Miami Daily News*, May 3, 1950.

In the Bag, daily column, *Miami Daily News*, May 17, 1950.

"Italy Needs Leader to Curb Commies, Worker Declares." Man in the Middle, *Miami Daily News*, April 11, 1951.

"The Man." *Miami News*, November 23, 1963.

"Miami's Growing Air Horizons." *Miami Daily News*, June 22, 1947.

"A Midnight Visit with Fidel Castro." *Miami News*, April 26, 1959.

"A Negro Man Was Worried." *Miami Daily News*, July 23, 1952.

"The Negro's Problem." *Miami Daily News*, December 7, 1954.

"The New World." *Miami Daily News*, August 10, 1954.

"An Offer." *Miami News*, May 16, 1965.

"Oil Refineries." View of the News, *Miami News*, August 27, 1962.

"Opening Minds." View of the News, *Miami News*, March 10, 1961.

"Operation Bootstrap." *Miami Daily News*, November 13, 1952.

"Operation Bootstrap in Puerto Rico." View of the News, *Miami Daily News*, September 10, 1957.

"Orr's Plan Might Be Answer." *Miami News*, September 25, 1958.

"Our Bay a Great Asset." View of the News, *Miami News*, June 23, 1960.

Paul Crouch series. *Miami Daily News*, May 9–16, 1949.

"Peace." *Miami News*, February 21, 1965.

"Photograph Raises Intriguing Questions on 'Flying Saucers.'" *Miami Daily News*, March 29, 1950.

"Preserve Cape Florida Light." Unsigned editorial, *Miami News*, July 26, 1958.

"Press Has a Great Duty to Tell Both Sides." View of the News, *Miami Daily News*, October 8, 1957.

"The Profound Neglect of Duty." *Miami Daily News*, December 31, 1951.

"Reapportionment." View of the News, *Miami News*, September 7, 1962.

"Red Schoolhouses." *Miami News*, May 25, 1961.

"Reds Face Ouster as Union Leaders Plan Housecleaning." *Miami Daily News*, June 14, 1948.

"Reds Pull Out of Geneva Peace Conference." *Miami News*, March 29, 1967.

"RFK Myth." *Miami News*, June 12, 1968.

"Robert Francis Kennedy, Man of Courage." *Miami News*, June 6, 1968.

"The Sad Story of Castro." View of the News, *Miami News*, November 3, 1959.

"Saigon's Tail Wags the U.S. Policy Dog." *Miami News*, December 26, 1968.

"Segregation, Dollars & Sense." *Miami News*, February 8, 1959.

"A Spiritual Leader's Down-to-Earth Plea." *Miami News*, April 11, 1963.

"Statement by Bill Baggs." *Miami News*, July 29, 1966.

"Stubborn Enough to Exist." *Miami News*, June 14, 1966.

"Testing Ground." View of the News, *Miami News*, October 13, 1962.

"There Is Indeed This Santa Clause," *Miami Daily News*, December 24, 1951.

"Unnecessary Risks." View of the News, *Miami News*, April 25, 1963.

"U.N. Reports 1–4." View of the News, *Miami News*, October 15–18, 1962.

"Video Begins Here Tomorrow Night on Station WTVJ." Television Edition, *Miami Daily News*, March 20, 1949.

"The Violent Hucksters." *Miami News*, August 9, 1968.

"Want to Debate This?," *Miami Daily News*, May 17, 1954.

"War and Discipline." View of the News, *Miami News*, April 21, 1961.

"The Ways of Peace Searched." *Miami News*, February 19, 1965.

"We Can Save the Lighthouse." Signed editorial, *Miami News*, August 24, 1958.

"Why Not Re-Do City from Ghetto to Bay." *Miami News*, December 27, 1968.

"The Worst Dressed." *Miami Daily News*, February 9, 1955.

"You Could Call It 'Bedsheet Fiction.'" *Miami Daily News*, April 21, 1957.

"You Just Grab the Rattlesnake." *Miami Daily News*, July 27, 1947.

"Yugoslavian Editor Points with Pride to Paper's 'Freedom.'" Man in the Middle, *Miami Daily News*, April 19, 1951.

"Yugoslavs Struggle against High Prices, Food Shortages." Man in the Middle, *Miami Daily News*, April 15, 1951.

Other Newspaper, Journal, Magazine, and Internet Articles

Anderson, Maria. "Pedro Pan: A Children's Exodus from Cuba." *Smithsonian Insider* (blog), July 11, 2017. https://insider.si.edu/2017/07/pedro-pan-childrens-exodus-cuba.

"Announcement." *Miami Daily News*, July 28, 1957.

"Announcement." *Miller County Liberal*, May 23, 1941.

"Another Editor in the Baggs-McGill Tradition." Special Anniversary Section, *Miami News*, May 14, 1971.

Ash, Clarke. "Miami Crawled with CIA Men." *Palm Beach Post*, October 18, 1987.

Ashmore, Harry S. "The Ashmore Controversy." Letters to the Editor, *Baltimore Sun*, October 11, 1967.

Bernstein, Carl. "The CIA and the Media." *Rolling Stone*, October 20, 1977.

"Bill Baggs, 48, Dies of Pneumonia." *Miami News*, January 8, 1969.

"Bill Baggs to Attend Caribbean Conference." *Miami News*, September 3, 1961.

Bookman, Todd. "John F. Kennedy Diary Reveals Shift from Journalist to Budding Politician." NPR, April 25, 2017. https://www.npr.org/2017/04/25/525604352/john -f-kennedy-diary-reveals-shift-from-journalist-to-budding-politician.

Brigham, Robert K. "A Lost Chance for Peace in Vietnam." *New York Times*, June 16, 2017. https://www.nytimes.com/2017/06/16/opinion/a-lost-chance-for-peace-in -vietnam.html.

Clampitt, Fred. "Odds, Ends about that Guy Baggs." *Miami Daily News*, February 12, 1951.

Colbert, Haines. "Don Wright Took Just Four Years to Win Pulitzer." *Miami News*, May 3, 1966.

———. "Eldridge Tops Orr, But Debate Still On." *Miami News*, October 1, 1958.

Corchoran, Bob. "Cape Florida Deed Presented to Burns." *Miami News*, April 5, 1965.

"Cox Buys the Metropolis." 75th Anniversary Special Section, *Miami News*, May 14, 1971.

Cox, E. E. "Congressman Cox Resents Passage of the Unjust Bill." *Miller County Liberal*, January 31, 1940.

"Crawford Baggs Dies at Wesley Memorial." *Atlanta Constitution*, October 19, 1923.

"Cuba Raps U.S. in Wild U.N. Session." *Miami News*, October 8, 1962.

"Cuban Missile Crisis." Special Section, *Miami News*, October 15, 1982.

"Editor Charges LBJ-Hanoi Deal," *Pensacola Times*, November 1, 1968.

"Editor Raps News Control." *Miami News*, February 20, 1963.

Eyerdam, Rick. "Baggs Park OK'd by House." *Miami News*, April 13, 1973.

Farrell, John A. "When a Candidate Conspired with a Foreign Power to Win an Election." *Politico*, August 6, 2017. https://www.politico.com/magazine/story/2017 /08/06/nixon-vietnam-candidate-conspired-with-foreign-power-win-election -215461.

Garvin, Glenn. "The Miami Herald, the CIA, and the Bay of Pigs Scoop That Didn't Run." *Miami Herald*, April 17, 2015. https://www.miamiherald.com/news/local /community/miami-dade/article18792675.html.

Gehrke, Donna, and Christensen, Dan. "'Like a Death in the Family,' Reader Says." *Miami News*, October 15, 1988.

Glass, Ian. "Your Impossible Dream Has Come True, Bill Baggs." *Miami News*, March 13, 1974.

Golden Anniversary Special Section, *Miami Daily News*, May 12, 1946.

Goldstein, Gordon M. "'Marigold: The Lost Chance for Peace in Vietnam,' by James G. Hershberg." *The Washington Post*, January 27, 2012. https://www .washingtonpost.com/entertainment/books/marigold-the-lost-chance-for -peace-in-vietnam-by-james-g-hershberg/2012/01/27/gIQAiUMWYR_story .html?utm_term=.43166e7b8796.

Grace, Art. "Bill Baggs and the News." Gracefully Yours, *Miami News*, June 24, 1959.

Hendrix, Hal. "Firm U.S. Policy Is Urged to Discourage Dictators." *Miami News*, August 16, 1958.

Hesser, Charles F. "Baggs Urges Nonpartisan Constitution." *Miami News*, July 13, 1967.

"Hoke Welch, Former Managing Editor of Miami News." UPI Archives, July 11, 1981. https://www.upi.com/Archives/1981/07/11/Hoke-Welch-former-managing-editor -of-the-Miami-News/4174363672000.

Hurricane Donna Special Section. *Miami News*, September 16, 1960.

"It's Our Third Pulitzer." *Miami News*, May 7, 1963.

"James M. Cox Dies at 87." *Dayton Daily News*, July 15, 1957.

Jessup, John K. "Peace on Earth?" *Life*, March 5, 1965, 32A–36A, 92A.

"JFK Greets Emerging Caribbean." *Miami News*, September 7, 1961.

Kassewitz, Jack. "Covenant of Brotherhood." *Miami News*, January 10, 1969.

———. "New City Commissioner Offers Political Paradox." *Miami News*, April 20, 1972.

Keasler, John. "The Man—Littered, Literate, Unique; Waystop between a Wild Irreverence and a Deep Belief." *Miami News*, January 8, 1969.

"King Suspect Is Arrested." *Miami News*, June 8, 1968.

Kleinberg, Howard. "History of *The Miami News* 1896–1987." *Tequesta*, no. 47 (1987): 5–29. http://digitalcollections.fiu.edu/tequesta/files/1987/87_1_01.pdf.

———. "Littered and Literate—and a Force for Positive Change." *Miami Herald*, October 25, 1994.

———. "The Miami News Ends; The Causes Continue." *Miami News*, December 31, 1988.

———. "Other Great Lives Tied to King's Memory." *Miami News*, January 17, 1987.

"Lower Vote Age, Says Bill Baggs." *Miami News*, November 30, 1966.

Lucas, Robert W. "Maybe Ashmore 'Goof' was Planned," *Press and Sun-Bulletin*, September 19, 1967.

Mahoney, Dan. "The Publisher's Corner," *Miami Daily News*, December 30, 1950.

———. "The Publisher's Corner." *Miami Daily News*, April 21, 1951,

Maier, Thomas. "Inside the CIA's Plot to Kill Fidel Castro—with Mafia Help." *Politico*, February 24, 2018. https://www.politico.com/magazine/story/2018/02/24/fidel -castro-cia-mafia-plot-216977.

"A Man of Considerable Dimensions." *Miami Daily News*, January 24, 1953.

Mann, Jack. "The Defender . . . In Priestly Garb." *Miami News*, December 4, 1968.

———. "Gibson Breaks Witch Hunt in State Led by Johns." *Miami News*, December 5, 1968.

———. "Gibson Firm on Ideals—But He Was 'Hurt Inside.'" *Miami News*, December 6, 1968.

Masur, Louis P. "Why it Took a Century to Pass an Anti-lynching Law." *Washington Post*, December 28, 2018. https://www.washingtonpost.com/outlook/2018/12/28/why-it-took-century-pass-an-anti-lynching-law/?utm_term=.b7e49577e59a.

McGill, Ralph. "A Hi, a Smile, and a Joke." *Miami News* and *Atlanta Constitution*, January 8, 1969.

———. "A Thin Wail in the Night." *Atlanta Constitution*, February 19, 1953.

"Miamian Wins Merit Award, Fellowship." *Tampa Bay (St. Petersburg) Times*, June 25, 1952.

"Miss Baggs, Mr. Beers Take Vows Wednesday." *Miller County Liberal*, June 7, 1939.

Mohl, Raymond A. "'South of the South?' Jews, Blacks, and the Civil Rights Movement in Miami, 1945–1960." *Journal of American Ethnic History* 18, no. 2 (Winter 1999): 3–26. http://www.jstor.org/stable/27502414.

Montayne, Carlton. "A Day Spent in Lauderdale." Monty Says, *Miami Daily News*, January 23, 1953.

Mormino, Gary R. "Midas Returns: Miami Goes to War, 1941–1945." *Tequesta*, no. 57 (1997): 5–51. http://digitalcollections.fiu.edu/tequesta/files/1997/97_1_01.pdf.

Morris, Mercedes K. "The *Star & Herald*—An Epitaph." *Canal Record*, December 1988, 81–82. http://ufdc.ufl.edu/AA00010871/00153/94j.

"News Will Sponsor TV's 'Meet the Press.'" *Miami Daily News*, August 31, 1956.

"News' Jay Mallin Scores Cuban Beat." *Miami News*, January 2, 1959.

Ochs, Martin S. "The Sage of Atlanta." *Virginia Quarterly Review* 75, no. 3 (Summer 1999): 589.

Oppel, Rich. "Voting at 18 Up for Debate." *Tallahassee Democrat*, December 1, 1966.

"Palm Tree Politics." *Tampa Bay (St. Petersburg) Times*, July 23, 1955.

"The Press: Meet the Press." *Time*, September 15, 1958. http://content.time.com/time/subscriber/article/0,33009,863834,00.html.

"Prisoner Airlift Awaited." *Miami News*, October 8, 1962.

"R. C. Orr Dies at 71; Landscaper." *Atlanta Constitution*, December 10, 1962.

Renick, Ralph. "Bill Baggs Had 2 Idols: Lincoln and John XXIII." The Voice of Ralph Renick, *The Voice* (Archdiocese of Miami), January 17, 1969. Private collection.

Roberts, Gene, and Hank Klibanoff. "The Embrace of Principled Stands." *Neiman Reports* 60, no. 2 (Summer 2006): 88.

Robinson, Arthur. "Miami's Fast Air Growth Started from Daring Pioneer Flight in 1911." Golden Anniversary Special Section, *Miami News*, May 12, 1946.

Robinson, Greg, and Maxime Minne. "The Unknown History of Japanese Internment in Panama." Discover Nikkei (website), April 26, 2018. http://www.discovernikkei.org/en/journal/2018/4/26/japanese-internment-panama.

Schneider, Ben. "Developers Buy on Key Biscayne." *Miami News*, February 3, 1958.

"Second in Miami; First on Cuba." *Time*, November 16, 1962.

Staff Report. "The Dayton Daily News Turns 120." *Dayton Daily News*, August 23, 1998.https://www.mydaytondailynews.com/news/the-dayton-daily-news-turns-120-the-story-its-founding-and-connection-the-community/L56kcwazoNFzi XsaCZRnXI.

"Statement by Bill Baggs," *Miami News*, July 29, 1966.

"Statement by John S. Knight." *Miami News*, July 29, 1966.

Taylor, Alan. "The 1939 New York World's Fair." *Atlantic*, November 1, 2013. https://www.theatlantic.com/photo/2013/11/the-1939-new-york-worlds-fair/100620.

"That Long, Long Line." *Globe-Gazette* (Mason City, Iowa), September 21, 1962.

Theoharis, Jeanne. "Don't Forget That Martin Luther King Jr. Was Once Denounced as an Extremist." *Time*, January 12, 2018.

Tucker, William. "Hoke Welch Ends 15 Years as County Aide." *Miami News*, October 7, 1975.

———, William. "We'll Hit All Ships to Cuba, Alpha 66 Threatens." *Miami News*, October 11, 1962.

"Vipers Created a Furor." *Miami News*, October 25, 1971.

Warren, Fuller. Letters to the Editor. *Miami Daily News*, February 15, 1955.

Wilson, Earl. "One Society." *Springfield Leader and Press*, March 6, 1958.

Wylie, Philip. "Wylie Bats for Baggs." *Miami Daily News*, February 8, 1951.

Official Records and Government Documents

Ball, George (Undersecretary of State). LBJ Oral History Collection, LBJ Presidential Library, Austin, Texas. National Archives and Records Administration.

Baggs, William C. Military Records. National Personnel Records Center, St. Louis, Missouri. National Archives and Records Administration.

Bundy, William P. (Assistant Secretary for East Asian and Pacific Affairs). LBJ Oral History Collection, LBJ Presidential Library, Austin, Texas. National Archives and Records Administration.

Correspondence between Vice President Richard M. Nixon and Bill Baggs. Richard Nixon Pre-Presidential Materials (Laguna Niguel), Richard Nixon Presidential Library and Museum, Yorba Linda, California. National Archives and Records Administration.

Katzenbach, Nicholas (Undersecretary of State). LBJ Oral History Collection, LBJ Presidential Library, Austin, Texas. National Archives and Records Administration.

Kennedy, John F. Presidential Papers. Presidential Office Files, John F. Kennedy Presidential Library and Museum, Boston, Massachusetts. National Archives and Records Administration.

Read, Benjamin H. (Executive Secretary of the Department of State and Special Assistant to the Secretary). LBJ Oral History Collection, LBJ Presidential Library, Austin, Texas. National Archives and Records Administration.

Rostow, Walt W. (Special Assistant for National Security Affairs). LBJ Oral History Collection, LBJ Presidential Library, Austin, Texas. National Archives and Records Administration.

Salisbury, Harrison (Managing Editor of *New York Times*). LBJ Oral History Collection, LBJ Presidential Library, Austin, Texas. National Archives and Records Administration.

Sullivan, William H. (U.S. Ambassador to Laos). LBJ Oral History Collection, LBJ Presidential Library, Austin, Texas. National Archives and Records Administration.

Warnke, Paul C. (Assistant Secretary of Defense for International Security Affairs). LBJ Oral History Collection, LBJ Presidential Library, Austin, Texas. National Archives and Records Administration.

Books Used for Historical Background

Egerton, John. *Speak Now against the Day: The Generation before the Civil Rights Movement in the South*. New York: Knopf, 1994.

Isaacson, Walter, and Evan Thomas. *The Wise Men: Six Friends and the World They Made*. New York: Simon and Schuster, 2012.

Roberts, Gene, and Hank Klibanoff. *The Race Beat: The Press, the Civil Rights Struggle, and the Awakening of a Nation*. New York: Vintage Books, 2007.

Rose, Chanelle N. *The Struggle for Black Freedom in Miami: Civil Rights and America's Tourist Paradise, 1896–1968*. Baton Rouge: Louisiana State University Press, 2015.

Teel, Leonard Ray. *Ralph Emerson McGill: Voice of the Southern Conscience*. Knoxville: University of Tennessee Press, 2001.

———. *Reporting the Cuban Revolution: How Castro Manipulated American Journalists*. Baton Rouge: Louisiana State University Press, 2015.

Vonk, Carita Swanson. *Theodore R. Gibson: Priest, Prophet and Politician*. Miami, Fla.: Little River, 1997.

INDEX

ABOUT THE AUTHOR

An award-winning freelance writer, journalist, and editor, Amy Paige Condon is founder of the community creative writing workshop The Refinery Writing Studio in Savannah, Georgia. She co-authored the bestselling *Back in the Day Bakery Cookbook* (Artisan, 2012) and *Wiley's Championship Barbecue Cookbook* (Gibbs Smith, 2014). She lives in Savannah with her husband, three dogs, and a talkative pig named Gus.

amypaigecondon.com
therefinerywritingstudio.com
Twitter: @RefineryWriting
Instagram: @TheRefineryWrites